Historiography: An Introductory Guide

# Historiography

## *An Introductory Guide*

Eileen Ka-May Cheng

continuum

**Continuum International Publishing Group**

The Tower Building          80 Maiden Lane
11 York Road                Suite 704
London SE1 7NX              New York NY 10038

www.continuumbooks.com

First published 2012

**British Library Cataloguing-in-Publication Data**
A catalogue record for this book is available from the British Library.

ISBN:   HB:  978-1-4411-0966-8
        PB:  978-1-4411-7767-4

**Library of Congress Cataloging-in-Publication Data**
A catalog record for this book is available from the Library of Congress.

Typeset by Fakenham Prepress Solutions Ltd, Fakenham, Norfolk NR21 8NN
Printed and bound in India

# Contents

Acknowledgements    vi
Introduction    1

1   Art and Science in Renaissance and Early Modern
Historical Writing    4

2   Enlightenment and Philosophical History    29

3   Romantic and Critical History    61

4   Scientific History and Its Challengers    91

5   Social History, Fragmentation, and the Revival of
Narrative    112

6   History and Historiography in Global Perspective    133

Notes    147
Appendix – American and European Historians from the
Renaissance to the Twentieth Century    174
Suggestions for Further Reading    204
Bibliography    211
Index    226

# Acknowledgments

I would first like to thank Michael Greenwood for inviting me to do this project and for his supportive attitude throughout the writing of the book. I would also like to acknowledge the helpful suggestions of Daniel Woolf on the initial proposal for the book. Finally, I would like to acknowledge the aid of my research assistants Caitlin Durham in creating and compiling the table of historians in the appendix, and J. T. Jamieson in proofreading the text and checking the appendix.

Eileen Ka-May Cheng
Historiography: An Introductory Guide

# Introduction

"What is historiography?" asked the American historian Carl Becker in 1938. Readers may well ask that question since professional historians have themselves differed over the meaning of the term, defining it variously to mean the writing of history, the study of historical methodology, the analysis of the different schools of interpretation on a particular historical topic, or the history of historical writing.[1] It is not surprising that many readers are either unfamiliar with the concept of historiography altogether, or at best view it as a dry and esoteric subject, of interest only to specialists, when even historians have often treated historiography in this way. The English historian G. R. Elton articulated the view of historiography as a narrow subfield that is somehow different from "real" historical study when he declared, "There are times when work on the history of history must appear distinctly narcissistic, especially when it deals with ages which did not regard history very highly."[2]

The aim of this book is to challenge this view of historiography – defined to mean the study of the history of historical writing – by presenting an accessible and concise overview of the history of historical writing from the Renaissance to the present, focusing primarily on the United States and Western Europe.[3] The book not only describes the major schools of historical writing and the different approaches taken by historians from the Renaissance to the present, but explains the emergence of these approaches by placing them in the context of their time and showing how they reflected broader social and cultural developments. Far from treating historiography as a subject distinct from real history, then, the approach of this book is based on the assumption that historical writing is as much a product of its time as any other historical development, and can therefore serve as a lens into major trends and developments in the history of Western civilization.

By taking this approach, the book also seeks to avoid falling into the trap that has been all too common, especially in older surveys of historiography, of presenting the history of historical writing as a linear progression of improvement from the backward and simplistic outlook of earlier historians to the more sophisticated and complex perspective of modern scholars, or what the historian Peter Novick has called a "Whig" interpretation of historiography.[4] Accordingly, while following a chronological structure, beginning with the Renaissance and ending with the rise of global history in recent historical scholarship, with each chapter devoted to a major stage in the development of historical writing, the book tries as much as possible to analyze its subjects on their own terms and as the products of their context, rather than judging them according to modern standards of scholarship.

To better achieve this goal, the book focuses on selected case studies of individual historians who illustrate important trends and developments for each chapter. While the individuals chosen for these case studies were not necessarily the most important or representative of their time, taken together they show something of the diversity that characterized historical writing in each of the periods examined in the book. The book quotes more extensively from the subjects of these case studies than is often the case with general surveys of historiography, both as a way of presenting these historians in their own words – and thus, in some sense, on their own terms – and to illustrate how to analyze their writings. Unlike many other general works on historiography, then, the book does not try to provide a comprehensive overview of the subject, but instead takes a more conceptual approach aimed at conveying broad themes and trends to readers.[5] The goal of the book is therefore to give readers a framework for analyzing historiography, which they can then apply to the study of other historians not covered in the book.

To this end, the book includes a listing in the appendix of some of the most important European and American historians for each of the eras it covers. Although this listing is necessarily also selective, it should give readers a starting point for further research and show them how the individual historians examined by the book were part of a much larger constellation of thinkers, demonstrating the diverse range of possibilities available to historians of different eras. And when we consider this range of possibilities, and the conflicts they engendered, the sense of fragmentation that some modern historians have bemoaned in current historical scholarship appears less new – and less threatening – than they have feared. And so, what a study of historiography demonstrates is that far from being a threat to the integrity and vitality of the discipline, conflict has been a defining feature of it from the Renaissance to the present, just as it has been of history itself.

In turn, there can be no better way of challenging the widely held misperception of history as simply a dry chronicle of facts and dates than by examining how widely historians have differed not only in their interpretations of historical events, but in their very definitions of history. Thus, rather than being something distinct from "regular" history, historiography can illuminate an integral aspect of historical analysis – its subjective and inter-pretive character – and in so doing demonstrate to readers what makes history such an interesting and complex subject.

# Chapter One

## *Art and Science in Renaissance and Early Modern Historical Writing*

The period from the Renaissance to the early seventeenth century was a time of great change for Europe, bringing with it not only the cultural changes associated with the Renaissance, but also the Scientific Revolution and the colonization of the Americas. These changes both stimulated greater interest in history and transformed the nature of that interest. With the growth of interest in history also came greater conflicts over how to approach it. Even as historians began to align history with science by making its study more systematic, the view of history as an art or as a branch of rhetoric and literature gained added life from the influence of Renaissance humanism. And so, while this was the time when the critical methods that would come to define history as a discipline first developed, historians varied widely in their willingness to embrace these methods and put them into practice.

Jean Bodin, Francis Bacon, and John Selden demonstrated in different ways both the growing importance of such critical methods, and the limits to which historians actually incorporated these methods into their historical writing, illuminating more generally both the extent of and limits to the transformation that the Renaissance brought about in the writing of history. And so, while Bodin, Bacon, and Selden all expressed a more secular outlook than their medieval predecessors did in their approach to history, they differed widely in how far they were willing to challenge religion. The persisting influence of religion was most apparent in the colonial American historian William Bradford's work. Yet paradoxically, Bradford shared his European contemporaries' concern with truth and historical complexity, not despite but because of his religious perspective.

## THE RENAISSANCE "SENSE OF THE PAST"

First emerging in Italy during the late fourteenth century, the intellectual and cultural transformations that would come to be known as the Renaissance gradually spread to Northern Europe, where they took on their own distinctive form during the fifteenth and sixteenth centuries. Meaning "rebirth," the Renaissance revived classical learning as an alternative to medieval scholastic thought. More than just a literary and artistic movement, the Renaissance encompassed a much broader set of cultural changes that grew out of the revival of classical learning. Although not as much of a departure from medieval assumptions as the term Renaissance suggested (and indeed, this term would not be widely used until the nineteenth century), or as its adherents claimed, this movement did mark an important shift of emphasis away from a world-view centered on the Church, in favor of a more humanistic and secular perspective.

The Renaissance stimulated interest in history in many different ways. The Renaissance fascination with classical antiquity contributed specifically to a greater interest in the history of ancient Greece and Rome. Viewing the ancient Roman past as the pinnacle of civilization, the Italian poet and scholar Petrarch (1304–74) – who played a leading role in the revival of classical learning during the Renaissance – contrasted the greatness of Rome to what he considered the dark ages of his own time. Petrarch expressed his desire to return to and revive the classical past in the series of letters he wrote to ancient authors, declaring in a letter to Livy, "I should wish (if it were permitted from on high) either that I had been born in Thine age or thou in ours; in the latter case our age itself, and in the former I personally, should have been the better for it."[1] Petrarch revealed how his belief in the superiority of ancient Rome to the present contributed to his interest in history when he stated, "In order to forget my own time, I have constantly striven to place myself in spirit in other ages, and consequently I delighted in history."[2]

His desire to use the past to forget the present also pointed to a belief in the difference between past and present that was another distinguishing feature of the Renaissance view of history. Whereas medieval thinkers had emphasized the likeness between past and present, imposing their contemporary perspective on the past, Renaissance thinkers showed a greater recognition of how alien the past was from the present. This sense of disjunction between past and present in turn contributed to a fascination with history, as Renaissance thinkers sought to recover and hold on to a past that seemed increasingly distant from them.[3] Thus, not only did the Renaissance contribute to a greater interest in history, but it also changed the nature of that interest.

Yet if Renaissance thinkers held up classical antiquity as a pinnacle from which their contemporaries had fallen away, this did not mean that they viewed the past as inherently superior to the present. On the contrary, part of their purpose in celebrating classical antiquity was to revive its greatness in the present so that their contemporaries could achieve a rebirth of the civilization that they associated with the classical world. And so, the Renaissance fascination with classical antiquity did not mean that they uncritically celebrated ancient Greece and Rome as an unattainable ideal.[4] In their assumption that it was possible to change the present for the better by reviving classical antiquity, Renaissance thinkers revealed a willingness to challenge traditional authority – specifically, that of medieval learning and Christian theology. Paradoxically, then, their desire to revive classical tradition contributed to a greater willingness to question tradition. Consequently, where the medieval conception of the universe as a hierarchical and stable order that was complete in itself left little room for even the idea of change or innovation, Renaissance thinkers showed a greater acceptance of the possibility – and desirability – of change and newness.[5] Renaissance historical thinkers took this acceptance of newness and this willingness to depart from tradition into their choice of historical subjects, as many of them wrote about the history of their own times in the belief that the present was more important and relevant than the distant past. Thus, for all their fascination with classical antiquity, Renaissance historical thinkers by no means confined themselves to the history of ancient Greece and Rome.[6]

The Florentine historian Francesco Guicciardini revealed this concern with the recent past in his history of Italy (1540), declaring that his purpose was to provide an account of "those events which have occurred in Italy within our memory." Far from viewing classical antiquity as a golden age, Guicciardini portrayed the recent history of Florence as a golden age that had come to an end in 1494.[7] In his effort to explain the invasions that helped bring about an end to Florence's golden age, Guicciardini pointed to yet another trait that differentiated Renaissance from medieval historical writing – its greater concern with historical explanations. Whereas medieval historians showed only a limited interest in explanation, attributing events either to individuals or to God, Renaissance historians examined a wider range of causes, devoting much more attention to the complex relationship between them. And so, while Guicciardini attributed the problems that Italy suffered after 1492 partly to the role of individuals, he also considered structural factors like the balance of power. Likewise, Guicciardini's better-known contemporary, the Florentine historian and political thinker Niccolo Machiavelli, revealed his concern with going beyond the individual or the divine to explain historical events in his use of Fortune to refer to impersonal secular forces. While the role of Fortune revealed the limits to human control, Machiavelli at the same time made clear his view of Fortune as a secular force that was subject to human influence when he pointed out that it was possible to "take precautions" which would protect against the potentially destructive power of Fortune. Not only, then, did Machiavelli and Guicciardini show a greater interest in causation than their medieval predecessors did; they also revealed the more secular character of Renaissance historical explanations in their emphasis on material and human forces.[8]

All of these developments both reflected and furthered the growing prestige of history as a discipline, which resulted in an outpouring of historical writing in Europe during the fifteenth and sixteenth centuries. Challenging Aristotle's categorization of history as inferior to poetry, Renaissance scholars not only claimed that history was equal to the other liberal arts disciplines, but even argued that it should be the foundation for them.[9] Yet far from unifying historians, the increasing regard for history actually divided them. Just as the Renaissance took different forms in different places, its effects on the writing of history varied by place and time. Even historians from the same society differed sharply from one another. Thus, for example, while both Machiavelli and Guicciardini wrote about the history of Florence and lamented its decline after 1494, and both looked to history as a source of political lessons for the present, Guicciardini showed a greater awareness of the limits to the kinds of lessons that could be drawn from history. While expressing his hope that readers would "draw many useful lessons both for themselves and for the public good" from his history of Italy, he also suggested the limits to how much people could use those lessons to shape the course of events in his emphasis on the uncertainty and unpredictability of human affairs, noting "countless examples" of how "unstable" they were.[10] Guicciardini revealed even more clearly his doubts about the value of such historical lessons when he criticized the widespread tendency to look to ancient Roman history as a source of examples for the present. In direct contrast to Machiavelli, who drew extensively from Roman history for lessons that could serve as a basis for the science of politics, Guicciardini questioned the usefulness of examples that came from a society so different from his present one as that of ancient Rome when he declared,"How wrong it is to cite the Romans at every turn." As he explained,

> For any comparison to be valid, it would be necessary to have a city with conditions like theirs, and then to govern it according to their example. In the case of a city with different qualities, the

comparison is as much out of order as it would be to expect a jackass to race like a horse.[11]

One of the most important sources of division in Renaissance historical writing was over the question of whether history was a science or an art. On the one hand, following ancient models of historical writing, Renaissance historical writers, like their classical predecessors, treated history as an art or a branch of rhetoric and literature. Hence their main goal was to offer a coherent literary narrative that could serve as a source of political lessons for the present, making issues of style and form more important to them than scholarship and research. Yet if the traditional view of history as a form of art gained added life from the influence of Renaissance humanism, Renaissance scholars at the same time increasingly viewed history as a science that was based on a systematic and empirical analysis of the past.[12]

The emerging view of history as a science both reflected and furthered changes in historical methodology, contributing to a transformation of the way in which scholars approached the study of history, as Renaissance scholars developed the critical methods that eventually came to define history as a discipline. These methods originated largely in fields outside of history such as antiquarianism and the law. The fascination with classical antiquity fueled antiquarian interest in material artifacts from the ancient past such as ruins and coins. In order to date these artifacts and verify their authenticity, antiquarians had to subject them to systematic critical analysis. Not only did antiquarianism broaden the kinds of sources available to historians by promoting an appreciation for the historical value of non-textual sources; it also contributed to a more critical way of viewing those sources, which could then be applied to documentary sources as well. Developments in the legal realm contributed even more directly to a recognition of the need for a critical analysis of documentary sources, particularly among French historians, as legal scholars gave primacy to the value of primary sources over secondhand

accounts and emphasized the importance of assessing the reliability of sources as the basis for truth. Ironically, then, the very
trait that would eventually come to distinguish history as a discipline – the critical analysis of primary sources – had roots in areas
outside history.[13]

## JEAN BODIN AND THE *ARS HISTORICA*

As part of their desire to establish the status of history as a
science, Renaissance scholars not only adopted new methods of
historical study, but became increasingly self-conscious about the
need to articulate a method that would make the study of history
more uniform and systematic. Consequently, a literary genre
known as the *ars historica* – meaning the art of history – came
into its own between the late fifteenth and early seventeenth
centuries. Exponents of this genre came from many different
nationalities, varying widely in their concerns and their doctrines.
Yet what they had in common was the desire to reflect broadly on
the theory of history, discussing such issues as the purpose and
form of history and offering principles of historical criticism and
analysis. Hence many of the authors associated with this genre
devoted extensive attention to commenting on and criticizing
earlier historians in order to demonstrate how to assess the reliability of different sources and bring together conflicting accounts
of the same subject. In this way, the *ars historica* laid the basis for
the critical methods of analysis that would later come to define
history as a discipline.[14]

   Yet as the French jurist and historian Jean Bodin (1530–96) – one
of the most influential contributors to the *ars historica* – revealed,
the view of history as an art and the view of history as a science
were not mutually exclusive. The publication of Bodin's *Method
for the Easy Comprehension of History* in 1566 brought him international renown – and notoriety – at once turning him into the
leading authority of this time on the *ars historica* and provoking
heated controversy over his specific historical claims and their

implications. The controversy over his work demonstrated the contested nature of Renaissance historical writing, revealing both the extent of and limits to the changes brought about by the Renaissance.[15]

Bodin expressed his appreciation for the artistic element to history when he complained about how few of the historical works he had read had "reported their findings artistically and logically," noting, "I see no one who has compressed into graceful form the scattered and disjointed material found."[16] Declaring that his purpose was to explain both "the art and the method" of history, Bodin revealed his belief that his desire to make the study of history more systematic and scientific was entirely compatible with his view of history as an art.[17] Bodin sought to achieve this goal by offering detailed guidelines on many different aspects of historical study, beginning with a definition of history that broke the subject down into different categories. He then went on to provide instructions not only on which historians to read and how to assess them, but even on the order in which they should be read.[18]

What made his work so controversial was its secular approach and its use of a critical analysis to challenge a theological under-standing of history. In his definition of history, Bodin did not repudiate a belief in the divine altogether, but differentiated between three different forms of history – human, natural, and divine – arguing that since human history "explains the actions of man as he lives in society," the study of the divine should be left to the realm of theologians. In making this separation between human and divine history, Bodin suggested that the purpose of the historian should be to understand human history in terms of human action, without reference to divine intervention.[19] Bodin took his secular perspective into his analysis of specific historical theories that were current in his time, resulting in one of the most controversial of his claims – his attack on the theory of the four empires. Based on a biblical prophecy taken from the Book of Daniel, the theory of the four empires postulated the view that history was supposed to follow a progression through rule by four different empires – beginning with the Babylonian and ending with the Roman – as decreed by God, before the coming of the millennium brought history itself to an end.[20] Bodin questioned the assumption that there had been only four empires in the history of the world, arguing that the world had seen "almost an infinitude" of great empires over the course of its history and naming specific empires like those of the Arabs and the Tartars that were excluded by the theory of the four empires.[21] In addition, he attacked the widely held belief that the Roman Empire still existed in the form of the Holy Roman Empire, which made the Holy Roman Empire the last of the four empires. Declaring that to claim "that the Germans have the most powerful monarchy in the world is absurd, and it is even more absurd to pretend that this is the Roman Empire," Bodin mocked such claims by arguing that a stronger case could be made for considering the Turkish Empire the current incarnation of the Roman Empire.[22] Consequently, German scholars in particular hotly contested Bodin's attack on the theory of the four empires, viewing it as an affront to their belief in the greatness and importance of Germany to the unfolding of world history.[23]

Even more controversial was Bodin's challenge to the myth of the golden age. Drawn from the same prophetic vision in the Book of Daniel that provided the basis for the theory of the four empires, the myth of the golden age portrayed human history as a process of decline through a series of stages from its earliest beginnings as a golden age of purity and innocence into the corruption of the present and last stage of human history. Bodin derided the view that earlier ages were superior to and more pure than the present, pointing to what he believed was the savagery described by the Old Testament and by such ancient Greek historians as Thucydides.[24] As he exclaimed,

There you have your famous centuries of Gold and Silver! Men lived dispersed in the fields and forests like wild beasts, and had no private property except that which they could hang on to by force and crime: it has taken a long time to pull them away from this savage and barbarous way of life and to accustom them to civilized behavior and to a well-regulated society such as we now have everywhere.[25]

What made Bodin's attacks on both the theory of the four empires and the myth of the golden age so threatening to his contemporaries was his challenge to the authority of the Bible as a historical source that provided an accurate account of the past and future direction of history. More fundamentally, by portraying human history as a process of change that was amenable to human action and improvement, Bodin undermined the traditional view of history as the direct manifestation and unfolding of divine will – and the assumption that the historian's purpose was simply to uncover that will. The heated opposition to Bodin's views from other historians of the time who continued to uphold this understanding of the historian's purpose revealed the persisting influence of religion in this period and the limits to the changes brought about by the Renaissance. Bodin himself illustrated those limits, eventually turning away from his conception of history as the product of human action to embrace a species of Jewish mysticism and to support witch-hunting in the belief that he was following a personal spirit that guided his actions by tapping him on the shoulder.[26]

## FRANCIS BACON AND THE SCIENTIFIC REVOLUTION

Both the extent of and limits to the transformation in Renaissance historical writing were even more clear with the English scientist and historian Francis Bacon (1561–1626). Far from viewing science and religion as opposed to one another, he believed that his desire to place history on a more scientific basis would actually further religion. And even as he sought to apply scientific principles to the writing of history, he did not put those principles into practice in his own historical work, following instead the classical tradition of history as a form of literature or art. Thus, Bacon revealed his ambivalence about the relationship between history and science, at once aligning them with one another and differentiating between them.

Better known for his contributions to the Scientific Revolution as a leading proponent of the scientific method than he was for his work as a historian, Bacon revealed the close connection between the Scientific Revolution and the emerging view of history as a science. The Scientific Revolution is a term that has been used to designate a whole set of changes in scientific understanding that occurred very gradually over the course of the sixteenth and seventeenth centuries. These changes were so gradual that some scholars have questioned whether they should even be described as a revolution, particularly since the term Scientific Revolution was not one that scientific thinkers at the time would have used. Whether or not the Scientific Revolution was truly a revolution, it did bring about a transformation of scientific understanding on two levels. First, through the accumulation of new discoveries and knowledge about the natural world and the development of new theories that would account for these discoveries, the Scientific Revolution resulted in a changed understanding of how the universe worked. Beginning with the publication of the Polish astronomer Nicolaus Copernicus's *On the Revolutions of the Heavenly Spheres* in 1543, which challenged the medieval view of the universe by placing the sun rather than the earth at the center of the universe, the Scientific Revolution culminated with the publication of the Englishman Sir Isaac Newton's *Mathematical Principles of Natural Philosophy* in 1687. Bringing together the discoveries and theories of his predecessors, Newton explained the orderly movement of the planets and other heavenly bodies according to the universal law of gravitation. By explaining natural phenomena in terms of uniform and regular laws, Newton proffered a vision of a rational and mechanistic universe that made it possible to explain the natural world without reference to divine or supernatural intervention. Second, as Newton revealed in bringing together induction with deduction, the Scientific Revolution also involved a transformation in the methods of scientific inquiry that emphasized the use of reason and the need to test theories through direct experiment and observation.[27]

Through his role as a leading proponent of induction, Francis Bacon was instrumental to this transformation. Ironically, although most famous for his contribution to the Scientific Revolution, Bacon was not really a practicing scientist and did not even accept the findings of Copernicus. Yet his arguments for the value of science and for the need to place science on a more empirical basis played an important role in fostering a spirit favorable to scientific inquiry, and his works achieved wide influence not only among the educated elites in England but also throughout Europe. Sharply attacking the scholastic emphasis on received authority and tradition, Bacon disagreed with the scholastic view that there were no new truths to be discovered. Instead, he emphasized the need for individuals to reach their own conclusions, based on empirical evidence and observation. Bacon urged that they do so through induction – that is, by going from the particular to the general. Scientists should make general conclusions only after making and collecting many particular observations and experiments. Believing strongly in the practical uses of science, Bacon argued that induction from empirical evidence would in turn contribute new knowledge that could benefit humankind. Active in many different arenas, Bacon was also a lawyer and royal official who served as Lord Chancellor under James I. A strong supporter of the English monarchy and a staunch Protestant, Bacon revealed the breadth of his intellectual concerns in his *Advancement of Learning* (1605), which he wrote to promote a more general renovation and reform of learning in England. Among the many topics he discussed in this work, Bacon commented broadly on the value of history and offered his own prescriptions for how to approach history in a more methodical and systematic way.[28]

These prescriptions revealed Bacon's desire to apply a scientific approach to the study of history. Dividing, like Bodin, history into different categories, such as civil and ecclesiastical, and then further dividing these categories into subcategories such as memorials and antiquities, Bacon sought to make the study of history more orderly and rational, and thus more scientific, through this system of classification. As a rational form of inquiry, history, like science, had to be based on an objective account of the facts for Bacon. Hence he urged the importance of "simply narrating the fact historically, with but slight intermixture of private judgment." His emphasis on the need for the historian to simply describe facts without making judgments of "praise and blame" was consistent with the principle of induction in giving primacy to the particular over the general. Like the scientist, Bacon suggested, the historian was supposed to first collect the facts before drawing any larger conclusions from them, rather than imposing his theories on the facts. Just as he believed that science had to be based on observation and experiment, in his argument for the value of examining "the principal books written in each century," rather than relying on the works of other historians, Bacon revealed his desire to place history on an empirical basis and his belief in the importance of validating facts through firsthand observation from sources contemporaneous with the events they described. And in his unwillingness to accept the claims of other historians without verification, Bacon displayed the same kind of critical and questioning attitude that he urged scientists to adopt.[29]

As was the case with Bodin, Bacon's desire to place history on a more scientific basis reflected a secular outlook that threatened the authority of religion. Like Bodin, Bacon suggested the need to understand history in terms of human action without repudiating a belief in the divine altogether by dividing history into three different categories – the ecclesiastical, the literary, and civil. Simply by separating civil and literary history into a different realm from the ecclesiastical, and placing these two types of history on an equal level to the ecclesiastical, Bacon challenged the primacy traditionally given to religious history and implied a separation between the sacred and secular that went counter to the assumption that all of human history represented the working out of divine will. And in his claims for the value of religious history as a source of wisdom for the clergy, Bacon not only questioned the authority of saints, but suggested that clerical authority was something that required human effort and study rather than being divinely ordained, when he declared, "For the works of St. Ambrose or St. Augustine will not make so wise a bishop or divine as a diligent examination and study of Ecclesiastical History."[30]

Yet Bacon would only go so far in his challenge to religion. He made clear his belief in the providential basis for human history when he explained why the tendency to focus on great public actions and individuals at the expense of "smaller passages and motions of men in matters" was so misleading. In neglecting the more obscure aspects of history, the historian would lose sight of "the true and inward springs and resorts thereof," for "such being the workmanship of God, that he hangs the greatest weights upon the smallest wires."[31] And while Bacon urged the need to examine biblical prophecies in a more logical and systematic way, he did not question the reality of such prophecies. On the contrary, he believed that a more careful analysis of these prophecies would result in a more accurate understanding of their meaning, which would actually strengthen rather than undermine religious faith. Thus he urged the value of writing the history of prophecy "both for the better confirmation of faith, and for better instruction and skill in the interpretation of those parts of prophecies which are yet unfulfilled." More specifically, Bacon thought that in promoting the advancement of science and learning, he was fulfilling a prophecy given in the Book of Daniel that the restoration of human control over nature through the development of science and technology was a necessary precursor to the advent of the millennium. Claiming that it was part of God's plan for the advancement of navigation and discovery and the improvement of the sciences "to meet in one age," Bacon supported his claim by citing Daniel's statement "that many shall go to and fro on the Earth, and knowledge shall be increased." And so, far from viewing his advocacy of science and learning as a threat to religion, Bacon believed that he was furthering God's will and helping to bring about the millennium.[32]

While Bacon sought to place history on a more scientific basis, he at the same time differentiated between history and science in the role he gave to history in his vision for the reformation of learning. On the one hand, Bacon assigned to history an equal place to science in his vision for the renovation of learning. On the other hand, Bacon subordinated history to science by claiming that history provided the raw data that scientists could use for the purposes of induction, without being a science itself, declaring that "[k]nowledges are pyramids, whereof history is the basis."[33] Hence, he did not fully put his own precepts for a more scientific and methodical approach to history into practice in the actual history he wrote on the life of Henry VII, which adhered instead to the classical tradition of history as a form of art. Written after Bacon had been impeached from his position as Lord Chancellor, the history was published in 1622, taking Bacon no more than 14 weeks to write. Bacon was able to produce a history so quickly partly because of the limited research he did for it. While he did examine some archival sources for this work, he relied primarily on published sources. Nor did he subject these sources to the kind of systematic critical analysis that he urged, even replicating some of their errors in his own work. The result was that his work contained numerous factual inaccuracies, including so basic a fact as the date of Henry VII's death.[34]

Yet Bacon's failure to engage in the kind of research and critical analysis that he prescribed was not just a matter of carelessness or poor scholarship. Rather, in his disregard for critical scholarship, Bacon adhered to a belief in the distinction between history and antiquarian scholarship that had become more firmly estab-lished in England by the 1570s, partly in response to the growing number of antiquarian works that were being published in this period. According to this distinction, history was not seen as an academic discipline that required scholarly training or knowledge to write. On the contrary, as the study of past politics, history was supposed to be the preserve of those involved in politics and public affairs, as Bacon had been in his capacity as a royal official, who possessed the experience that would qualify them to write about this subject. The writing of history therefore did not require extensive research in primary sources; the historian's role was to take the facts that he believed had already been established by other historians' accounts and bring them together into a coherent narrative. Research in manuscript and archaeological sources was supposed to be the preserve of antiquaries, whose role it was to critically assess these sources for their accuracy and authenticity.[35]

For this reason, Bacon saw nothing wrong with relying so heavily on published sources, and did not think it incumbent upon him as a historian to systematically assess their accuracy. Instead, reflecting the influence of Renaissance humanism, Bacon looked to ancient historians – in particular Tacitus – as his models, sharing their goal of creating an elegant literary narrative. Drawing from Tacitus the concern with explaining historical events in terms of human action that differentiated so much of Renaissance historical writing from its medieval predecessor, Bacon emphasized the importance of psychological factors in explaining Henry VII's policies and actions. For Bacon, the most important of these factors were the insecurity created by the uncertain basis for Henry's claims to be king, his imprudence, and his avarice.[36]

## JOHN SELDEN: THE SYNTHESIS OF HISTORY WITH ANTIQUARIAN SCHOLARSHIP

Yet even as Bacon reflected the solidification of the distinction between history and antiquarianism, his contemporary John Selden blurred that distinction by bringing together these two forms of historical writing in his *Historie of Tithes* (1618). Known as one of the most learned men in England during his time, Selden was, like Bacon, active in politics, taking part in the parliamentary opposition to the early Stuart kings and supporting Parliament during the English civil wars. Selden was therefore in a position to put his learning to practical uses, as both other scholars and politicians of his time consulted him on a wide range of legal and historical issues.[37] Selden took this desire to bring together the scholarly with the practical into his own historical writing as he demonstrated the practical uses of antiquarian scholarship by integrating it into history.

A lawyer by training, Selden focused on legal history in his early works, while at the same time showing a concern with relating the history of law to its broader social context, as he used the law to illuminate such topics as the history of social distinctions in his *Titles of Honour* (1614).[38] Well versed in the legal scholarship of Continental – and particularly French – humanists, Selden derived his appreciation for philology from them. Taking his extensive research and knowledge of philology and other disciplines that were considered the realm of the antiquarian into his early works on legal history, Selden adhered to the distinction between history and antiquarianism in his unwillingness to characterize these works as histories. Yet his belief that the goal of all learning was supposed to be truth led him into a growing recognition of the interconnections between different disciplines.[39] Selden expressed this recognition in the preface to his *Titles of Honour* when he declared,

> It is said that all isles and continents (which are indeed but greater isles) are so seated, that there is none, but that, from some shore of it, another may be discovered. . . . Certainly the severed parts of good arts and learning, have that kind of site. And, as all are to be diligently sought to be possessed by mankind, so every one hath so much relation to some other, that it hath not only use often of the aid of what is next it, but, through that, also of what is out of ken to it.[40]

While recognizing the boundaries that divided different disciplines from one another, Selden also allowed for the crossing of those boundaries if it was necessary to further the cause of truth.[41] Although Selden did not claim for this work the status of history, he did portray it as a work of truth "in matter of story and philologie," revealing his belief that it was possible to bring together a realm associated with history – story – with a realm that had been considered the preserve of antiquaries – philology.[42] Defining philology broadly to encompass not only the study of language but also the historical context for social customs and institutions, Selden looked to philology as a medium for bridging disciplinary boundaries and determining truth. Making coherence the test of validity, Selden believed that it was possible to ascertain the truthfulness of a claim by using philology to see if it was consistent with all that was known about its context – a principle that he termed synchronism.[43]

Selden used this technique to greatest effect in his most famous and controversial work, his *Historie of Tithes* (1618), which went even further than his *Titles of Honour* in crossing disciplinary boundaries and integrating history with antiquarian scholarship. Offering a detailed history of tithes in England and other countries from biblical times to the late sixteenth century, this work provoked sharp criticism for its challenge to religious authority. Writing at a time when the practice of tithing was increasingly under attack in England, Selden disputed the Church's claims that this practice was grounded in divine right by showing how the payment of tithes had historically been rooted in the secular laws and customs of each country that had adopted this practice. Not only did Selden's work question the authority of the Church on the specific issue of tithes. More fundamentally, in analyzing the history of a religious practice in secular terms, his work suggested that religious history was not the purview of the divine, but was subject to the same kind of analysis – and influenced by the same kinds of forces – as other realms of history.[44]

Selden's decision to call this work a history was partly a political one, using the term history to make it appear to be a disinterested study of a subject that was highly charged in his time. Yet his characterization of this work as history was more than just a rhetorical strategy. Selden presented the results of his extensive research in chronological form, thereby imposing a narrative structure on his account that aligned his work with history, rather than with antiquarian scholarship. At the same time, in emphasizing the importance of philology to validating the truthfulness of his narrative, Selden revealed his belief in the compatibility between history and antiquarian scholarship. Far from viewing such scholarship as opposed to history, Selden suggested that it could actually enhance the value of history by giving history a firmer basis in truth. Yet Selden was not fully able to integrate all of his scholarship into a chronological narrative, revealing the difficulties involved in synthesizing history with antiquarianism.[45]

Accordingly, although Selden's work laid the basis for a synthesis of these two realms, that synthesis was by no means complete by the seventeenth century. While Selden's history was sharply attacked by supporters of the clergy who feared its erudition as a threat to the claims of the Church, those very attacks added to the prominence of the work, enabling it to serve as a model to the growing number of English scholars seeking to integrate history with antiquarian scholarship. As a result, English scholars showed an increasing recognition by the 1630s of the affinity between history and antiquarianism, without completely abandoning the distinction between the two realms.[46]

## WILLIAM BRADFORD AND PURITAN HISTORY

Even as Selden and Bacon illustrated the rise of a secular mode of historical analysis by the early seventeenth century, the heated opposition to Selden's work revealed the persisting power of religious categories of thought in the writing of history. That power was especially evident in the work of the Puritan historian William Bradford. One of the many accounts chronicling the history of American colonization by European settlers during the seventeenth and eighteenth centuries, Bradford's history of Plymouth demonstrated how important the writing of history was in justifying colonization and defining colonial identity.[47] A process that began with Columbus's "discovery" of America in 1492, European colonization of the Americas took many different forms, reflecting the varied motives that gave rise to this development. Although Columbus did not actually discover America, since he could not be said to discover an area already inhabited by Native Americans, Europeans came to understand their exploration and settlement of the Americas in these terms. And while Columbus was not even the first European to "discover" America, his voyages did mark the beginning of a period of sustained European contact with and settlement of this region. Partly a product of the changes brought about by the Renaissance, European exploration of the Americas both reflected and furthered the spirit of inquiry and the acceptance of the possibility of the new and unknown that characterized Renaissance thought. At the same time, European responses to the "New World" revealed the persistence of tradition and the ambivalence about the idea of newness that also marked this period.[48]

William Bradford reflected this ambivalence in his account of the early history of the Plymouth colony, simultaneously departing from tradition in the very act of colonization and appealing to tradition in likening the Pilgrim colonists of Plymouth to the early Christians. Founded in 1620, soon after the establishment of England's first permanent North American colony at Jamestown in 1607, the Plymouth colony differed sharply from its Jamestown predecessor both in character and the motives for its settlement. Where the motives of the Jamestown colonists were primarily economic, the Pilgrims who founded Plymouth were motivated mainly by religious concerns. Bradford took these religious concerns into his history, analyzing his subject in terms of a

providential framework and using his work to express his uncertainties about whether the colony had succeeded in its religious
mission. Yet rather than detracting from his analysis, Bradford's
religious perspective actually contributed to his concern with
accuracy and impartiality and to his recognition of the complexity
of historical causation.

The first and one of the most highly regarded of the Puritan
histories of New England, Bradford's history of Plymouth was
not published until 1856. The work was widely used by other
colonial historians, who were able to access the first book of the
history in manuscript form. Bradford wrote the first book of the
history in 1630, which covered the origins of the Plymouth colony
to its arrival in 1620. Bradford returned to the history in 1644
or 1645 and worked on it until 1650, covering the period until
1646. Bradford's prominence rested not only on his work as a
historian but also on his role as governor of Plymouth from 1621
to 1654. Bradford came from unstable beginnings, moving among
different relatives during his childhood as a result of the early
death of his parents. While living near Scrooby, England, Bradford
joined the Puritan congregation there. Unlike other Puritan historians such as John Winthrop and Cotton Mather, who came
from the Massachusetts Bay colony, founded in 1630, Bradford,
like the rest of the Pilgrim settlers of Plymouth, embraced a
separatist form of Puritanism. Both the non-separatist Puritans
of Massachusetts Bay and the separatists of Plymouth challenged
the authority of the Anglican Church, criticizing it for retaining
too much of the hierarchy and rituals of the Catholic Church.
Instead, the Puritans wished to return to the simplicity and purity
that they believed characterized the early Christian church. But
whereas the Puritans of Massachusetts Bay wished to purify and
reform the Anglican Church, the separatist Puritans of Plymouth
believed that the Anglican Church had become so corrupt that
it was beyond redemption, and for this reason wanted to break
away entirely from the Anglican Church. Subjected to persecution by English authorities on account of their challenge to the

established English Church, Bradford and his fellow pilgrims sought to escape such persecution first by going to Amsterdam in 1608, and then by establishing the Plymouth colony as a refuge where they could freely practice their religion.[49]

Portraying the Pilgrims as the "Lord's free people" whose role was to serve as the carriers of the "right worship of God and discipline of Christ" "according to the simplicity of the gospel," Bradford believed that they were enacting the will of God in founding Plymouth.[50] Embracing the Puritan belief in the total omnipotence of God and the powerlessness and sinfulness of man before God, Bradford viewed all of human history as the product of a divine plan. And so, whereas Bradford's contemporaries Bacon and Selden sought to interpret religious history in secular terms, Bradford interpreted secular events in religious terms, attributing even seemingly minor incidents to the hand of Providence, as in the case of the fate of a sailor on the Pilgrims' voyage to Plymouth who had continually mocked and cursed those suffering from seasickness. Bradford thus explained the sailor's death from a "grievous disease" as a "special work of God's providence" which reflected "the just hand of God upon him."[51] Where, then, Bradford portrayed the sufferings of the ungodly as the product of divine displeasure, he treated the successes and achievements of the Pilgrims as a sign of divine favor. Accordingly, while Bradford expressed compassion for the sufferings of Native Americans afflicted by a smallpox epidemic, he in the end justified those sufferings as the outcome of God's will, declaring that "it pleased God" to bring this sickness down upon them. The Pilgrims' immunity to the disease was in Bradford's eyes equally the product of God's will. Thus he noted, "by the marvelous goodness and providence of God, not one of the English was so much as sick or in the least measure tainted with this disease."[52]

While Bradford differed from Selden and Bacon in his providential interpretation of history, he shared their appreciation for the complexity of historical causation, offering, like Bacon, multi-causal explanations for the developments he examined. For example, he attributed the apparent degeneration of the colony from the purity of its religious ideals into what he considered sinfulness and immorality by 1642 to several different factors. In his view, part of the reason for the rise of such "wickedness" as adultery and bestiality among the Plymouth colonists "may be that the devil may carry a greater spite against the churches of Christ and the Gospel here" precisely because of their religious purity, leading the devil to make Plymouth a special target for corruption "that he might cast a blemish and stain upon them in the eyes of [the] world." At the same time, Bradford also recognized the secular forces that could have contributed to the "wickedness" he described. Like streams that burst forth all the more violently when dammed up, "so wickedness being here more stopped by strict laws … it searches everywhere and at last breaks out where it gets vent." For Bradford, the severity of the corruption he perceived was the product of the severity of the Pilgrims' religious ideals, which in imposing such tight restrictions for the suppression of even the slightest sign of immorality created a pressure that made outbursts of immorality all the more extreme. Finally, Bradford suggested that the severity of the corruption he described was no worse – and indeed better – than anywhere else, but only appeared worse because the Pilgrims placed themselves under closer moral scrutiny and made their lapses more public than was the case in other societies.[53]

Here, then, while Bradford did appeal to the supernatural as part of his explanation when he referred to the role of the devil, he did not view the supernatural as a substitute for more secular forms of explanation. On the contrary, Bradford's belief in the providential basis for all human history contributed to his interest in secular causes since he thought that Providence often worked indirectly through secular agents. Therefore, to understand the workings of Providence, it was also necessary to understand the secular forces that Providence used as its instrument. And because in Puritan belief the will of Providence was often inscrutable and difficult to grasp, it was all the more important for Bradford to closely examine history and take into account all of its complexity and uncertainty to come to a better understanding of the mysterious ways in which Providence worked. And so, ultimately for Bradford, an appreciation for the complexity of historical causation was a way to express his reverence for the omnipotence of God.[54]

Bradford's effort to account for all the problems that Plymouth faced in the latter part of his history also pointed to his uncertainties about the colony's ability to stay true to its original religious ideals. Such uncertainties were products of both the internal conflicts created by the growth of the colony and the founding of the larger and more powerful Puritan colony of Massachusetts Bay in 1630. Through his narrative of the Plymouth colony's decline away from its original ideals, Bradford at once expressed his fears that its earlier purity had been irreparably lost, and sought to combat those fears. By drawing a contrast between the purity of the colony's early years and its later fragmentation and corruption, Bradford sought to remind his readers of what they had lost and provide them with a model that would inspire them to revive that earlier purity.[55]

Bradford also shared Selden's concern with accuracy and truth not just despite, but because of his religious perspective. Owing to his assumption that all of history was the product of God's will, Bradford believed that it was necessary to record the colony's past as accurately as possible in order to understand that will and be true to it. For this reason, Bradford did not just rely on his own memory to write his work, but used letters and other manuscript sources to verify his account, including lengthy excerpts from the letters of his subjects in the body of his text. By providing such excerpts even from figures whom he sharply criticized for working against the interests of the colony, such as Thomas Weston, he was able to incorporate opposing points of view into the history, thereby revealing his sense of impartiality and allowing readers to decide for themselves if they agreed with his analysis. As Bradford put it when explaining his decision to include so many extracts from letters by his subjects, "I would not be partial to either, but deliver the truth in all, and as near as I can in their own words and passages. And so leave it to the impartial judgment of any that shall come to read or view these things."[56]

Thus, while Bradford, Selden, Bacon, and Bodin all shared a commitment to critical methods of historical writing, they differed both over the sources of their commitment and the extent to which they put those methods into practice. If, on the one hand, Selden and Bodin revealed how a commitment to such methods threatened religion, Bradford demonstrated their compatibility with his religious beliefs. And where Selden went the furthest in integrating antiquarian scholarship with history, Bacon revealed the persisting ambivalence about the relationship between these two forms of historical writing in the disparity between his prescriptions for writing history and the way in which he actually wrote his history. That ambivalence would deepen with the rise of the Enlightenment ideal of philosophical history in the eighteenth century.

# Chapter Two

## *Enlightenment and Philosophical History*

Divisions among historians took new form with the rise of the Enlightenment in the eighteenth century. Far from leading to a rejection of history, Enlightenment ideals of reason and progress gave added importance to the study of history, as Enlightenment thinkers turned to history as an important means of effecting those ideals. The notion of philosophical history that was a defining feature of Enlightenment historical writing embodied this belief in the social utility of history. Even as Enlightenment historians shared widely in the ideal of philosophical history, they differed both over the application of this ideal and its relationship to other traditions of historical writing, combining philosophical history with both the classical tradition of exemplary history and the tradition of antiquarian scholarship in different ways.

Voltaire, William Robertson, Edward Gibbon, and Mercy Otis Warren illustrated both the diversity and commonalities of Enlightenment historical writing as they put the ideal of philosophical history into practice in different ways and used it for different purposes. And so, if Voltaire used philosophical history as a weapon against organized religion, Robertson viewed religion and philosophical history as compatible with one another. And if Voltaire embodied the opposition between erudition and philosophical history, Gibbon represented the synthesis of these two approaches. Finally, while sharing many of the same assumptions about the nature and purpose of history, Mercy Otis Warren went much farther than any of these three historians in challenging the established political order, revealing both the extent of and limits to the radicalism of the Enlightenment.

## WHAT IS ENLIGHTENMENT?

The Enlightenment is a term that has been broadly used to describe the intellectual transformations of the eighteenth century, but modern scholars have hotly debated the meaning and character of this transformation, reflecting the differences among Enlightenment thinkers themselves. These differences were such that it might be more accurate to speak of the eighteenth century as a time of many Enlightenments in the plural, rather than of the Enlightenment as a unified movement.[1] The German philosopher Immanuel Kant offered an influential definition of the Enlightenment in his well-known essay, "What is Enlightenment?" Declaring that for him, Enlightenment was "man's release from his self-imposed tutelage," Kant pointed to the belief in human ability and reason that many Enlightenment thinkers shared and that accounted for why they have been grouped together into a movement, when he proclaimed that tutelage was

> man's inability to make use of his understanding without direction from another. Self-incurred is this tutelage when its cause lies not in lack of reason but in lack of resolution and courage to use it without direction from another. *Sapere aude!* "Have courage to use your own reason!"- that is the motto of enlightenment.

Kant thus urged individuals to use their own reason and think for themselves, rather than follow the dictates of tradition and established authority.[2] While, as Kant himself revealed when he pointed to how often man's tutelage was the result of his own "lack of resolution and courage," Enlightenment thinkers recognized the limits to reason and the many other forces that worked against the operation of reason in human behavior, they for the most part maintained a faith in the importance of reason as an ideal.[3]

Reason was so important to Enlightenment thinkers because

they believed it was necessary to achieve progress. Specifically, influenced by the Scientific Revolution, Enlightenment thinkers applied its understanding of the natural world to human society. Believing that human society was governed, like the natural world, by universal laws, Enlightenment thinkers assumed that it was possible for human beings to understand the workings of those laws through the exercise of their reason, and by using that understanding to improve society, Enlightenment thinkers hoped to further the progress of humanity as a whole.[4] The term *philosophe*, which Enlightenment thinkers adopted to describe themselves, revealed the social dimension to their thought, differentiating them from formal philosophers, who in their minds were more concerned with ideas for their own sake than with using them to criticize and reform society.[5] And so, while Enlightenment thinkers did not completely abandon religion, overall, they embraced a more secular perspective in which religion played a less central role than it had in the seventeenth century and placed more faith in human ability to effect historical change.[6]

Enlightenment ideas therefore had mixed effects on the study of history. While the Enlightenment rejection of traditional authority and faith in progress seemed to orient Enlightenment thinkers away from a concern with the past toward the present and future, Enlightenment thinkers actually took a great interest in history and wrote extensively about it. Hence many of the leading Enlightenment philosophes – including Voltaire, David Hume, and Diderot, to name just a few – produced works of history, or wrote broadly about their theories of history in their philosophical works, as in the case of Kant and Condorcet. Yet Enlightenment thinkers have often been criticized for being anti-historical in their approach to the past, writing about history only to condemn it and use it to further their belief in progress.[7] Viewing history as a branch of philosophy rather than as an autonomous field of inquiry, Enlightenment thinkers believed that history was by definition supposed to serve a social function. As a result, they were unable to understand the past on its own terms, imposing their belief in a universal human nature on the past and measuring historical actors according to the standards of their own time. The English philosopher and politician Lord Bolingbroke encapsulated the view of history as a form of philosophy with his widely quoted precept, taken from Dionysius of Halicarnassus, that history was "philosophy teaching by example." For Bolingbroke and other Enlightenment thinkers, the value of history rested on its ability to promote virtue by providing readers with moral examples to imitate or avoid. As Bolingbroke's reference to Dionysius of Halicarnassus revealed, this exemplary theory of history did not originate with the Enlightenment, but was firmly rooted in classical tradition.[8] A part of that tradition which attached particular importance to the moral function of history was that of civic humanism or classical republicanism, as modern scholars have labeled a constellation of ideas that gained widespread currency in eighteenth-century Anglo-American political culture. Looking to ancient Greece and Rome as models, classical republicanism was the product of a long train of development, coalescing ideas derived from such diverse sources as the classical historian Tacitus, the Renaissance political thinker Machiavelli, and eighteenth-century English opposition writers. In classical republican ideology, a healthy republic depended on virtue, for the preservation of liberty against the encroachments of power required citizens to sacrifice for the public good. Virtue was public, not private, for citizens could realize the republican ideal of civic virtue only through political or military activity – that is, either through their willingness to participate in public affairs or through their willingness to give up their lives in war. Classical republican thinkers thus looked to the examples proffered by history as an important means of instilling virtue. Among the lessons that history taught, however, was how fragile liberty was in the face of the constant encroachments of power. The more prosperous a society, the more susceptible it was to the dangers of corruption. The result was that in classical republican theory, all republics followed a cyclical pattern of rise and decline into corruption and tyranny, in which success contained the seeds of its own decay.[9]

Enlightenment historians also revealed their assumption of a universal human nature and their desire to use the past for the sake of the present in their conception of philosophical history, by which they meant a history that provided a systematic inquiry into the general laws and principles that governed human nature. Through such an analysis, they hoped to lay the basis for a science of society that would both explain and further the progress of humanity. This understanding of the historian's purpose revealed how the Enlightenment belief in human agency and efficacy laid the basis for the emergence of history as a form of rational inquiry whose purpose was to analyze and explain historical events in terms of human, rather than divine, action.[10] And so, whereas the purpose of the historian in the classical tradition of exemplary history was to narrate and relate lessons of virtue or vice, the purpose of the historian in Enlightenment philosophical history was to explain and systematize. Enlightenment historians thus aligned history with philosophy in two different senses, bringing together these various modes of historical writing in different ways.[11]

Enlightenment historians likewise varied over the relationship between philosophical history and the antiquarian tradition of scholarship that they inherited from the Renaissance. While history and antiquarian scholarship had traditionally been seen as distinct, and even opposed to one another, historians became increasingly ambivalent about the relationship between these two genres by the eighteenth century. The traditional distinction between historians and antiquarians, or érudits as they were sometimes known, was premised on the belief that history did not require any special training or even extensive research in the field. On the contrary, the most important qualification for a historian was experience in politics, while research in manuscripts or archaeological sources was considered the province of antiquaries.[12] Yet by the eighteenth century, historians showed an increasing regard for antiquarian scholarship, as the Göttingen school of German historians took the lead in developing what would become one of the distinguishing features of history as a profession – its commitment to a critical analysis of primary sources. Not only did this ideal of critical scholarship privilege the authority of primary sources; it required the historian to both verify his claims by citing his sources, and to determine their reliability by weighing them against one another for inaccuracies and inconsistencies, making the kind of manuscript research and techniques of source criticism associated with antiquarian scholarship increasingly important. A center for the study of philology and statistics, Göttingen contributed to the development of history into a science by placing the discipline on an empirical basis and providing historians with the technical skills necessary to collect and analyze their empirical data. With their training in philology and statistics, and in what were considered the "auxiliary sciences" of paleography and numismatics, the Göttingen historians were able to bring together the scholarship of the érudits with the synthetic perspective of the philosophic historians.[13]

Likewise, although by no means universal or consistent in their use of primary documents, British historians in the eighteenth century increasingly emphasized the importance of documentary research to their work. While David Hume, for example, relied on published sources for his *History of England* (1754–62) and showed little interest in original documents, William Robertson was scrupulous about using and citing primary sources, and many of his contemporaries included lengthy excerpts from such sources in their histories.[14] But even as critical scholarship became increasingly important to the writing of history, philosophical historians like Voltaire spoke all the more derisively of such scholarship in their disparagement of the "érudits" as pedantic and esoteric, a view encapsulated by Voltaire's famous maxim "Woe to details!"[15]

## "WOE TO DETAILS!": VOLTAIRE AS PHILOSOPHICAL HISTORIAN

One of the best known and most influential of the Enlightenment philosophes, Voltaire (1694–1778) revealed the importance of history to Enlightenment thinkers and played a leading role in putting the ideal of philosophical history into practice with the publication of his *Essay on Manners* in 1754, one of the first works to be considered a philosophical history.[16] From a middle-class background, Voltaire was imprisoned in the Bastille, and later exiled to England for challenging an aristocrat who had insulted him to a duel. His residence in England led to the publication of his *Philosophical Letters* (1734), his first major work of political and social criticism. Although it was suppressed in France, the success of this work and the controversy it provoked helped establish his reputation as a leading exponent of Enlightenment ideals. While his subversive views – especially when it came to religion – often put him at odds with French authorities, his talent for popularizing Enlightenment ideas and his stinging attacks on religious intolerance would also bring him renown as a man of letters throughout Europe, turning him into one of the most prominent and widely heralded of the philosophes. Consequently, he benefited from the support of wealthy patrons, including even so august a figure as Frederick the Great of Prussia, who invited Voltaire to live at his court.[17]

Voltaire took his talent for popularization into the study of history, contributing to a revival of interest in history, which had been undermined in France by the Pyrrhonists' skepticism about the usefulness and reliability of historical knowledge.[18] Voltaire first turned to this subject with the publication of his history of Charles XII of Sweden in 1731. Following the tradition of exemplary history, this work used the contrast between Charles and Peter the Great to instruct his readers in the attributes of good leadership and to illustrate the evils of war. Praising Peter the Great for his self-control and his efforts to reform and civilize

Russia, Voltaire criticized Charles for his excessive devotion to military glory. As this contrast made clear, Voltaire did not object to monarchy as a system of government in and of itself; what he criticized in Charles was his failure to use his power for the benefit of his people. As much as he urged the need to challenge traditional authority, then, Voltaire was far from democratic in his views, as he, like most of the other Enlightenment philosophes in Europe, directed his challenge against the power of established religion, not against monarchy. Viewing the power of organized religion and the aristocracy as the real threats to the advance of Enlightenment ideals, Voltaire looked to monarchs for aid in combating these forces, hoping to harness the power of monarchy to promote the progress of Enlightenment ideals. His royalist sympathies were therefore more a matter of practicality than principle.[19]

Voltaire revealed both the extent of and limits to his sympathy for monarchy in his *Age of Louis XIV* (1751). While Voltaire spoke admiringly of Louis XIV's rule as an absolute monarch, he by no means uncritically glorified Louis, condemning, for example, his revocation of the Edict of Nantes and the destructive effects of the wars upon which Louis had embarked. In addition, as he made clear in his title and his statement of purpose, his praise was ultimately directed toward the achievements of the age of Louis XIV, not of Louis as an individual. While Louis's policies played a part in those achievements, Voltaire did not attribute them solely to Louis.[20] What for Voltaire made this period "the most enlightened century that ever was" was the flourishing of the arts that took place during that era, "which, by marking an epoch in the greatness of the human mind, stand as examples to posterity."[21] The cultivation of the arts was so important to Voltaire because, as products of the mind, the state of the arts marked the progress of human reason, and were thus a sign of and means to achieving Enlightenment ideals. To illustrate and explain the development of the arts, Voltaire directed his attention to the history of manners, meaning the history of social and cultural life. In doing so, he expanded the boundaries of history, departing from the traditional emphasis on the history of politics and military affairs. For this reason, he warned his readers that his work would not provide "the exhaustive detail of wars, towns besieged, taken and retaken by force of arms, given and regained by treaty," since his concern was with "that which merits the attention of the ages," namely "that which depicts the genius and manners of men, or which serves to instruct and inculcate the love of country, of virtue, and of art." Consequently, while the first half of the work offered a chronological account of military and political developments, the second half focused on the history of manners, examining developments in areas like the economy and the arts and sciences.[22]

Voltaire went even further in departing from the traditional boundaries of history by making the history of social and cultural life the main subject of his *Essay on Manners*, the most influential of his historical works, first published in 1754 and repeatedly revised by him, with the final edition appearing posthumously in 1785. Covering a broad geographic and temporal span, this work traced the emergence of European civilization from the time of Charlemagne to the beginning of the age of Louis XIV. Wishing to transcend national prejudices in favor of a more cosmopolitan perspective, Voltaire sought to look at the development of Europe as a whole by incorporating the histories of many different European nations and their contributions to civilization. While in making Europe the focus of his analysis, he revealed his assumption that civilization was a European attribute, he placed his discussion of European history in a broader context by devoting substantial attention to areas of the world outside Europe, beginning the work with accounts of Asian and Arab history.[23]

While he did not succeed fully in integrating all of the different national histories he included into a unified narrative of the development of European civilization, he was the first of the Enlightenment historians to make such a narrative his goal, thus establishing a model of philosophical history that would have an important influence on other Enlightenment historians.[24] The *Essay* was a philosophical history in offering a broad perspective that sought to explain the rise of civilization in secular terms and to use this explanation to draw wider conclusions about the nature and causes of human progress. Recognizing the many different forces that contributed to the progress of civilization, Voltaire revealed his secular perspective and his desire to look beyond the political and military realm in the emphasis that he placed on economic factors. In his account, the growth of towns – and the commercial development they fostered – together with the growing power of monarchy played an important part in creating the stability and prosperity necessary for cultural advancement. While these conditions were largely in place by the sixteenth century, the persisting influence of religious fanaticism and conflict had destructive effects that limited and offset the progress of culture during this period. Only with the diminishing power of such fanaticism by the beginning of the age of Louis XIV was Europe – and in particular France – ready to fulfill that progress with the cultural flowering that occurred in this period.[25] In identifying the growth of civilization with the declining power of Christianity, Voltaire both reflected and furthered his hostility to organized religion. This hostility would become increasingly apparent in the later editions of his work, as he revised the *Essay* to place more emphasis on the harmful effects of religious fanaticism, with the result that the later editions took on a more polemical tone and employed more simplistic categories of analysis to describe the conflicts between the forces of civilization and its opponents. Thus, if Voltaire's desire to promote Enlightenment ideals contributed to his interest in history and his innovative approach to the subject, it also in the end led him to turn away from history in favor of philosophy.[26]

## WILLIAM ROBERTSON: STADIAL HISTORY AND THE SCOTTISH ENLIGHTENMENT

Sharing Voltaire's desire to broaden the boundaries of history into the social and cultural realm, the Scottish historian William Robertson at the same time revealed the varied forms that philosophical history could take and the different social purposes it could serve. Accordingly, while partly influenced by Voltaire, Robertson's interest in the history of manners also stemmed from his commitment to what has become known as the four-stage theory of history, or Scottish stadial theory, so-called because it was a theory of history closely identified with the Scottish Enlightenment. In its analysis of how societies followed the same laws of development, the four-stage theory of history embodied the broad perspective of philosophical history. While, then, Robertson shared Voltaire's aspirations to philosophical history, as a Presbyterian clergyman who held a leading position in the Church of Scotland, he differed from Voltaire in seeing no conflict between this ideal and a faith in organized religion.

Robertson was part of a larger circle of Scottish Enlightenment thinkers that included such figures as Adam Smith, David Hume, and Adam Ferguson. The emergence of this circle and its influence on Enlightenment thought pointed to the development of Scotland into a major center for learning and culture during this period. Paradoxically, the rise of Scotland as an intellectual center came at a time when Scotland had lost its political autonomy with the Act of Union in 1707, which officially unified England, Scotland, and Wales into one kingdom with one political system and an integrated economy that allowed free trade within the United Kingdom. While Scottish elites welcomed the economic benefits that the Act of Union brought for Scotland as well as the broader scope and audience for their views which closer ties with England gave them, they were also uneasy about the loss of political independence that came with the elimination of their own parliament under the Act of Union. The primacy that classical republican ideals gave to political participation as the ultimate expression of virtue and the basis for citizenship made the loss of political autonomy all the more cause for anxiety to Scottish elites during this period. One way in which Scottish Enlightenment thinkers adapted to this transformation was by turning away from the formal political arena in favor of the institutions of civil society – commerce, literature and the arts, and social clubs – as arenas for the exercise of virtue. Scottish moralists could in this way base their own claims to citizenship and civic morality on their participation in commercial and cultural activities, rather than on their political involvement. The greater regard that Scottish Enlightenment thinkers gave to cultural endeavor helped foster the intellectual flowering that occurred in this period and shaped its content.[27]

Scottish Enlightenment historians took their regard for the civic value of commercial and cultural activity and extended it to their study of the past through their interest in the history of manners. The most notable expression of their interest in this topic was the four-stage theory of history that Scottish conjectural historians used to explain the rise of commercial society. According to this theory, all human societies followed the same natural laws of social development to progress through a series of stages – the hunter, the pastoral, the agricultural, and the commercial (in the most common variant of this scheme) – with each stage defined by its mode of subsistence, and each one more civilized and advanced than the last.[28] This understanding of social development contributed to the growing interest in the history of manners and social life by making commerce the engine and culmination of human progress. Because of this assumption, the Scottish conjectural historians devoted substantial attention to the development and effects of commerce in their histories.[29]

This four-stage theory of history has come to be closely associated with the Scottish Enlightenment because its leading exponents included Scottish philosophers and historians like John Millar, Adam Ferguson, William Robertson, and Adam Smith.

While most of these historians would not themselves have used the term "conjectural" to speak of their work, the Scottish moral philosopher Dugald Stewart first used the term "conjectural history" to describe this school of historical writing. The work of these historians came to be known as conjectural history owing to their belief that the gaps in the historical record and the lack of historical documents for the earlier stages in their theory required them to conjecture about what had happened in those earlier stages. Believing that the purpose of history was to contribute to a science of society, these historians did not consider their conjectures to be a form of speculation, since they based their conclusions on what they believed were larger universal truths about human nature. By using what they knew about human nature to explain human behavior in earlier periods of history, they could fill in the gaps in their factual knowledge about the past. In turn, by explaining human development in this way, these historians hoped to make knowledge about human nature and society more systematic and scientific.[30]

One of the most influential and successful exponents of Scottish stadial theory was William Robertson (1721–93). The son of a minister, Robertson became a minister himself, achieving an influential position as leader of the moderate wing of the Church of Scotland. After publishing his first historical work – his *History of Scotland* – in 1759 to great popular and critical success, Robertson was appointed Historiographer Royal of Scotland and Principal of Edinburgh University, a position that made him a leading figure in Scottish intellectual life.[31] Robertson's reputation as a historian would only grow with the publication of his next historical work in 1769, *The History of the Reign of the Emperor Charles V*. As was the case with Voltaire's *Age of Louis XIV*, Robertson's *History of Charles V* was not meant simply to be the biography of an individual, but aimed to give a portrait of the times in which Charles lived. Robertson revealed his desire to examine Charles's reign from a broader perspective by preceding his account of Charles himself with "A View of the Progress of

Society in Europe" – the best-known and most influential section of the work – which gave a more general analysis of the development of feudal society in Europe. Robertson pointed both to the influence of Voltaire's *Essay on Manners* on his analysis and his differences from Voltaire in one of his notes for the "View."[32] Explaining why he had not cited Voltaire's *Essay* earlier in his work, Robertson praised Voltaire for the versatility of his literary talents, adding,

> In all, if he had left religion untouched, he is instructive and agreeable. But as he seldom imitates the example of the modern historians in citing the authors from whom they derive their information, I could not, with propriety, appeal to his authority in confirmation of any doubtful or unknown fact. I have often, however, followed him as my guide in these researches; and he has not only pointed out the facts with respect to which it was of importance to inquire, but the conclusions which it was proper to draw from them.[33]

While sharing Voltaire's interest in manners and his cosmopolitan perspective, Robertson revealed his greater regard for religion in his criticism of Voltaire's treatment of this subject. And as his criticism of Voltaire's carelessness about citing sources demonstrated, Robertson was much more scrupulous and systematic in his research than Voltaire was, not only basing his works on extensive research in primary sources but providing citations to his sources.[34]

Following the lead of Voltaire's *Essay*, Robertson sought to explain the progress of civilization in his "View of the Progress of Society," and like Voltaire, Robertson associated civilization with a cosmopolitan viewpoint. For this reason, a central theme in the "View" was the process by which European nations moved away from a view of themselves as self-contained entities isolated from one another to a recognition of their interconnections and interdependence on one another. The role that Robertson assigned to the

Crusades in this transformation revealed the complex relationship between religion and Enlightenment ideals in his work. While, in keeping with Enlightenment hostility to religious extremism, Robertson was critical of the folly and fanaticism of the Crusades, Robertson also believed that they had unintentionally contributed to progress by broadening the perspectives of its participants and stimulating commerce, which in turn played an important role in refining and softening the manners of medieval Europeans. If, in the role that he gave to commerce as an agent of refinement, Robertson adhered to the assumptions of stadial history and its desire to explain historical development in terms of material forces, he at the same time revealed his own religious sympathies in giving religion a constructive role – however unintentional – in furthering commerce and the refinement of manners.[35]

Robertson likewise brought together religion with his commitment to stadial theory in the main text of his history of Charles V through the role he gave to the Reformation in bringing Europe out of what he believed was the darkness and superstition of medieval society. Interpreting the Reformation as an instrument of "peculiar providence," Robertson revealed the providential element in his theory of historical causation. While, as a devout Presbyterian, Robertson adhered firmly to the view that history was the expression of divine will, he believed that Providence generally expressed its will through secondary causes that were secular in character. For this reason, he saw no conflict between his providential perspective and his Enlightenment view of history as a form of rational inquiry into secular causes. Believing that such an inquiry would indirectly illuminate the workings of Providence, he did not consider it necessary to make frequent reference to providential supervision over human affairs. The Reformation was for Robertson an important such secondary cause. In his view, for all their destructiveness and fanaticism, the religious conflicts provoked by the Reformation also had a beneficial effect in energizing and freeing the human mind from its previous acceptance of established authority, thereby contributing to a desire for liberty which Robertson associated with the progress of commercial society. The division between Catholic and Protestant, while destructive in the short term, in the long run contributed to the rise of religious toleration and resulted in a more humane and moderate form of Christianity based on an acceptance of religious pluralism.[36]

Building on the analysis of his "View of the Progress of Society," Robertson articulated most clearly the assumptions of Scottish stadial theory in his next work, the *History of America*, first published in 1777. Although Robertson had intended to cover the entire history of European colonization of the Americas, he did not complete his history of America, publishing only the sections dealing with Spanish colonization, and leaving the sections he had written on British colonization of North America unpublished on his death. Robertson attributed this decision to the outbreak of the American Revolution, which in his view made "inquiries and speculations" about the history of the British colonies no longer of interest. The volumes that he did publish examined Spanish colonization from the time of Columbus's "discovery" of America to the conquest of Mexico and Peru, concluding with an analysis of the overall effects of Spanish and Portuguese colonization that extended into the eighteenth century. Revealing his belief in the importance of commerce to historical development, Robertson began his work with a history of commerce that went back to ancient Greece and Rome. In keeping with the assumptions of Scottish stadial theory, Robertson pointed to the power of commerce as a civilizing force when he spoke of how it broadened perspectives and promoted a spirit of intellectual curiosity and enterprise that gave rise to European exploration and colonization of the Americas.[37]

Robertson revealed how the four-stage theory served to justify the conquest and dispossession of Native Americans by Europeans as he directly applied its assumptions to his analysis of Native Americans. Interpreting the conflict between the Spanish and Native Americans as one between two societies in different stages of development, Robertson justified and explained Spanish conquest over Native Americans by identifying the Spanish with a more advanced stage of commercial development. Characterizing Native Americans as belonging to the more primitive pastoral stage of development, Robertson continually disparaged them as backward and inferior to Europeans, even while expressing sympathy for their sufferings at the hands of the Spanish and criticizing the Spanish for their cruelty. Yet in pointing to how such cruelty forced Native Americans out of their indolence and contributed to the economic growth and prosperity of the colonies, he suggested that the dispossession and destruction of Native Americans, however tragic, was a necessary stage in the progress of commercial society. For all his disparagement of Native Americans, Robertson at the same time displayed a certain fascination with them, devoting book 4 of his history to a discussion of their manners and customs. Robertson likewise took his interest in the history of manners into his analysis of the Incas and Aztecs, offering a lengthy discussion of their social and cultural history in book 7 of his work. In this way, Robertson demonstrated how stadial theory at once contributed to the denigration of these cultures as inferior to Europeans and stimulated an interest in them as a way of shedding light on the earlier stages of social development that stadialists believed all cultures had gone through.[38]

## EDWARD GIBBON: ERUDITION AND PHILOSOPHICAL HISTORY

The ideas of Voltaire and Robertson came together with the influence of other historiographical traditions in the work of Edward Gibbon (1737–94). One of the most highly regarded Enlightenment historians, Gibbon contributed to the development of historical writing through his ability to synthesize the broad perspective of philosophical history and its concern with making larger generalizations about human nature with the scholarship and research of the érudits in his *Decline and Fall of the Roman Empire* (1776–88).[39] While viewing himself as a philosophical historian whose purpose was to unify his research into a coherent narrative that would enable him to draw larger generalizations about the past, he at the same time departed from its assumptions of universality to show a greater recognition of historical diversity and of the differences between past and present.[40]

Financially dependent on his father, Gibbon converted to Catholicism while at Oxford, but eventually renounced his conversion to Catholicism and reconverted to Protestantism after his father sent him to Switzerland for this purpose. His studies during his time in Lausanne played an important role in his intellectual development, contributing to his decision to become a writer and providing him with the education and training that laid the foundations for his historical scholarship. While in Lausanne, Gibbon also met Voltaire. After his return to England, he published his first essay on literature in 1761. His decision to write the *Decline and Fall* came during his first trip to Rome in 1764.[41] As Gibbon described this moment, "It was at Rome, on the fifteenth of October, 1764, as I sat musing amidst the ruins of the Capitol, while the barefooted fryars were singing Vespers in the temple of Jupiter, that the idea of writing the decline and fall of the City first started to my mind."[42] He did not begin working on the *Decline and Fall* until 1773, however, publishing the first volume in 1776, the next two volumes in 1781, and the final three in 1788. Like his contemporaries, Gibbon did not view history as an enterprise that required his exclusive attention, or as a field of study separate from politics and other areas of endeavor. Hence, while working on the *Decline and Fall*, he also entered politics, successfully running for Parliament in 1774, where he served until 1780. Gibbon himself pointed to this experience and to his service in the militia between 1760 and 1762 as important influences on his perspective as a historian.[43]

Gibbon made his name with the publication of the *Decline and Fall*. Although the first volume stirred sharp controversy for its critique of religion, it was highly successful, going through three editions within a year of publication.[44] The product of vast research in a wide variety of sources, ranging from ancient Greek and Roman histories to the works of seventeenth-century French ecclesiastical scholars, Gibbon's history relied heavily on what was then considered antiquarian research in such subjects as chronology and the study of coins and medals. Gibbon attested to his research and his commitment to a critical analysis of sources in the footnotes for which his work has been famed, using them to comment on the reliability of his sources and to point out their inaccuracies. What made his footnotes so famous was the ironic wit that he displayed in them, since he used them not just to cite his sources but to offer mocking jibes exposing instances of human frailty and hypocrisy, directed especially against religion.[45]

Rather than seeing such research as opposed to philosophical history, Gibbon combined his erudition with the broad perspective of a philosophical historian as he sought to explain the causes of the decline of the Roman Empire. While recognizing the many different forces that contributed to the destruction of the Roman Empire, Gibbon emphasized in particular the twin forces of "barbarism and religion" in bringing down the empire. Accordingly, a major organizing theme throughout the work was the opposition between barbarism and civilization. In his use of these categories, Gibbon reflected the influence of Scottish stadial history and its assumption that some cultures were at a more advanced stage of development than others. At the same time, while sharing its faith in commerce as an engine of progress, he questioned the primacy that Scottish stadial theory gave to economic factors as the driving force in social development. And while his language echoed that of Scottish stadial theory, describing ancient European tribes in terms very similar to those used by Scottish stadial thinkers to speak of the hunter and pastoral stages of development, Gibbon questioned their assumption that all societies followed the same universal laws of development, differentiating, for example, between Africans, whom he believed were unable to improve, and the early Germanic tribes, whom he believed possessed this capacity.[46]

Referring to the ancient European tribes that would eventually overrun Rome as barbarians, Gibbon revealed his view of them as backward and primitive through the terms he used to describe them. Speaking of the "fierce savagery" of these tribes, he associated barbarism with irrationality and a lawless freedom when he contrasted the discipline of Roman armies with the "impetuous and irregular passions of barbarians."[47] For Gibbon, then, to be barbaric was to follow instinct and do whatever one wanted without thinking about others or about long-term consequences. By contrast, he suggested, civilization was defined by self-control and a concern for others. Even while this contrast privileged civilized society as superior to barbarism, Gibbon did not completely denigrate the early European tribes. The very qualities that made them barbaric also gave them an independence and strength that more civilized societies lacked and enabled them to eventually conquer Rome. His description of the ancient Britons as possessing "valor without conduct" and "love of freedom without a spirit of union" thus mixed disparagement with a certain respect for their virtues.[48]

Conversely, while Gibbon identified ancient Rome with civilization, he did not uncritically glorify Roman society, recognizing how its very greatness contained the seeds of its own decay. Even at his most celebratory in the opening to his work, when he enthused that "in the second century of the Christian Æra, the empire of Rome comprehended the fairest part of the earth, and the most civilized portion of mankind," he subtly punctured Roman claims to greatness by immediately pointing to the underlying threats to that greatness when he spoke of how its inhabitants "enjoyed and abused the advantages of wealth and luxury," and of how "the image of a free constitution was preserved with decent reverence. The Roman Senate appeared to possess the sovereign authority, and devolved on the emperors all the executive powers of government."[49] In pointing to how imperial Rome maintained only the appearance of freedom, Gibbon revealed his belief that the decline of Rome was the product of a long process that had already begun with the overthrow of the republic.[50] Although Rome enjoyed a golden age of prosperity during the reign of the Antonines, that prosperity was tenuous, dependent as it was on the will of a single individual, and in its own way laid the basis for Roman decline. As Gibbon explained,

> This long peace, and the uniform government of the Romans, introduced a slow and secret poison into the vitals of the empire. The minds of men were gradually reduced to the same level, the fire of genius was extinguished, and even the military spirit evaporated.[51]

Ultimately for Gibbon, the decline of Rome was the product of its own success, as the long period of peace and prosperity it enjoyed under the Antonines softened and corrupted its inhabitants, depriving them of the vigor that was necessary to maintain their liberty against both internal and external threats. This explanation for Roman decline reflected the influence of classical republican ideals on Gibbon. While his concern with the corrupting effects of prosperity adhered to the classical republican belief in the need for civic virtue and its fear of power and luxury as threats to virtue, his analysis of how the prosperity of Rome brought with it the seeds of its own decay was consistent with the cyclical view of history that classical republican thinkers had long used to explain the rise and fall of republican governments.[52]

Yet if he seemed to embrace a cyclical theory of history in his analysis of Roman decline, Gibbon also shared in the Enlightenment belief in progress. He affirmed his belief in progress and revealed his awareness of the differences between past and present in the contrast he set between ancient Rome and the Europe of his own time, declaring,

> It is the duty of the patriot to prefer and promote the exclusive interest and glory of his native country: but a philosopher may

be permitted to enlarge his views, and to consider Europe as one great republic, whose various inhabitants have attained almost the same level of politeness and cultivation. The balance of power will continue to fluctuate, and the prosperity of our own, or the neighboring kingdoms may be alternately exalted or depressed; but these partial events cannot essentially injure our general state of happiness, the system of arts, and laws, and manners, which so advantageously distinguish, above the rest of mankind, the Europeans and their colonies.[53]

In pointing to the progress of Europe as a whole rather than singling out that of a particular nation, Gibbon revealed the cosmopolitan perspective that characterized so much of Enlightenment philosophical history. While recognizing the importance of nations, this cosmopolitan viewpoint emphasized the need to look beyond nationalistic prejudices and acknowledge the interdependence and interconnectedness of European nations with one another. In addition, in attributing the prosperity of Europe to its balance of power, Gibbon pointed to another reason for the decline of Rome – its imperial conquests, which turned it into a universal monarchy that controlled all of Europe. Not only was this system oppressive, making it impossible to escape from the power of Rome, but the homogenization and uniformity that resulted from imperial expansion had a stultifying effect, discouraging the kind of diversity and interdependence that would promote intellectual growth and civilization. At the same time that he affirmed his belief in progress, then, Gibbon's analysis of Roman decline highlighted its fragility, offering an implicit warning to his contemporaries that if one power conquered in his own time like Rome did, Europe could suffer the same fate as Rome.[54]

In pairing religion with barbarism as the two most important forces in the decline of Rome, Gibbon also shared in the Enlightenment challenge to the authority of established religion. This pairing put Christianity in a negative light by reversing the traditional association between Christianity and civilization, and turning it into a force that had destroyed rather than furthered Roman civilization. In promoting an ascetic mindset that directed attention away from this world to the next, and giving primacy to such qualities as submission and humility, Christianity weakened the attachment of its adherents to the empire and undermined the martial virtue and concern for social usefulness that Gibbon believed were necessary for a healthy society.[55] Gibbon thus turned Christian assumptions on their head, taking the qualities lauded by Christianity as virtues and showing how they had helped destroy the Roman Empire. One of the main techniques that Gibbon used to further his critique of religion was irony. Although Gibbon revealed his ironic perspective throughout his work, making the disparity between appearance and reality a central theme in his analysis, he used irony to greatest effect in his critique of Christianity.[56] Gibbon's use of irony reflected and furthered the ambiguity in his own religious views after his reconversion to Protestantism. Because of that ambiguity, modern scholars have differed over whether his critique of Christianity was that of a Deist who was totally anti-Christian or that of a Christian who believed that the organized church had departed from true Christianity.[57] Regardless of what his actual religious views were, his treatment of the rise of Christianity in chapters 15 and 16 was seen as anti-religious, causing such controversy that he had to soften his critique in later editions of the chapters, even though he did not directly attack Christianity in these chapters. Critical of Voltaire and some of the other philosophes for being too extreme in their attacks on religion, Gibbon turned to irony as an effective strategy for excoriating religion while maintaining a posture of rational distance and detachment that avoided the excesses he criticized in Voltaire.[58] Gibbon used irony on many different levels throughout chapter 15. The whole purpose and structure of the chapter was ironic in that its goal was really the opposite of what he claimed it was.[59]

Beginning the chapter by paying obeisance to the traditional Christian explanation for the rise of this faith, Gibbon pointed to the "obvious but satisfactory answer" "that it was owing to the convincing evidence of the doctrine itself, and to the ruling Providence of its great author," and characterized the secular forces he described merely as "secondary causes." Yet in focusing his analysis on these secular forces, he made them seem primary, not secondary, implicitly challenging the assumption that the explanation for the rise of Christianity was the inherent validity of its doctrines and the role of God in promoting them. In his account, then, there was nothing special or divine about the rise of Christianity, directly contrary to his opening statement; it was just an important historical force that needed to be explained just like any other historical force.[60] He further undermined Christianity through the nature of his explanation. Even while purporting to defend Christianity against the stigma of its appeal to the poor and uneducated, he reinforced that stigma by pointing to all the learned and respected philosophers who rejected the religion. While seeming to lament that such a great thinker as Seneca had not seen fit to adopt Christianity, he actually implied the opposite, suggesting that the rejection of Christianity by someone as intelligent as Seneca was a sign that there was something wrong with the religion. Thus his explanation for the appeal of Christianity actually sought to highlight how unappealing it was as a religion.[61]

## MERCY OTIS WARREN: EXEMPLARY HISTORY AS REVOLUTIONARY HISTORY

In the same year that Gibbon published the first volume of his history, Americans declared their independence from Britain. Although colonial writers such as Thomas Hutchinson or Cotton Mather had already produced accounts of their colonies' histories before the American Revolution, the Revolution and the achievement of independence from Britain stimulated American interest in history and gave that interest new direction, as American revolutionary historians used history to justify the Revolution and define national identity. Among the best known of these historians, Mercy Otis Warren (1728–1814), like the other revolutionary historians, shared in the Enlightenment view of history as a form of philosophy. Warren and her fellow revolutionary historians differed, however, from most of their European counterparts in using this exemplary theory of history to challenge the belief in monarchy and the established political order. Warren revealed both the extent of and limits to that challenge as she sought to promote republican ideals in her history of the American Revolution.

Writing at a time when national bonds were still tenuous and uncertain, the revolutionary historians sought to promote a greater sense of national unity in their works by downplaying the differences that divided Americans. These historians had, for the most part, supported the Revolution, and many of them had actively participated in the Revolution. In addition to Warren, this generation of historians included David Ramsay, Edmund Randolph, Jeremy Belknap, John Daly Burk, Hugh McCall, George Minot, Hugh Williamson, and John Marshall. Like their European counterparts, the revolutionary historians for the most part came from the elites.[62] Predominantly Federalist in their political allegiances, the revolutionary historians also included staunch Republicans like Mercy Otis Warren and John Daly Burk. Although their histories at times served partisan purposes, the revolutionary historians for the most part sought to transcend partisan bias in their histories. Likewise, while their histories reflected their sectional loyalties, national unity took precedence over sectional allegiances. With the exception of Warren's and Ramsay's histories of the Revolution, these historians for the most part did not write about the nation's history as a whole. Coming from different regions of the country, the revolutionary historians revealed their own strong sense of regional and provincial identity in choosing to write primarily about their states and localities. Hence, the first history published in the new nation was Jeremy Belknap's *History of New Hampshire* (1784–92), and historians from other parts of the country followed suit by publishing studies of individual states, such as Burk's *History of Virginia* (1804–5) or Hugh Williamson's *History of North Carolina* (1812). Yet these historians saw no conflict between their local loyalties and their nationalistic purposes. They portrayed their region as the nation in miniature and projected their regional values onto the nation as a whole.[63]

The moral function of history was all the more important to these historians because they shared with many of their fellow revolutionaries a commitment to classical republican ideals. Because of the importance of virtue to republican ideals, these historians saw no conflict between their political concerns and the writing of history. The revolutionary historians viewed the writing of history as itself a revolutionary act since, by providing their readers with moral examples to follow, they hoped to instill the kind of virtue necessary for the preservation of liberty.[64]

Mercy Otis Warren both followed and departed from her contemporaries as she sought to promote republican virtue in her history. Born into one of the leading political families in Massachusetts, Warren was able to acquire an education at a time when women possessed very limited opportunities for education by learning from her brother James and the tutors to her brothers. With her marriage to James Warren, she joined another of the leading political families in the colony. Both her husband and her brother James Otis, Jr. were active figures in revolutionary resistance to British measures, while Warren vigorously supported the Revolution in her own right through the plays and propaganda she wrote. Her history of the Revolution, published in 1805, represented a continuation of her revolutionary activism.[65] Yet her gender gave that activism a different cast, since she wrote at a time when the belief in women's inferiority to men generally excluded them from both participation in politics and the writing of history. Because virtue was considered a quality that was based on reason, women, as beings governed by the passions, in classical republican theory inherently lacked the capacity to live up to its requirements for citizenship. Women were by the same token excluded from the writing of history as an intellectual enterprise that required the exercise of reason. Because history had been traditionally defined to entail the study of politics and war, the exclusion of women from these arenas further disqualified them from the writing of history on the basis that they lacked the experience necessary to discuss these subjects.[66] Despite such prohibitions, some women in the eighteenth century were able to publish on historical subjects, either in a formal history as in the case of Catharine Macaulay or in other formats such as memoirs and travel writing.[67] Although unusual, then, Warren's history was not entirely unprecedented. In the preface to her history of the American Revolution, Warren simultaneously upheld the assumptions that had excluded women from the writing of history and challenged those assumptions when she apologized for her foray into this male sphere, admitting that "it is the more peculiar province of masculine strength, not only to repel the bold invader of the rights of his country and of mankind, but in the nervous style of manly eloquence, to describe the blood-stained field, and relate the story of slaughtered armies." Here, Warren reasoned that it fell to men to write about history, for they were the actors in the events that she considered the proper subject matter of history – war and political affairs. When she spoke of "manly eloquence," Warren suggested that the very ability to recount and describe these events was a male attribute. For this reason, Warren expressed great trepidation at the thought of writing a history herself and spoke of how "the trembling heart has recoiled at the magnitude of the undertaking." In emphasizing her "trembling heart," Warren reaffirmed the association between women and emotion that had traditionally disqualified women from writing about history.[68]

Yet because the Revolution had affected women too, Warren believed that she had both a right and a responsibility to write about this event. As she explained, "recollecting that every domestic enjoyment depends on the unimpaired possession of civil and religious liberty, that a concern for the welfare of society ought equally to glow in every human breast," she could not abandon her history despite her qualms about entering a traditionally male sphere. While firmly committed to the prevailing belief in women's domestic role, Warren did not think that this role precluded an interest in public affairs. On the contrary, because liberty was as necessary to the domestic as it was to the political realm, it was incumbent upon women to do what they could to promote it. Thus, even though she did not question the subordination of women in her analysis of the Revolution, simply in writing a history at all, Warren challenged the traditional exclusion of women from participation in the political sphere.[69]

Following classical republican precepts in her fear of power as a constant threat to liberty, Warren identified avarice and ambition as the "leading springs" in human action and cited ancient Rome and Britain to illustrate how "[t]he love of domination and an uncontrolled lust of arbitrary power have prevailed among all nations, and perhaps in proportion to the degrees of civilization." Interpreting the American Revolution as a struggle between British corruption and American virtue, Warren viewed the taxes imposed by the British on the colonists as part of a plot to enslave Americans and destroy their liberty. She therefore saw revolutionary resistance to such measures as both a sign and means of preserving American virtue. Emphasizing the unified and orderly character of revolutionary protests against British policy, Warren argued that such unity had enabled the revolutionaries to prevail against Britain and win their independence.[70]

Yet for Warren the achievement of independence did not mean that republican ideals were secure. Herself a staunch Jeffersonian Republican, writing at a time when partisan divisions between Republicans and Federalists were emerging, Warren feared that republican ideals were yet again in danger – this time from Americans themselves, as the political partisanship of this period and what appeared to be a growing absorption in material gain threatened to undermine the republican ideals of virtue and self-sacrifice that the revolutionaries had fought to preserve. Warren expressed such fears when she commented on how the achievements of the revolutionaries had been forgotten and the principles for which they had fought "nearly annihilated" "amidst the rage of the accumulation and the taste for expensive pleasures that have since prevailed; a taste that has abolished that mediocrity which once satisfied, and that contentment which long smiled in every countenance."[71] Through her history, Warren not only hoped to remind her contemporaries of revolutionary achievements and principles; she also sought to revive those principles by holding the revolutionaries up as exemplars of republican virtue for present-day Americans to emulate.[72]

Calling for "an undeviating adherence to the principles that produced the revolution," Warren expressed her firm commitment to the ideal of equality when she declared that those principles "were grounded on the natural equality of man, their right of adopting their own modes of government, the dignity of the people, and that sovereignty which cannot be ceded either to representatives or to kings."[73] While, then, Warren went much further in her challenge to monarchy than did her European counterparts, her disparaging references to the "incendiary and turbulent set of people" who took part in such popular protests as Shays Rebellion at the same time demonstrated the elite bias to her understanding of equality. Although she based the authority of government on the sovereignty of the people, she also, in keeping with classical republican assumptions, expected them to defer to gentlemen like her husband who possessed the independence and education to know best what would serve the public good.[74]

Warren's portrayal of Native Americans revealed even more clearly the limits to her understanding of equality. Like Robertson, her depiction of Native Americans contained a certain duality that reflected the influence of Scottish stadial theory on her work. As much as she celebrated the Revolution, she recognized the costs it exacted from Native Americans, expressing sympathy for their dispossession and sufferings, and criticizing white brutality against them. Echoing the language that Gibbon used to describe the "pastoral nations" of Europe, Warren portrayed Native Americans as savages who belonged to a more primitive stage of society than European Americans, while recognizing their merits, when she declared, "[I]f they have not civilization they have valor; if they have not patriotism they have a predilection to country." For this reason, she lamented, "however the generous or humane mind may revolt at the idea, there appears a probability, that they will be hunted from the vast American continent, if not from off the face of the globe" by Europeans, "aided by the interested Americans." In Warren's view, the only alternative to extermination was to "civilize" Native Americans, which for her meant teaching them to adopt the practices and ideals of white American culture. She drew directly on the assumptions of Scottish stadial theory to explain why she believed Native Americans were capable of being civilized in this way. The evolution of "the most refined and polite modern nations" from their earlier state of "rude, ignorant" savagery demonstrated that it was possible for Native Americans to likewise evolve from their savage state to a more civilized one, since "there is no difference in the moral or intellectual capacity of nations, but what arises from adventitious circumstances." For Warren, then, the progression "from the rude states of nature to the highest pitch of refinement" was a universal one that all societies went through.[75] As she in this analysis expressed the broad perspective of a philosophical historian, she revealed both the extent of and limits to her understanding of equality. If on the one hand she affirmed a belief in the equality of Native Americans in her claims that they possessed the same capacity for civilization as Europeans and white Americans, on the other hand she still judged Native Americans according to white standards of civilization, revealing her inability to understand Native American culture on its own terms.[76]

Warren also lived up to the precepts of philosophical history in providing a secular explanation for the Revolution. But even as she overall placed more emphasis than her predecessors did on the role of human agency in shaping the historical process, she did not deny a role for Providence altogether. Thus, for Warren, the embrace of Enlightenment ideals did not require a repudiation of religion. Warren reconciled the role she gave to Providence with her belief in human agency by portraying Providence as a general guiding force in history, rather than as a being that intervened directly in historical events. While suggesting that the Revolution was part of a divine plan, she also believed that it was up to human beings to realize that plan. Warren expressed this sense of divine mission in the conclusion to her work when she spoke of how the United States could serve as an example to the world "of peace, liberty, righteousness, and truth," bringing civilization to the "western wilds" so that

> this last civilized quarter of the globe may exhibit striking traits of grandeur and magnificence, which the Divine Economist may have reserved to crown the closing scene, when the angel of his presence will stand upon the sea and upon the earth, lift up his hand to heaven, and swear by Him that liveth forever and ever, that there shall be time no longer.[77]

Warren's imagery here brought together a traditional Christian vision of the millennium with an Enlightenment view of Providence as "the Divine Economist," a characterization that put Providence on an almost human level, making Providence seem simply like a figure whose purpose was to systematize and order human affairs in the way that an economist would.

Thus, Warren, Gibbon, Robertson, and Voltaire in different ways brought together seemingly opposed ideals – reason and religion, erudition and philosophical history, and a belief in the value of history with a faith in progress. As they did so, these historians revealed both the extent of and limits to their departure from their Renaissance and seventeenth-century predecessors. While they embraced overall a more secular view of history that gave primacy to human agency as a causal force, Warren and Robertson revealed the persistence of a providential view of history. And while Gibbon went much further in integrating erudition and history than did his predecessors, Voltaire's disparagement of erudite scholarship revealed the persisting opposition between these two forms of historical writing. Just as Enlightenment historians followed and departed from their predecessors, so too would their successors of the nineteenth century both build upon and break away from their ideas.

# Chapter Three

## *Romantic and Critical History*

The nineteenth century was a time when history seemed to come into its own, fueled by the reaction against the French Revolution – in particular by the rise of nationalism and Romanticism. The writing of history grew even more politicized during this period as interest in history became an increasingly pervasive presence in European and American culture, making it a powerful source of legitimacy for historians and thinkers of strikingly different political persuasions and backgrounds.[1] Paradoxically, the nineteenth century was also the time when historians showed a growing interest in the past for its own sake with the rise of two seemingly opposed approaches to history – the view of history as a form of Romantic art, in which the historian's purpose was to make the past come alive for the reader, and the view of history as science, whose purpose was to recover the objective truth of the past.

Yet the examples of George Bancroft, generally seen as the quintessential Romantic historian, and Leopold von Ranke, one of the pioneers of scientific history, demonstrate that these two views of history were not mutually exclusive, as both historians in different ways brought together elements of Romantic and scientific history. In addition, while they differed in their understanding of nationalism, both historians alike used their work for nationalist purposes. On the other side, while drawing from the same tradition of German idealism as did Ranke and Bancroft, Karl Marx repudiated their nationalist framework and used his theory of historical materialism to challenge the social order that Ranke and Bancroft sought to uphold. From a very different perspective, Jacob Burckhardt likewise dissented from the growing power of nationalism, while in his own way sharing Ranke's desire to bring together scientific history with the view of history as art.

## THE LEGACY OF THE FRENCH REVOLUTION: THE RISE OF ROMANTICISM AND NATIONALISM

Although the restoration of the Bourbon monarchy in 1815 officially brought the French Revolution to a close, the French Revolution had far-reaching effects on European culture that extended well into the nineteenth century. The leading intellectual and political developments of this period came about in large part as a reaction against the French Revolution and the Enlightenment ideas that many thinkers believed were responsible for the Revolution. In England, Edmund Burke took the lead in articulating the main lines of the conservative reaction against the French Revolution in 1790, even before the French Revolution had entered its radical phase and embarked upon the Reign of Terror, when he condemned the Revolution for repudiating tradition and emotion as the basis for political allegiance in favor of abstract reason. While not entirely opposed to change, he revealed his respect for tradition in arguing that such change had to be gradual and organic. As Burke revealed in his critique of reason, the reaction against the French Revolution entailed a more fundamental repudiation of the Enlightenment ideals that he and many thinkers of the time believed had brought about the Revolution. This turn away from Enlightenment ideals extended beyond the political realm into the intellectual and aesthetic arena with the rise of Romanticism.[2] *Immanuel Kant*

The rise of Romanticism both contributed to a greater interest in the past for its own sake and shaped the way in which historians expressed that interest. Romanticism was a broad term that encompassed artists and thinkers of many different persuasions. Hence the meaning of this term has been subject to sharp debate both among modern commentators and among Romantic thinkers themselves. Yet these thinkers did share certain concerns and beliefs that account for why they have been grouped together as part of the same movement. Specifically, one of the defining features of Romantic thought was the rejection of the Enlightenment faith in reason in favor of a belief in the value of emotion. Another important theme in Romantic thought was a belief in the primacy of the individual, which entailed a regard for the uniqueness of each person and an emphasis on the importance of cultivating and expressing that uniqueness. The glorification of nature as the place where human beings could best access the divine was also central to Romantic thought. Finally, Romanticism was defined by a cult of the artist that privileged the artist as a figure who possessed a special ability to communicate with the divine and access higher truths through the use of the imagination and emotion.[3]

Romantic thinkers differed from their eighteenth-century predecessors not just in the status that they accorded to the artist but also in their view of how the artist was supposed to convey higher truths. The Romantic artist was, to use M. H. Abrams's famous distinction, not a mirror but a lamp. Where in eighteenth-century neoclassical aesthetics, the artist was simply supposed to reflect or copy external reality in the way that a mirror did, Romantic aesthetic theory viewed the artist as a lamp, who would illuminate truth by expressing his own perspective and inner feelings in the way that a lamp did through the light it sent out. Rather than simply reflecting the outer world, then, the artist actively shaped perceptions of reality through the use of his own imagination and transformed what he perceived by projecting his own vitality and passion into his perception of the world. Romantic thinkers in this way defined truth itself differently from their Enlightenment predecessors. Departing from the Enlightenment belief in external, objective truths that were waiting to be discovered by the artist or historian, Romantic thinkers viewed truth as something that came from within the individual, giving the artist a more active, interpretive role in creating truth.[4]

This understanding of the artist's role had an important influence on the writing of history in the nineteenth century, as historians came to view themselves as artists and tried to achieve the same goals as Romantic artists did in their work. American historians shared with their European counterparts this view of history as a form of literary art, repeatedly using metaphors of painting and portraiture to describe their work. The American philosopher and historical writer Francis Bowen summed up this artistic conception of history when he asserted,

> The little facts thus made known seem to me to be rather the materials for history, than history itself; they should be expanded into broad pictures, and worked up with high coloring. After all, imagination is as necessary for the historian as research; only it must be imagination based on facts.

In urging the need for "broad pictures" and "high coloring" in history, Bowen likened history to art; and like art, history had to be dramatic and vivid, hence the need for "high coloring." For this reason, Bowen believed that facts were a necessary but not a sufficient basis for history. Rather than just cataloging endless facts and details, the historian's goal was to enable readers to visualize the past as they would a painting. The historian could only do this by using the imagination to describe and connect those facts into a coherent and vivid narrative that would recreate historical scenes and events in graphic detail for readers.[5]

Yet, as Bowen's reference to facts revealed, unlike artists, historians had to balance the Romantic premium on the imagination with a commitment to fact and scholarship. Romantic historians reconciled these goals through their belief that to convey the truth of an event, the historian could not just relate what had happened in the past; he also had to recreate his subjects' experience of that event and enable readers to relive that experience. The historian's role, then, was to use the imagination to enter into the feelings of his subjects and enable readers to experience those feelings for themselves, not to project his own feelings and perspective into his account of the past.[6]

Because another recurring theme in Romantic thought was a

fascination with the past, Romanticism not only shaped how historians approached history, but also contributed more generally to the widespread interest in history that characterized nineteenth-century European and American culture. While Enlightenment thinkers had also displayed a concern with history, the nature of Romantic interest in this topic differed in several ways. Where Enlightenment philosophes had turned their attention to ancient Greece and Rome, disparaging what they believed was the backward religiosity of the Middle Ages, Romantic thinkers in direct contrast were fascinated with the Middle Ages. Not only did Romantic thinkers focus on different aspects of the past; they also differed from their Enlightenment predecessors in their attitude toward the past. Unlike Enlightenment philosophes, whose belief in a universal human nature and desire to use the past to progress beyond it limited their ability to understand the past on its own terms, Romantic thinkers showed a greater recognition of how different the past was from the present and a greater interest in understanding that differentness for its own sake.[7]

Yet this interest in the past for its own sake did not mean that Romantic historians abandoned their predecessors' belief in the political purpose to history. While part of a more general reaction against the French Revolution, Romanticism had mixed political implications. And so, even as some nineteenth-century historians used the Romantic nostalgia for the past for conservative purposes, other historians during this period found the Romantic emphasis on the primacy of the individual appealing as a basis for challenging the established social order. The double-edged political implications of Romanticism were especially apparent in the complex relationship between this movement and the rise of nationalism – the other major development of the nineteenth century.[8]

Although the countries that would form the basis for modern nations such as England or France had existed long before this period, the rise of nationalism entailed a change in the way that inhabitants of those countries understood their relationship to one another and to the polity. While scholars have differed sharply over both the origins and meaning of nationalism, they have generally agreed that nationalism in the broad sense of a community defined and united by an attachment to the nation as an abstract entity did not come to fruition in Europe and the United States until the nineteenth century. Before this point, the ties that bound inhabitants of a nation to one another were more personal and local, and people for the most part obeyed their government out of loyalty to a particular monarch or leader, often feeling a stronger sense of connection to their region or locality than to the nation as a whole. While a sense of nationalism had already begun to develop in England and France during the eighteenth century, the French Revolution galvanized this development in France as well as in other nations. If in France, the sense of promise and idealistic fervor created by the French Revolution, and later the sense of pride created by Napoleon's conquests, helped fuel the development of nationalism, the process of resisting Napoleon's invasions contributed to a stronger sense of national unity and identity throughout other European nations. This development in turn made history an imperative, as both Americans and Europeans during this period used history as a vehicle for defining and legitimizing their nations. Consequently, the nation increasingly became the focus and basic unit of analysis in historical writing during this period.[9]

If, in some ways, the Romantic premium on the individual seemed directly opposed to the growing emphasis on national unity, Romantic ideals in other ways reinforced nationalism. Hence, many of the leading Romantic historians of the nineteenth century, including among them Thomas Macaulay (1800–59) in England and Jules Michelet (1798–1874) in France, were also fervent nationalists. While both men lived up to Romantic ideals in their artistic and dramatic approach to history, the differences between them at the same time illustrated how those ideals could be used for opposing political purposes.

The son of a poor printer with republican sympathies who had been persecuted and censored by Napoleon, Michelet began his career as a secondary schoolteacher of history, making his name with his *History of France*, whose first volume was published in 1833. The success and acclaim for this work gave Michelet the standing which led to his appointment as chair of history at the Collège de France. Although Michelet based much of his work on archival research, he also saw his role as that of a revolutionary poet and prophet, writing in a dramatic and emotional style that made no attempt to hide his political sympathies. An ardent nationalist who viewed this quality as "the life of the world," Michelet saw no conflict between his nationalism and his revolutionary sympathies because he identified the nation with the people.[10]

Influenced by his father's anti-clericalism in his rejection of traditional Christianity, Michelet turned history into a religion of sorts, portraying the French Revolution as a sacred event that was different from ordinary events. Accordingly, describing history as a form of "resurrection," he believed that his role as a historian was to write a gospel of the Revolution that would resurrect its spirit and convert people to a worship of its ideals in the same way that Christians were supposed to worship the Bible.[11] For this reason, he focused in his work on re-creating the experience and feelings of the French Revolution, viewing himself as an instrument of communion who could collapse the distance between past and present and unite the French people by rekindling the spirit of the French Revolution among his contemporaries. Michelet expressed this understanding of his role when he declared in his preface,

> I commune with my own mind. I interrogate myself as to my teaching, my history, and its all-powerful interpreter – the spirit of the Revolution … The Revolution lives in ourselves – in our souls; it has no outward monument. Living spirit of France, where shall I seize thee, but within myself?[12]

In his desire to revive the spirit of the French Revolution, Michelet was responding to his own political context – specifically to the French Revolutions of 1830 and 1848. Increasingly unhappy with the bourgeois monarchy that had been established by the Revolution of 1830, Michelet expressed that disillusionment in his history of the French Revolution, which he began writing in 1846. By the time he finished this work in 1853, the outcome of the French Revolution of 1848, which ended with Louis Napoleon's seizure of power (and the loss of his position at the Collège de France because of what Louis Napoleon deemed his subversive political views), only gave him further cause for despair. Thus his exhortations to resurrect the spirit of the French Revolution contained a mixture of increasing doubts that such a resurrection was possible with a persisting hope that it could still be realized.[13]

If, for Michelet, the problem with the revolutions of 1830 and 1848 was that they did not go far enough in overturning the established social order, for Macaulay, the problem with them was that they had gone too far in their radicalism. And so, in direct contrast to Michelet, Macaulay wrote his history to maintain the established social order, holding up England as a model of gradual, orderly change in opposition to what he considered the destructive extremism of the revolutions of 1848. Unlike Michelet, then, Macaulay was very much part of the political establishment in Britain, serving in Parliament as a member of the Whig Party and helping to rewrite India's penal code during his time as a British official in India. Even more successful and influential as a historian than he was a politician, Macaulay published the first two volumes of his history of England in 1848, following with two other volumes in 1855 and leaving the fifth volume incomplete on his death in 1859. His history was so popular that he was able to make a fortune from the copies that he sold. Living up to his own injunctions for the historian to give "to truth those attractions which have been usurped by fiction," Macaulay wrote in a novelistic style that dramatized his subject through the vivid character sketches he provided.[14]

While the popularity of his work was partly the product of his dramatic literary style, it also stemmed from the celebratory nationalism that characterized the history, as he used his account of the Glorious Revolution to show how the England of his time represented the pinnacle of progress, describing the period from the Glorious Revolution to the present as "eminently the history of physical, of moral, and intellectual improvement."[15] Identifying progress with the liberal ideals he embraced, Macaulay believed that the Glorious Revolution marked an important turning point in advancing that progress by establishing these ideals on a secure basis. Specifically for Macaulay, liberalism meant respect for the primacy of the individual in the form of guarantees for individual rights such as freedom of expression, freedom of religion, and the security of individual property. Yet there was a conservative cast to Macaulay's liberalism. Depicting the Glorious Revolution as an event characterized by respect for order and tradition, Macaulay legitimized the liberal ideals he championed by showing how deeply rooted they were in English tradition and how they had developed as a result of a gradual evolution. Drawing an implicit contrast between England and the Continent to explain why England had been spared the destructive radicalism of the revolutions of 1848, Macaulay concluded,

> It is because we had a preserving revolution in the seventeenth century that we have not had a destroying revolution in the nineteenth. It is because we had freedom in the midst of servitude that we have order in the midst of anarchy.[16]

## LEOPOLD VON RANKE: HISTORY AS SCIENCE AND ART

As the German historian Leopold von Ranke (1795–1886) revealed, however, Romantic history coexisted with other approaches to historical writing in the nineteenth century. Often considered the founder of scientific history, Ranke embraced a view of history as an objective account of facts that seemed to go directly counter to the ideals of Romantic history. Yet rather than viewing Romantic and scientific history as opposed to one another, Ranke brought together both of these approaches in his work. In addition, as much as he proclaimed the importance of objectivity, Ranke paradoxically furthered his political purposes in his formulation of this ideal, sharing Macaulay's desire to preserve the established social order and in his own way sanctifying the rise of nationalism as the product of history.

Although often portrayed as the "founder" of scientific history, Ranke drew on an earlier tradition of critical scholarship established by his predecessors at Göttingen in the eighteenth century. Barthold Georg Niebuhr (1776–1831), a professor of history at the newly established University of Berlin, carried that tradition forward, as he applied the methods of textual criticism taken from philology to the study of Roman history.[17] Through a systematic and critical examination of classical texts, especially poetic sources, for inaccuracies and inconsistencies, Niebuhr believed that it was possible to piece together the fragments of early Roman history and construct a more complete and reliable version of this subject than that provided by existing accounts.[18] Niebuhr in turn directly influenced Ranke. Introduced to Niebuhr's *History of Rome* (1811–12) while studying theology and classical literature at the University of Leipzig, Ranke developed his interest in history as a result of his experiences as a schoolteacher of classical literature. The publication of his first book *Histories of the Latin and Germanic Nations from 1494–1514* in 1824 brought Ranke almost immediate recognition as a historian. Consequently, the following year, Ranke received an appointment as professor of history at the University of Berlin, which, partly through his influence, became a center for historical scholarship in the nineteenth century. Ranke followed with the publication of his two best-known works – his *History of the Popes* (1834–6) and his *German History in the Time of the Reformation* (1839–43).[19]

Both in his definition of the purpose of history and in the

methods he prescribed, Ranke sought to differentiate history from other areas of endeavor by defining history as a science whose goal was supposed to be the disinterested pursuit of objective truth. Rather than viewing history as a branch of philosophy whose function was to provide moral examples for society, Ranke believed that the historian could achieve truth only if it was divorced from any social purpose and if the historian avoided making any moral judgments – an ideal that was encapsulated by the famous declaration he made in the introduction to his *Histories of the Latin and Germanic Nations* that the goal of the historian was to show "what actually happened" in the past. In order to achieve this goal, Ranke believed, the historian had to conduct archival research and critically analyze primary sources. Although his predecessors at Göttingen had also urged the need for a critical analysis of primary sources, Ranke went much further than they did in putting these prescriptions into practice and was more successful than they were in synthesizing his research into a coherent narrative. The appendix to his history of the Latin and Germanic nations revealed his commitment to critical scholarship, providing an extensive analysis of the inaccuracies and distortions of the secondary sources on the subject, while the broad scope of this work demonstrated his ability to integrate his research.[20]

What distinguished Ranke from his predecessors and accounts for his influence was not just the extent to which he put critical methods into practice, but the graduate seminars that he established to train students in those methods, which became part of the required training for historians at all German-speaking universities by 1848. Not only did these seminars enable Ranke to disseminate his methods, but in his assumption that history was a science that required specialized training, Ranke also laid the basis for the development of history into a professionalized discipline.[21]

At the same time, Ranke was very much influenced by Romantic ideals in his approach to history. Thus he combined his commitment to scientific history with a firm belief in the artistic element to history, urging the importance of form as well as content in the writing of history.[22] He expressed his view of history as a form of literary art in his use of dramatic techniques to create suspense and bring the characters in his historical works to life.[23] The emotional language he used to speak of his fascination with documentary sources demonstrated how his commitment to archival research brought together Romantic ideals with a view of history as a science. Speaking in erotic terms of his attachment to manuscripts, he described one archive, for example, as "still absolutely a virgin. I long for the moment I shall have access to her and make my declaration of love, whether she is pretty or not."[24] While, then, he shared the desire of Romantic historians to bring the past to life for readers, he believed that research in primary sources was necessary to achieve this goal since they provided the most direct access to the vital reality of the past. Primary sources for Ranke were thus both a scientific means of validating truth and a way to make that truth vivid for readers.[25]

Ranke likewise brought together Romantic and scientific ideals of historical writing in his emphasis on the need for the historian to make the particular, rather than the universal or abstract, the object of study. While his interest in the particular reflected in part a scientific concern with empirical facts, his fascination with studying the particular in all its uniqueness was also consistent with the premium that Romantic thinkers placed on the individuality and diversity of human experience. He revealed the Romantic element to his concern with the particular when he argued that the "true historian" had to possess a pleasure in the particular for its own sake that was aesthetic and emotional in character, exclaiming,

> If he has a real affection for this human race in all its manifold variety to which we ourselves belong, an affection for this creature that is always the same yet forever different, so good and so evil, so noble and so bestial, so cultured and so brutal, striving for

eternity yet enslaved by the moment, so happy and so wretched, content with so little and yet craving so much![26]

In his emphasis on studying the particular for its own sake, Ranke revealed another way in which he helped lay the basis for the professionalization of history – through his commitment to historicism. While the term historicism has taken on many different meanings, the form identified with Ranke and the one that has come to be a defining assumption of the historical profession referred to the idea that everything that happened in history was the product of historical forces, which meant that historical events could be explained without resort to extra-historical forces such as God, and that all individuals and events were influenced and conditioned by their historical context. Hence each historical era possessed an integrity and uniqueness that made it important in and of itself, rather than serving merely as a stepping stone to the present, and the goal of the historian was to understand what made each era distinct by examining events in the context of their own time – a view encapsulated by Ranke's famous statement that "every epoch is immediate to God."[27]

Ranke's reference to God here revealed that he saw no conflict between his historicist perspective and his religious beliefs.[28] A devout Lutheran, Ranke took his religiosity into his view that all of history represented the emanation of divine will. Ranke's belief in the spiritual basis for all history also revealed the influence of German idealist philosophy on his thought. Contrary to his reputation, Ranke did not define objectivity to mean the sheer accumulation of facts devoid of larger philosophical generalizations. The conventional perception of Ranke as an empiricist who rejected any speculation into higher causes was based on a misunderstanding of Ranke by American historians at the turn of the twentieth century. Rather than rejecting German philosophical idealism, Ranke was deeply influenced by this tradition, and, like German idealist philosophers, he embraced a pantheistic view that all of history represented the expression of God's will, proclaiming, "God dwells, lives, and can be known in all of history." Consequently, Ranke believed, "Every deed attests to Him, every moment preaches His name, but most of all, it seems to me, the connectedness of history in the large."[29]

Although in his famous injunction to study the past "wie es eigentlich gewesen (as it actually was)," the word "eigentlich" has conventionally been translated to mean "actually," the meaning of this term was ambiguous in the nineteenth century, since it could also mean "essentially." This translation suggests that Ranke's goal was not just to present the facts of history, but to uncover the spiritual essences behind those facts.[30] Ranke made his concern with the spiritual dimension to history clear when he declared, "No one could be more convinced than I that historical research requires the strictest method: criticism of the authors, the banning of all fable, the extraction of the pure facts … But I am also convinced that this fact has a spiritual content."[31] As this statement revealed, Ranke saw no conflict between his commitment to an ideal of objectivity that made history an account of empirically proven facts and his belief in an overarching spiritual force to history.[32] On the contrary, he attached such importance to objectivity partly because of his faith in the spiritual basis for history. Ultimately for Ranke, since God expressed himself through historical phenomena, thereby infusing all historical facts with a spiritual element, an impartial account of the facts of history would reveal the workings of divine will and show how all those facts were connected as part of a larger whole.[33] Thus, even as he urged the study of the particular for its own sake, he believed that such a study would illuminate the universal by giving "a knowledge of the objectively existing relatedness" in all things.[34]

Ranke's religious beliefs in turn provided the foundation for his conservative political outlook. A staunch supporter of monarchy, Ranke openly expressed his conservative political views as editor of the *Historisch-Politische Zeitschrift*, a journal whose purpose was to oppose the liberal tendencies that had been fomented by the revolutions of 1830 in France and Belgium, and in the memorials he wrote in opposition to the reforms advocated by the revolution of 1848. Consequently, Ranke was not as impartial as he claimed to be in his historical writing. Although seemingly contradictory, his conservatism and his commitment to objectivity actually went hand-in-hand with one another. Simply in urging the historian to avoid moral judgments and confine himself to a "strict presentation of the facts," Ranke assigned a conservative role to the historian that denied the possibility of using history as an instrument of social criticism. Further, by portraying everything that happened in history as the expression of God's will, Ranke gave divine sanction to the existing social order as the product of that historical process. Thus, he suggested, to overturn that order would not just be socially destructive; it would also be sacrilegious.[35]

And so, although Ranke was more qualified in his support for German unification than were many of his contemporaries, he came to accept the unification of Germany under Prussian auspices in 1870 as the necessary result of the historical process, viewing the Prussian monarchy and army as the only forces powerful enough to withstand the revolutionary upheavals that he believed threatened to destroy social order.[36] Ranke's conservatism also converged with the nationalist tendencies of his time in the primacy he accorded to the state. Describing states as "thoughts of God," Ranke spiritualized the power of the state, making states into leading actors in the historical process and the agents of God's will in the world. Ranke made explicit his belief in the spiritual character of power and located that power in the state when he declared that "in power itself there appears a spiritual substance" and that "no state has ever subsisted without a spiritual base and a spiritual substance."[37] This spiritualization of power not only favored the interests of established authority, but justified the use of force to maintain that authority.[38] At a time when the state was coming to be increasingly identified with the nation, Ranke's elevation of the state as a spiritual entity helped to sanctify the development of Germany from a loose confederation of principalities into a unified nation state, and the rise of nationalism in general, as the realization of divine will. Ranke contributed even more directly to the sanctification of nationalism through the role he gave to nations in history. Although he was himself uncertain about the relationship between the nation and the state, Ranke viewed nations, like states, as the active instruments of historical transformation, defining universal history as the study of the emergence of nations and their interactions with one another. And so, even as many of his histories covered a broad geographic scope that cut across national lines, he emphasized military and political developments in which the actions of nation states were paramount, turning the nation into a basic unit of historical analysis and legitimizing its development as the natural product of history.[39]

## GEORGE BANCROFT AND AMERICAN EXCEPTIONALISM

Although usually viewed as polar opposites, the American historian George Bancroft (1800–91) and Ranke had more in common than has often been assumed. One of the most influential American historians of his time, Bancroft both reflected and reinforced the increasingly chauvinistic nationalism that was developing among his contemporaries with his celebratory account of American history. Yet his Romantic writing style and his ardent nationalism did not mean that he was any less committed than Ranke was to the view of history as a science. Hence he, like Ranke, urged the importance of a critical analysis of primary sources, believing that an impartial account of the past would reveal the workings of divine will.

Born in Massachusetts, Bancroft's New England background pointed to the dominance of this region over the writing of history in the United States during this period. While Bancroft differed from his New England colleagues in his political sympathies, he, like many of them, embraced a vision of American history and of the historian's role that reflected his status as part of what modern scholars have termed the "Brahmin" elite. Writing before history had become a professionalized discipline, these historians believed that history was supposed to be the vocation of gentlemen amateurs. Thus, most of these historians did not make a living from historical writing; they were either independently wealthy or supported themselves by pursuing other occupations in addition to history.[40]

Accordingly, Bancroft combined his historical pursuits with an active political career, and in fact used his work as a historian to further his political goals. In 1831, the publication of an article supporting President Andrew Jackson's attack on the Bank of the United States brought Bancroft to political prominence and marked the beginning of his career as a leading figure in the Massachusetts Democratic Party. Bancroft's rise to political eminence coincided with his emergence as a historian, and his history reflected his political sympathies to such an extent that it provoked the famous charge that every volume "voted for Jackson."[41] With the publication of the first volume of his *History of the United States* in 1834, Bancroft immediately established his reputation as one of the nation's leading historians. Bancroft followed this volume with nine others at irregular intervals, with the last volume appearing in 1874. The most comprehensive account of American history to that point, Bancroft's work achieved a commanding influence over nineteenth-century American historical writing, winning both wide popular and critical acclaim. Viewing, like many of his contemporaries, history as a form of Romantic art, Bancroft was so successful partly because he wrote in a dramatic and vivid style that sought to make history come to life for his readers.[42]

Bancroft's success as a historian was a function not just of his style but also of his celebratory nationalism and his ability to articulate the belief in American exceptionalism so widespread among his contemporaries.[43] While, for this reason, modern scholars have often attributed to him a mythic and uncritically celebratory view of the nation's past, Bancroft was actually a more sophisticated historian than these scholars have acknowledged, and his work combined a fervent nationalism with a cosmopolitan perspective. Very much aware of the international context for American developments, Bancroft's extensive research included both colonial and European archival sources, and he in fact devoted much of his discussion to European events.[44]

Bancroft could take such a broad view of American history because he embraced a teleological perspective that treated the colonial past, and indeed all of human history, as precursors leading inexorably up to the Revolution. In Bancroft's words, "prepared by glorious forerunners," the Revolution "grew naturally and necessarily out of the series of past events by the formative principle of a living belief." Bancroft believed that the Revolution was inevitable because it had been decreed by the "grand design of Providence."[45] In his belief that America's historical development fulfilled a divine purpose, and his belief that the Revolution represented a turning point in human history, Bancroft articulated two of the central assumptions of American exceptionalism. The Revolution was, for Bancroft, a turning point because it had brought about the realization of America's destiny to advance the cause of liberty.[46] Structuring his analysis around the development of liberty in America, Bancroft dated this development back to the Reformation and began his history with the colonial era.[47] Bancroft emphasized the role of the New England Puritans in developing and transplanting the principles of democracy and liberty to America, for, as he put it, Puritanism was "religion struggling for the People."[48]

This account of the origins of liberty served political and social purposes. An ardent Jacksonian, Bancroft gave historical legitimacy to the democratic principles he espoused by tracing their roots in the past.[49] Bancroft's emphasis on the Puritan contribution to democracy reflected his own sectional loyalties, since, by locating the roots of democracy in New England, Bancroft asserted the primacy of his own region in American development and defined the nation in terms of New England. At the same time,

Bancroft's history also served nationalist purposes. Recognizing that Puritanism was just one of the many strands that contributed to American independence, Bancroft gave credit to victims of Puritan persecution like Roger Williams, and to William Penn and the settlers of Virginia for instituting the principles of liberty in their respective regions. Bancroft thus sought to instill national unity by giving each section a role in the advance of democracy, and the other major theme of Bancroft's history was the development of union in America.[50]

With the Revolution, Bancroft believed, America had embarked on a process of continual progress. While the principles of the Revolution did not require a dramatic change in the nation's social or political system, the vitality of the principles themselves made them a source of continual renovation and reform for Bancroft. In his belief that the nation could remain indefinitely in a state of revolution without undergoing fundamental change, Bancroft summed up the exceptionalist vision of America as a nation that was exempt from the normal processes of historical change and decay. In this vision, by virtue of its closeness to nature, the United States could remain in a state of perpetual innocence and simplicity, untouched by the social forces that had corrupted the Old World.[51]

For all the apparent partiality of his depiction of America as a chosen nation, Bancroft saw his work as impartial, and indeed his commitment to impartiality was integrally related to his belief in American exceptionalism. When Ranke noted of his history in 1867 that it was "written from the democratic point of view," Bancroft responded by declaring, "if there is democracy in the history it is not subjective, but objective as they say here." While this exchange has been taken to signify the contrast between Bancroft's Romantic idealism and Ranke's scientific approach, the two historians were more alike than many scholars have recognized, and Bancroft had in fact studied with Ranke. If, on the one hand, Ranke, like Bancroft, was influenced by German philosophical idealism in his belief in the divine essence to history, Bancroft, on the other hand, shared Ranke's commitment to impartiality.[52] Like Ranke, he saw no conflict between his claims to impartiality and his providential perspective, since he believed that an impartial view of American history would reveal the unfolding of providential design. Thus he could assert that a history written from a democratic point of view was objective owing to his assumption that democracy was part of that design.[53]

Bancroft revealed how he, like Ranke, combined his belief in the spiritual and moral basis for history with a scientific definition of truth as the accurate representation of objective reality when he elaborated on what he meant by historical impartiality. Affirming the vital importance of impartiality, he declared,

> The historian, not less than philosophers and naturalists, must bring to his pursuit the freedom of an unbiassed mind; in his case the submission of reason to prejudice would have a deeper criminality; for he cannot neglect to be impartial without at once falsifying nature and denying providence.

When he likened the historian to the naturalist and emphasized the importance of an "unbiassed mind," he embraced a scientific ideal of truth that required detachment from the historian. Yet in arguing that it would be criminal, and indeed irreligious, for the historian to do otherwise, he revealed at the same time a moral component to his conception of truth. Historical truth, for Bancroft, was not just a matter of fact, but consisted of moral verities established by providence. For Bancroft, these moral verities did not reflect the historian's own personal perspective, but represented objective truths external to the historian. For this reason, he saw no conflict between his emphasis on moral judgment and his desire for impartiality. On the contrary, only by being impartial could the historian recover those deeper truths.[54]

In keeping with his view of history as a science, Bancroft shared Ranke's belief that impartiality required the historian to engage in a critical analysis of primary sources. One of the first Americans to conduct graduate work in Germany, Bancroft had studied at Göttingen and was, as a result, influenced by the same tradition of critical scholarship that laid the basis for Ranke's ideas. An important figure in transmitting the influence of German idealism and German critical scholarship back to the United States, Bancroft had studied under A. H. L. Heeren – one of the leading pioneers of German critical scholarship – while at Göttingen, and a few years after his return to America he published American translations of Heeren's *Reflections on the Politics of Ancient Greece* (1824), his *History of the States of Antiquity* (1828), and his *History of the Political System of Europe* (1828–9).[55]

Bancroft expressed his commitment to critical methods of scholarship in the preface to his history when he declared,

> I have applied, as I have proceeded, the principles of historical scepticism, and, not allowing myself to grow weary in comparing witnesses or consulting codes of laws, I have endeavored to impart originality to my narrative, by deriving it entirely from writings and sources, which were the contemporaries of the events that are described.

As the term "historical scepticism" revealed, Bancroft believed that the historian had to take a critical and questioning view of his sources; he could not just accept their assertions at face value. This was why examining primary sources was so important. Like Ranke, Bancroft believed that only by comparing these sources to one another and to secondary accounts could the historian test and verify the claims of historical actors as well as those of other historians.[56] Although he relied primarily on published sources for his first three volumes, those sources included both the works of other historians like Abiel Holmes and Jeremy Belknap, and primary sources like William Hening's statutes of Virginia and John Winthrop's journal. As his history progressed, not only did Bancroft rely more heavily on primary sources for his analysis;

these primary sources also increasingly consisted of unpublished manuscripts and archival material.[57]

Like Ranke, Bancroft believed that footnotes were a necessary requisite for the kind of critical analysis he urged. For this reason, Bancroft supplied footnotes throughout most of his *History*, using them both to attest to his documentary research and to provide critical commentary on these sources.[58] The consistency of his notes varied from volume to volume, and his treatment of quotations was admittedly suspect. Bancroft often combined different quotes, or interpolated his own language into them, without indicating or distinguishing his modifications to the original quotation. Such changes often made these quotes corrrespond more closely with his own arguments and style, and grew out of his desire to give meaning and coherence to his narrative. Yet Bancroft was, overall, far more scrupulous about citation than his predecessors. For most of the first six volumes in the *History*, Bancroft provided regular, though not extensive, footnotes. These notes generally contained a brief citation of Bancroft's source, occasionally supplemented by commentary from Bancroft comparing different sources to one another and giving his assessment of their reliability.[59] In one such footnote to his discussion of Ferdinand de Soto's exploration of Mississippi, Bancroft declared,

> On Soto's expedition, by far the best account is that of the Portuguese Eye-witness, first published in 1557, and by Hakluyt, in English, in 1609 ... This narrative is remarkably good, and contains internal evidence of its credibility. Nuttall erroneously attributes it to Vega. In the work of Vega, numbers and distances are magnified; and every thing embellished with great boldness. His history is not without its value, but must be consulted with extreme caution. Herrera ... is not an original authority.

As Bancroft concluded, "I have compared all these authors: the account in Hakluyt, with good modern maps, can lead to firm conclusions."[60]

## MARX AS A HISTORIAN

Although differing sharply from Bancroft in his social purposes, Karl Marx shared Bancroft's teleological view of history, since he drew from the same tradition of German idealism as Bancroft did. Where Marx differed from Bancroft was in his view of the end toward which history was moving and in his explanation of how history would reach that end. If, for Bancroft, the realization of American democracy represented the culmination of history, for Marx, that culmination would only be achieved with the overthrow of capitalist society by a communist revolution. And where, for Bancroft, ideas were the forces that drove this process, Marx gave primacy to the role of material factors.

While not known as a historian, Marx's theory of communism was as much a theory of how history worked and where it was going as it was a political or economic theory. As a result, his ideas had an important influence on the writing of history. Other forms of socialism had existed before Marx, but his version was the most influential. Like Ranke, from Germany, Marx came from a relatively affluent background. The son of a civil servant, Marx studied philosophy at the University of Berlin, where he was heavily influenced by G. W. F. Hegel's ideas. Marx entered journalism as a career, leaving Germany for Paris in 1843 to pursue that career. After meeting Friedrich Engels in 1842, the two men began to articulate their theory of history in the *German Ideology*, which they worked on between 1845 and 1846. Although not published in their lifetimes, the *German Ideology* offered an important statement of the materialist conception of history that informed their later work and would influence later historians.[61] The *German Ideology* reflected both the influence of Hegel on Marx and Marx's repudiation of Hegel. Marx derived his concern with history partly from Hegel, while his conviction that class conflict was the driving force in history grew out of Hegel's belief that all of history was the working out of a dialectic – that is, a conflict of opposing forces – leading to the realization of human freedom. Marx, however, rejected Hegel's assumption that ideas were behind this opposition. For Marx, historical conflict and change were the product of material forces; ideas merely reflected those forces, serving as tools for those who owned the means of production to maintain their control over those who did not.[62] Marx made clear the difference between his theory of history and the idealism of Hegel when he declared,

> In direct contrast to German philosophy which descends from heaven to earth, here we ascend from earth to heaven ... Morality, religion, metaphysics, all the rest of ideology and their corresponding forms of consciousness, thus no longer retain the semblance of independence. They have no history, no development; but men, developing their material production and their material intercourse, alter, along with this their real existence, their thinking and the products of their thinking. Life is not determined by consciousness, but consciousness by life.[63]

Marx gave concrete expression to this theory of history in the *Communist Manifesto*, his most influential work, published in 1848. Written for the League of the Just, a radical German workers' party that would become the Communist League in 1847, and whose purpose it was to mobilize the development of a working-class movement, the *Communist Manifesto* offered a statement of the League's political program and principles.[64] Although the goal of the *Manifesto* was polemical, Marx used history to further his political objectives, giving a history of how capitalist society had developed to show why he believed that a communist revolution was both necessary and inevitable. Opening the *Manifesto* with his famous declaration that "the history of all hitherto existing society is the history of class struggles," Marx went on to show how the transformation from feudal to capitalist society was the product of such a struggle. Specifically, in his view, the bourgeoisie, by whom he meant those who owned the means of production, had "played a most revolutionary part" in this process by destroying the more complex class structure of the Middle Ages and bringing an end to the illusions that had masked the exploitative character of the feudal system. The result was that in capitalist society a new and simpler class division had emerged that involved only two classes, the bourgeoisie and proletariat, by whom Marx meant wage workers who did not own the means of production and had to support themselves by selling their labor. Consequently, members of the proletariat had become commodities, who "are daily and hourly enslaved by the machine, by the overlooker, and, above all, by the individual bourgeois manufacturer himself." Not only were workers in capitalist society denied the fruits of their labor by the low wages they received, but the mechanization and division of labor had turned work into a completely monotonous and unrewarding activity, taking away from workers the ability to express their creativity and humanity through their labor.[65]

While always in struggle with the bourgeoisie, the development of the proletariat into a class was itself the product of a gradual process in which the bourgeoisie played a crucial role. First, by appealing to the proletariat for help against its enemies, the aristocracy, for example, the bourgeoisie had helped raise the political consciousness of the proletariat, thereby giving the proletariat "weapons for fighting the bourgeoisie."[66] Second, as capitalist society became increasingly oppressive, with more and more people falling into the proletariat class and becoming more and more miserable, the proletariat would become stronger and more united as a class, coming into increasing conflict with the bourgeoisie, until the point when it would come together and overturn capitalist society as a whole in a working-class revolution. Ironically, then, by bringing together the working class through the development and growth of industry, the bourgeoisie laid the basis for its own destruction, thereby making "[i]ts fall and the victory of the proletariat ... equally inevitable."[67]

Only then would there be an end to class conflict, since by abolishing private property the communist revolution would eliminate the material basis for class conflict and oppression. While there would be an interim period when the proletariat would have to use its political power to eradicate any vestiges of bourgeois society through state control of the means of production, the proletariat would eventually lose its identity as a class, and "the public power will lose its political character." Since, for Marx, political power "is merely the organised power of one class for oppressing another," the elimination of class conflict would ultimately bring about an end to the need for government as well, and "[i]n place of the old bourgeois society, with its classes and class antagonisms, we shall have an association, in which the free development of each is the condition for the free development of all."[68]

By grounding his critique of capitalist society in history, Marx made his theory of communism appear to be descriptive rather than prescriptive, giving added credibility to his claims that his ideas represented the fruit of an empirical and scientific analysis, in contrast to what he believed was the utopian and unrealistic character of other forms of socialism. And by making the destruction of capitalism by a communist revolution seem inevitable, Marx suggested that to oppose it would not just be wrong but futile.[69]

Published in February 1848, just before the outbreak of the revolutions of 1848 in France and Germany, the *Communist Manifesto* reflected Marx's hope that the revolutionary upheaval it advocated was approaching. Rather than viewing the failure of these revolutions as a contradiction to his theory, Marx argued that their outcome actually confirmed his theory of history in his *The Class Struggles in France* and *The Eighteenth Brumaire of Louis Bonaparte*, published in 1850 and 1852. *The Eighteenth Brumaire* offered an important expression of Marx's views on history, as he sought to apply his theory to an analysis of a specific political event, namely Louis Napoleon's seizure of power in France in 1851. While Marx had claimed in *The Class Struggles in France* that the failure of the revolution of 1848 had furthered the advance of communism by making the working classes more aware of the realities of class conflict and exposing the illusions that disguised those realities, he had become increasingly aware by 1852 of the power of such illusions. Marx expressed that awareness in *The Eighteenth Brumaire* when he famously declared,

> Men make their own history, but they do not make it just as they please; they do not make it under circumstances chosen by themselves, but under circumstances directly encountered, given and transmitted from the past. The tradition of all the dead generations weighs like a nightmare on the brain of the living.

Consequently, Marx became more pessimistic that the working classes would realize of their own accord the realities of their class oppression, and placed a greater emphasis on the need for a deeper theoretical analysis that would inform and guide the proletariat to see through the illusions that hid their exploitation. Paradoxically, then, through his analysis of history, Marx increasingly came to question whether history alone was sufficient to explain and reveal the course of social development to his contemporaries.[70]

## JACOB BURCKHARDT: THE RENAISSANCE AND CULTURAL HISTORY

Where Marx challenged nationalism from a communist perspective, the Swiss historian Jacob Burckhardt (1818–97) questioned the growing power of nationalism from a very different point of view, seeing it as a threat to the kinds of local loyalties and the cultural diversity he favored. Not only did Burckhardt differ from Ranke in his critical view of nationalism; he also departed from Ranke in his approach to history, focusing on the cultural rather than the political and military realm. Yet, for all his differences with Ranke, he in his own way, like Ranke, demonstrated that scientific history and the view of history as art were not mutually exclusive.

Burckhardt had in fact been directly exposed to the influence of scientific history, studying under Ranke at the University of Berlin, and was even offered the position as Ranke's successor there. Burckhardt turned down this offer, however, and ended up teaching art history and history at the University of Basel, publishing his most influential work *The Civilization of the Renaissance in Italy* in 1860. With this work, Burckhardt established the now widely held view of the Renaissance as a time of great cultural transformation that laid the basis for a modern outlook. First used by the French historian Michelet, the term Renaissance referred narrowly to developments in the fine arts before Burckhardt's work broadened its meaning. What made Burckhardt's work so innovative was not just its interpretation of the Renaissance, but its approach to the subject. Departing from the political focus of Ranke's ideal of scientific history, Burckhardt provided an influential model for the study of cultural history in the attention he gave to Renaissance culture and everyday life. Although Voltaire had preceded Burckhardt in promoting the study of cultural history with his *Essay on Manners*, Burckhardt went much further in carrying out this imperative, covering many different aspects of Renaissance social and cultural history, including religion, festivals, fashion, literature, and class relations, to name only a few.[71]

Very much concerned with style, Burckhardt saw no conflict between his desire to make his writing accessible to readers and his commitment to truth, bringing together in his own way the scientific ideals of historical writing that he had learned from Ranke with his view of history as a form of art. Burckhardt expressed his commitment to research and truth when he wrote to a friend in 1860 of his hope that his friend could say of his work "that the author has energetically resisted many temptations to let his imagination roam, and has instead held fast to the testimony of the sources."[72] At the same time, Burckhardt sought to enliven his work through the inclusion of vivid anecdotes and stories, even when he was uncertain of their basis in fact, as in the case of "[a]n old story – one of those which are true and not true, every-where and nowhere" in which

> [t]he citizens of a certain town (Siena seems to be meant) had once an officer in their service who had freed them from foreign aggression; daily they took counsel how to recompense him, and concluded that no reward in their power was great enough, not even if they made him lord of the city. At last one of them rose and said, "Let us kill him and then worship him as our patron saint."[73]

While emphasizing the importance of the Renaissance, Burckhardt did not uncritically glorify it. Thus, even as he detailed its many cultural achievements, he also pointed to its capacity for brutality in his lurid descriptions of the cruelty and ruthlessness of Italian Renaissance despots. Even the sense of individualism that he believed was the most important characteristic and legacy of the Renaissance had mixed implications for Burckhardt. In his summation of the Italian character in this period, Burckhardt made clear his belief that the very individualism which made possible the cultural achievements of the Renaissance was also the source of its destructive features, declaring, "The fundamental vice of this character was at the same time the condition of its greatness, namely, excessive individualism." Therefore, what was important for Burckhardt was not to make moral judgments about this sense of individualism, but to understand its effects on modern Europe, since, as he explained, "In itself it is neither good nor bad, but necessary; within it has grown up a modern standard of good and evil – a sense of moral responsibility – which is essentially different from that which was familiar to the Middle Ages."[74]

Because of his belief in the importance of individualism to modern society, Burckhardt was much more hostile than his contemporaries Bancroft and Ranke were to the growing power of nationalism in his time. Viewing cosmopolitanism as "itself a high stage of individualism," Burkhardt feared the rise of nationalism and the emergence of powerful nation states – especially that of Germany – in his own time as a threat to this cosmopolitan spirit.[75] For Burckhardt, what made nationalism such a dangerous force was its homogenizing effects on both culture and the individual. Burckhardt favored instead the kind of local patriotism that characterized his home city of Basel, believing that this form of loyalty was more conducive than nationalism was to preserving the sense of diversity that was so important to him.[76]

And so, if Bancroft and Ranke illustrated the growing power of nationalism in the nineteenth century, Burckhardt and Marx demonstrated that this development was by no means uncontested. Yet as much as they differed from one another, Ranke, Marx, and Burckhardt all in different ways laid the basis for important developments in twentieth-century historical scholarship, as scientific history, Marx's historical materialism, and cultural history took greater hold among historians. Rather than being a result of professionalization, then, the conflicts that divided historians in the twentieth century had their roots in the nineteenth.

# Chapter Four

## Scientific History and Its Challengers

With the professionalization of history during the latter part of the nineteenth century came the consolidation of the ideal of scientific history, as European and American historians defined their discipline in terms of this ideal. Rather than resulting in greater unity, this consolidation produced new conflicts of its own, provoking challenges to scientific history on a wide variety of fronts. Yet these challenges were rooted in the ideas of the scientific historians themselves, revealing the internal tensions in their definition of history. Most important, even as the scientific historians based their view of history as a science on their commitment to objectivity – encapsulated by the notion that the goal of the historian was simply to present an unbiased account of history as it actually was – they at the same time recognized the subjective element to history. In their attacks on the ideal of objectivity, then, the New Historians in the United States and their counterparts in Europe were at once departing from and following the lead of the scientific historians themselves.

Thus both the American historian J. Franklin Jameson and the English historian J.B. Bury simultaneously embraced a commitment to scientific history and a recognition of the subjective character of historical analysis. On the other side, the American historian Charles Beard – one of the most influential of the New Historians – revealed a lingering attachment to objectivity, even as he defined himself in opposition to this ideal.

## PROFESSIONALIZATION AND THE RISE OF SCIENTIFIC HISTORY

The product of many different forces, the ideal of scientific history was more complex than its later critics claimed. Not only did historians define scientific history in different ways; but even the form of scientific history that prevailed, based on the Rankean ideal of objectivity, coexisted with seemingly contradictory assumptions about the social function of history and the subjective character of historical analysis. Capitalizing on the growing prestige of science during the second part of the nineteenth century, American and European historians during this period sought to claim the authority of science for their discipline by defining it as a science. Yet they differed over what it meant to view history as a science, resulting in the emergence of two different conceptions of scientific history. The first form defined history as a science in the sense that its exponents believed that history, like the natural world, was governed by universal laws, making the purpose of the historian to uncover those laws, just as scientists did in their study of nature. The English historian Henry Buckle (1821–62) exemplified this kind of scientific history in his *History of Civilization in England* (1856–61), as he sought to determine the laws that explained the development of civilization. While the success of his work attested to the appeal of this form of scientific history, it would ultimately be superseded by the ideal of scientific history associated with Leopold von Ranke. This conception of scientific history made the scientific character of history rest on its methodology, associating science with an objective description of facts. In this view, history was a science whose goal was supposed to be the disinterested pursuit of objective truth – an understanding of the historian's purpose that many historians of the time identified with Ranke. Since, according to the Rankean ideal of objectivity, truth was an entity independent of the observer, the historian would attain this goal only if he avoided making any judgments of his own and presented an unbiased account of the facts. To achieve this kind of objectivity, the historian had to engage in archival research and a critical analysis of primary sources, a process that required special training in the graduate seminars that Ranke had pioneered at the University of Berlin. Although this ideal was not inherently opposed to social history, its adherents, like Ranke, tended to focus on political and military history as the best way to realize truth. Historians of many different nationalities embraced this model of scientific history while adapting it in different ways. Among the leading proponents of these scientific methods were Lord Acton in Britain, Charles Langlois and Charles Seignobos in France, and Herbert Baxter Adams in the United States.[1]

In turn, the rise of a form of scientific history defined by the ideal of objectivity both reflected and furthered the development of history into a profession in the United States and Western Europe during the latter part of the nineteenth century, as professional historians used this ideal to differentiate their own discipline from its traditional affiliates – literature and philosophy. Professionalization meant that history was increasingly viewed as a specialized discipline requiring expert training and knowledge learned in graduate school, like medicine or law, rather than as a subject anyone could study and learn on his own. History also became a profession in the sense that historians could now make a living by devoting themselves full-time to its study, in contrast to their predecessors who had viewed history as a literary pursuit, not as an occupation.[2]

The professionalization of history also had an institutional basis, as changes in the system and function of university education were instrumental to this process. Until well into the nineteenth century, the main function of colleges and universities in the United States and most of Europe was to teach and to provide a broad liberal education. Consequently, although history was a part of the curriculum in most American and European universities, it was often taught as ancillary or subordinate to other subjects such as philosophy and rhetoric, rather than as an independent subject of its own. Only with the establishment of the university as a research institution in which history was recognized as a separate subject was it possible for historians to become professionals in the sense of making a living as scholars and teachers and to train students in the specialized techniques and knowledge that they believed defined history as a profession. For this reason, Germany – where the state had been the most active in sponsoring and directing the establishment of universities whose main purpose was research – was in the forefront of professionalization. The creation of the University of Berlin in 1810 served as a model for this kind of university, with its emphasis on training students to conduct research. France followed suit in reforming its university system along the German model after the Franco-Prussian War in 1870–1. Slower to embrace this model was Britain, which did not require university teachers of history to possess a Ph.D., even into the twentieth century. In the United States, the establishment of history as an academic discipline in universities came with the transformation from the classical curriculum to the elective system in American colleges during the late nineteenth century, while Johns Hopkins University led the way in transforming American universities along the model of the research university with the creation of the first Ph.D. program in history in 1876.[3]

The establishment of academic journals whose purpose was to publish the research produced by professional historians was also important in laying an institutional basis for professionalization, enabling historians to disseminate the fruits of their scholarship and providing a vehicle for maintaining shared standards for research. Germany took the lead in the creation of such journals with the founding of the *Historische Zeitschrift* in 1859. France followed in 1876 with the founding of the *Revue historique*, and Britain in 1886 with the *English Historical Review*, while in the United States the *American Historical Review* was established in 1895.[4] The editors of these journals revealed the importance of scientific history to professionalization in their initial statements of purpose. In the prefatory note to its first issue, the *English Historical Review* affirmed its commitment to a "scientific spirit," declaring that the "object of history is to discover and set forth facts." At the same time, the editor of the *Review* did not see any conflict between his injunctions to impartiality and the use of history for social purposes. As he explained, "Recognizing the value of the light which history may shed on practical problems, we shall not hesitate to let that light be reflected from our pages, whenever we can be sure that it is dry light, free from any tinge of partisanship."[5] Thus, as much as they urged the importance of objectivity, the scientific historians did not interpret objectivity to mean the study of history completely for its own sake, devoid of any social purpose.

In particular, the professionalization of the discipline based on the ideal of scientific history served nationalist imperatives for historians in the United States and Western Europe. By discouraging the overt expression of controversial or partisan views, the ideal of objectivity served to obscure the conflicts that divided these nations and to promote a greater sense of unity in them.[6] Accordingly, the editor of the *English Historical Review* declared his intention to avoid even the possibility of seeming to engage in partisan conflict by "refusing contributions which argue such questions with reference to present controversy."[7] The editors of the *Revue historique* made clear the nationalist function of scientific history in the preface to the first issue of the journal. Even as they called for "strictly scientific methods of exposition, with each assertion accompanied by proof, by source references and quotations," they at the same time declared their aim to promote "the study of France's past," an imperative they considered "of national importance." Through such a study, "We can give to our country the unity and moral strength she needs by revealing her historical traditions and, at the same time, the transformations these traditions have undergone."[8]

The American historian J. Franklin Jameson (1859–1937) illustrated the close relationship between nationalism and the professionalization of history on the basis of scientific ideals. The first student to receive a Ph.D. in history from Johns Hopkins University and the first editor of the *American Historical Review*, Jameson played a leading role in the professionalization of history by using the journal to establish uniform standards of scholarship for the profession and to serve as a forum for the works of professional historians. While firmly committed to scientific history, Jameson combined his belief in the ideal of objectivity with a recognition of the subjective element to historical analysis, revealing that the views of the scientific historians on the nature and purpose of history were more complex than their reputation as naïve positivists would suggest.[9] In his *History of Historical Writing in America*, published in 1891, Jameson identified the qualities that defined modern scientific history and revealed his commitment to factual accuracy when he cited Thomas Prince and William Stith as "the progenitors of modern American historiography," since Prince possessed "[t]he wide sweep of the search after materials, the patience and industry in investigation, the minute accuracy and fidelity which characterize the best of the moderns." Hence, Prince's work was the first American history "of value as a contribution to historical science rather than to historical literature."[10] Yet Jameson at the same time recognized the subjective character of history when he declared that while "[t]he history of every science is in some degree conditioned by the natural course of things in the world at large … this is in a peculiar degree the case with the science of history." Consequently, "[v]iews of the past, and ways of looking at it, change with the changing complexion of the present." Here then, far from portraying historians as objective compilers of facts immune to the influence of their context, Jameson characterized them as particularly subject to that influence.[11]

Jameson reconciled this recognition with his faith in objectivity through his belief in the progressive character of historical knowledge. While always subject to the influence of external historical circumstances and forces, historical writing had become in his view increasingly scientific and objective as a result of the changing character of those forces. One of the most important such forces in the United States for Jameson was nationalism. Attributing the increasingly scientific and objective character of American historical writing to the development of a more secure sense of nationality in the United States, Jameson explained, now that, with the Civil War, the United States had finally "become a self-reliant nation," American historians "have become more critical and discriminating, have learned more nearly to look upon the course of American history with an impartial eye, from the standpoint of an outsider."[12] As much as he recognized that historical writing was the product of its context, he revealed the limits to that recognition in holding up scientific history as the culmination of the development of historical knowledge. If, for Jameson, scientific history had developed as a result of a historical process, it also possessed a value which transcended that process and made it immune to future historical changes.[13]

In pointing to how nationalism had furthered, rather than hindered, the development of a more objective understanding of American history, Jameson sanctioned his nationalist perspective as compatible with and therefore grounded in truth. Like his European counterparts, then, Jameson paradoxically used the ideal of objectivity to further nationalist purposes, legitimizing his nationalist depiction of American history as the expression of scientific truth rather than merely the reflection of his subjective perspective.[14] Praising the American Historical Association, a professional organization for historians founded in 1884, for its "broad and national" perspective, Jameson contrasted it to the narrower perspective of traditional local historical societies, which he disparaged as a "counter-current" to the broader national viewpoint promoted by scientific history. Only by adopting this broader perspective would it be possible, in Jameson's view, for historians to achieve "the adjustment of the sphere of our historical writing into conformity with the actual facts, relations, and proportions of our national existence."[15]

For Jameson, not only was it necessary for American historians to widen their outlook beyond the local to the national; it was also necessary for them to look beyond the political realm into the realm of social and economic history. Jameson revealed how much his understanding of history was a product of nationalist imperatives in his explanation for why it was so important for American historians to expand the scope of history in this way. According to Jameson, the same sense of national self-confidence that had furthered the development of objectivity had also contributed to a greater recognition by American historians of the "need of emancipation from the traditions and conventions of European historiography" and the importance of broadening the scope of historical analysis to include social and economic history. Such a departure from the traditional emphasis on political history would correspond better to American circumstances. As Jameson explained, since "the field of influence of natural conditions upon our national destiny has been peculiarly great," and that "of great individuals far smaller than in the Old World," American historians

> do not properly reflect the life that they seek to reflect if they write solely of individual persons or groups of persons and their conscious efforts; they must cease blindly to follow European schemes, and study economic and natural conditions and developments, the unintended growth of institutions and modes of life, the unconscious movements and changes of masses of men.[16]

In claiming that such an approach to American history would be more true both to the nation's unique historical circumstances and to the stage of historical development that the discipline of history had reached in his time, Jameson legitimized the study of social and economic history by associating it with the nationalist belief in American exceptionalism.[17] In his emphasis on how America's "natural conditions" had differentiated the nation from Europe, Jameson affirmed his commitment to a key component of exceptionalist ideology – the belief that America's closeness to nature had exempted it from the normal processes of historical change. For Jameson, America was exceptional by virtue not only of its social conditions but of the historical approach that was necessary for an understanding of those conditions. In this way, even as his nationalist purposes contributed to his embrace of the Rankean ideal of objectivity, they at the same time led him to depart from its political emphasis.[18]

Not only did Jameson use history to further his political purposes; like his European counterparts, he did so as part of a conscious belief in the social value of history. Contrary to their reputation as exponents of an arcane ideal of historical scholarship interested only in truth for its own sake, Jameson and other scientific historians were concerned with making their work accessible to the general public and relevant to contemporary social problems. In their concern with reaching general readers, Jameson and other scientific historians in the United States were responding in part to the nationalization of publishing and cultural production after the Civil War, which enlarged the market for history by contributing to the rise of a "middlebrow culture" whose aim was to popularize elite or "high" culture. This development brought professional historians both greater opportunities for reaching general readers and greater competition for those readers, as the expanding audience for history stimulated the growth of non-academic historical writing by historical novelists and journalists.[19] Jameson thus urged the social value of scientific history and reconciled it with his commitment to objectivity by arguing that the qualities associated with objectivity were themselves socially useful. As he wrote, "The severity of its methods, its merciless sifting and dissection, and comparison of human statements, will always make it the invaluable foe of credulity, the steady propagator of that methodical doubt on which enlightenment so largely depends," while at the same time serving as "one of the principal promoters of fairness of mind, that chief lubricant of human affairs."[20]

## J. B. BURY AND THE "SCIENCE OF HISTORY"

Like Jameson, one of the leading advocates of the view of history as a science in Britain, J. B. Bury (1861–1927), at once expressed a commitment to the ideal of objectivity and recognized the subjective element to historical writing. Trained as a classical philologist, Bury became known both for his works on Roman and Byzantine history, and for his writing on the philosophy of history. Appointed in 1902 as Regius professor of modern history at Cambridge University, Bury presented as his inaugural address one of his best known works, "The Science of History." Criticized for endorsing a simplistic positivism in this address, Bury, like his American counterparts, actually embraced a more complex understanding of historical truth than his critics recognized.[21]

Firmly committed to promoting professionalization and the ideal of scientific history in Britain, where professionalization had been slower to take hold than was the case in other European countries, Bury used his inaugural address to further this goal, opening it with an unequivocal affirmation of the status of history as a science. After noting the continued resistance to this definition of history, Bury declared, "It has not yet become superfluous to insist that history is a science, no less and no more." As a science, history, in Bury's view, was "not a branch of literature." Neither did he consider it simply a form of philosophy as had many of his predecessors. What distinguished history as a science, according to Bury, was its commitment to an accurate recovery of facts through the use of critical methods of scholarship.[22] Bury pointed directly to the influence of Ranke on this conception of history when he quoted Ranke's famous statement that the goal of the historian was to reveal "what actually happened" in the past, lamenting that this goal

> was little accepted in the sense of a warning against transgressing the province of facts; it is a text which must still be preached, and when it has been fully taken to heart, though there be many

schools of political philosophy, there will no longer be divers schools of history.[23]

While in this injunction Bury seemed to adhere to the scientific ideal of objectivity, his definition of history as a science entailed more than just a collection of facts. In his view, history could only be considered a science when it also adopted a developmental understanding of the historical process that recognized how all historical periods were interconnected as part of a larger unity, including both the past and future.[24] For this reason, Bury believed that an objective view of history required the historian to appreciate the importance of all historical periods, rather than giving primacy to the modern era as the culmination of the past. Far from a culmination, the present, together with "[a]ll the epochs of the past are only a few of the front carriages, and probably the least wonderful, in the van of an interminable procession."[25]

Only by recognizing how the present represented just a small part of a much larger whole would the historian attain a truly objective understanding of the past. Not only would this recognition constitute "the scientifically truest point of view" for Bury; it was also necessary for history to be relevant and useful to the present, since people could most effectively use the past to shape the present and future if they possessed an accurate understanding of their place within it.[26] And so, like Jameson, Bury did not see any conflict between his commitment to a scientific ideal of objectivity and his desire to make history socially useful, declaring that the purpose of his address was "to indicate the close interconnexion between the elevation of history to the position of a science and the recognition of its practical significance."[27]

Yet Bury's developmental understanding of history revealed a certain duality in his view of objective truth. While, in associating a developmental view with objectivity, Bury affirmed a faith in the possibility of objective truth, he at the same time questioned the ability of present-day historians to achieve that ideal in his emphasis on the limits to their knowledge. Applying his developmental perspective to the study of history, Bury believed that just as the historical process represented a long course of development that spanned far into the future, so too was historical knowledge the product of a gradual evolutionary process. Thus, for Bury, objectivity was a goal for future historians to achieve; all he and his contemporaries could do was to collect material for future generations to use. In pointing to how historical knowledge was the product of change and evolution, Bury, like Jameson, recognized the subjective element to historical analysis and the way in which historical interpretations reflected their context.[28] He could therefore in his later writings distinguish between "truly objective facts" like dates and names, and "the reconstruction, which involves the discovery of causes and motives, which it is the historian's business to attempt," and which he believed "depends on subjective elements."[29]

Thus, even as he affirmed his belief in scientific history, he at the same time shared in the questioning of the Rankean ideal of objectivity that was beginning to emerge among his contemporaries on the Continent, as such figures as Karl Lamprecht in Germany and Benedetto Croce in Italy in different ways challenged the Rankean conception of scientific history. While Lamprecht criticized this ideal for its focus on political history, urging the need for historians to go beyond politics and give more attention to social and cultural history, Croce went even further to repudiate the notion of history as a science altogether. With his famous claim that "all history is contemporary history," Croce rejected the notion that it was possible or desirable for historians to provide an objective account of the past, arguing instead for the importance of contemporary relevance in shaping an understanding of history. Rather than distorting the past, in his view, the influence of contemporary context and circumstances on accounts of history gave meaning and purpose to those accounts.[30]

## THE NEW HISTORIANS: CHARLES BEARD AND HISTORICAL RELATIVISM

The New Historians in the United States brought together both of these imperatives in their challenge to scientific history. Defining themselves in opposition to the scientific historians, the New Historians pointed to their view of themselves as exponents of a new approach with the publication of James Harvey Robinson's *The New History* in 1912. While the New Historians varied among themselves, what in their minds distinguished them from their predecessors was their shared commitment to making history relevant to the present, their desire to expand the scope of history beyond politics to include other realms of society, and their faith that they could achieve these goals by incorporating the methods of social science into history. Yet, as the case of Charles Beard (1874–1948) revealed, the New Historians were not as new as they claimed to be. If, on the one hand, scientific historians like Jameson had preceded them in recognizing the limits to objectivity and the importance of social history, Beard, on the other hand, revealed the persisting influence of the ideal of objectivity on the New History.[31]

Part of what Morton White has termed the "revolt against formalism," New Historians like Robinson repudiated abstract and, in their eyes, artificial systems of thought in favor of a perspective that emphasized the seamlessness and interconnectedness of human affairs and thus gave primacy to history and experience as the basis for knowledge. For anti-formalists, nothing could be understood apart from its context, and that context itself was always subject to change, enmeshed as it was in a complex series of connections across space and time. Therefore, according to the New Historians, each generation writes its own history, since the writing of history was itself contingent on its context. Consequently, the historian's task was to adapt his work so that it would best reflect the needs and concerns of the present.[32] Robinson summed up this understanding of the historian's purpose when he wrote in 1912, "The present has hitherto been the willing victim of the past; the time has now come when it should turn on the past and exploit it in the interests of advance."[33]

In their emphasis on making history useful, the New Historians reflected in particular the influence of pragmatism, a philosophy that based truth on usefulness, taking part in what one modern scholar has termed "the pragmatic revolt in American history." Part of the revolt against formalism, pragmatism rejected both the Romantic belief in the existence of absolute, eternal truths that reflected a higher reality and the view of truth as an objective external reality that was independent of the observer's perspective. Emphasizing the instrumental character of truth, pragmatism made truth a function of consequences; in this way of thinking, the test of whether a belief was true was its usefulness. Because of the emphasis on the practical function of truth, the American philosopher William James, one of the leading exponents of this theory, labeled it pragmatism.[34]

One of the ways in which the New Historians sought to make history relevant to the present was by using it to further the reform goals of the Progressive movement – hence many of the New Historians have also come to be known as Progressive historians. While the New History and Progressive history differed in emphasis, with the New History focusing more on methodological issues and Progressive history focusing more on the interpretive content of American history, there was considerable overlap between the two categories.[35] The Progressive movement was itself not a unified movement but is a term used to refer broadly to the movement for social reform that emerged in the United States roughly from 1890 to the 1920s. While the Progressives varied in their approaches and goals, they did share certain concerns, which is why they have been grouped together as part of the same movement. Specifically, they shared a concern with the social problems brought about by the rapid industrialization of this period, among the most important of which were the growing disparities of wealth that had resulted from this development, the poor living and working conditions experienced by factory workers, and the difficulty cities had in coping with the large influx of newcomers they attracted. Although they differed in their solutions to these problems, Progressive reformers agreed that the existing industrial order needed some kind of change and reform, and emphasized the importance of government regulation as an instrument of reform, urging the need for a greater sense of community and cooperation as an antidote to the dangers of unchecked individualism.[36]

Charles Beard was an influential figure who illustrated the convergence of the New History with Progressive history. Beard came from a prosperous middle-class background, the son of a successful Indiana mill owner and contractor. After training at Columbia for his graduate work, Beard taught there in the political science department until his resignation in 1917. Very much committed to the New Historians' program of making history relevant to the present, Beard was also an outspoken social critic and reformer, joining in the Progressive crusade to remedy the ills of industrial society.[37] He published his most influential work, *An Economic Interpretation of the Constitution*, in 1913. The book stirred sharp controversy with its challenge to conventional patriotic views of the founding fathers as motivated by disinterested principles in the creation of the Constitution. Far from being disinterested, Beard argued, both supporters and opponents of the Constitution were motivated by economic self-interest. This argument was so inflammatory that the book was banned from public schools in Seattle, while Warren Harding used the headline "Scavengers, Hyena-like, Desecrate the Graves of the Dead Patriots We Revere" to condemn the book in an Ohio newspaper. Despite such attacks, the book ended up becoming very influential and helped establish Beard's reputation as one of the leading American historians of his time.[38]

Although Beard disclaimed any overt political purpose to his work, his economic interpretation served indirectly to promote his Progressive reform goals. By portraying the Constitution as a document that was the product of historical forces just like any other document, Beard desacralized both the Constitution itself and the men who created it, thereby discrediting Supreme Court challenges to Progressive reforms as unconstitutional. Rather than a betrayal of the sacred principles established by the Constitution, changing the Constitution to allow for such reforms would actually be more true to the spirit of the founders than following it uncritically as an immutable form of scripture. Just as the founders created a Constitution that was suited to their interests, Beard suggested, his contemporaries had to adapt the Constitution to reflect their own circumstances and concerns. And by showing how the founders recognized that they could achieve their goal only by appealing to self-interest, Beard revealed to Progressive reformers the strategy they needed to follow to effect their reform purposes; rather than appealing to higher ideals and principles, they had to convince the public that it was in their interest to support it. Beard thus expressed in his book an ambivalence about the founders, demonstrating that he was by no means the subversive radical that his critics feared. Even while he sought to bring them down from their pedestal by revealing their self-interested motives, he at the same time admired them for their practicality and realism.[39]

Likewise, he was not as revolutionary in his economic approach as the designation "New Historian" suggested. In his emphasis on the economic factors behind the Constitution, Beard put into practice the injunctions of the New Historians to expand the scope of history beyond the traditional preoccupation with the political realm. Yet, in doing so, as Beard himself acknowledged, he was following earlier precedents. In making politics and law a function of economic interest, Beard revealed his debt to Marx's historical materialism. Unlike Marx, however, Beard did not attribute conflicts over the Constitution to conflicts between different classes; rather, the conflict in Beard's view was one within the propertied class, between those who owned landed, or what Beard called real property, and those who owned, in Beard's terms, personal property, meaning bonds and securities.[40] Beard was also ambivalent about Marx's belief in economic determinism, urging the need to analyze American history in terms of this theory while disavowing it in the introduction to the 1935 edition of the book, where he argued to the contrary that only by understanding the role of economic interest in politics could his contemporaries determine their own fate as the framers of the Constitution had done.[41] Accordingly, while Beard acknowledged his respect for Marx, he claimed that other thinkers – the most important of whom was James Madison – had a much greater influence on his economic interpretation.[42]

Adding to the ambiguities and inconsistencies in Beard's analysis of economic determinism was his turn toward historical relativism during the 1930s. In calling his *Economic Interpretation* "an interpretation" in the introduction to the 1935 edition of this work, Beard seemed to recognize the subjective element to historical analysis. At the same time he maintained a belief in objectivity when he indignantly repudiated criticisms of his work as partisan, arguing that his economic interpretation was more scientific and impartial than that of his opponents – where he differed from his scientific predecessors was over how to achieve this goal. Yet overall, by the 1930s, Beard became increasingly willing to question the ideal of objectivity, as he and other New Historians turned to historical relativism, not only criticizing the scientific historians' faith in objectivity for making history irrelevant to the present, but also challenging the validity of the ideal itself.[43]

As with his economic interpretation, Beard's challenge to objectivity had earlier roots. Long before Beard, his friend and fellow historian Carl Becker had begun to question the ideal of objectivity as early as 1910. The first of the New Historians to challenge the ideal of objectivity, Becker also went much further than most of the other New Historians in his relativism. Known for his ambivalence and ambiguity on the subject, Becker was himself wary of using the label "relativist" to describe his views on historical truth. Yet Becker could be considered a relativist if relativism is defined broadly to mean the belief that because historical interpretations were always a function of their context, there could be no absolute or universal standard of truth.[44] Hence, while Becker acknowledged the existence of an objective reality, not only did he believe that it was impossible for historians to transcend their own subjectivity and directly access that reality, he also questioned the desirability of objectivity as an ideal. Because, in his view, facts themselves were subjective entities, the writing of history was, by definition, an interpretive enterprise.[45] Yet, differentiating between relativism and skepticism, the scholar Peter Novick argues that Becker and other American relativists of his time were not complete skeptics who repudiated the possibility of true knowledge altogether, but instead emphasized the "plurality of criteria" for determining what is true. In other words, while they did not think that it was possible to achieve a unitary absolute truth, they did believe that some truths were better than others. Because it maintained a belief in the existence of standards of truth – however varied and contingent they were – relativism in this sense did not preclude the possibility of error or falsehood when those standards were violated.[46]

Yet these ideas would not take wider hold until after World War I, coming to fruition during the 1930s with the presentation of Becker's influential formulation of historical relativism, "Everyman His Own Historian," to the American Historical Association in 1931, and with Beard's equally influential exposition of this theory – in his 1933 American Historical Association address "Written History as an Act of Faith," and his 1935 article "That Noble Dream."[47] The evolution of Beard's ideas on the subject revealed the importance of World War I in contributing to the growing acceptance of historical relativism. Seen as a subversive and radical figure on account of his willingness to question the idealization of the founding fathers, Beard was also an ardent supporter of American intervention during World War I, actively participating in the propaganda effort to mobilize public support for the war. Yet even during the war, Beard maintained the nonconformist posture that made him such a controversial figure, resigning from Columbia in October 1917 to protest the firing by President Nicholas Murray Butler of professors who had expressed pacifist views or opposed conscription. However, like Becker and many other of the New Historians, within a few years after the war, by 1922, Beard had repudiated his support for American intervention owing to his disillusionment with the outcome of the war, which had not in his view brought about the better world he had hoped it would.[48]

The war also brought about a deeper disillusionment for Beard and many of his American contemporaries – with the faith in the possibility of objective truth itself. The war undermined their faith in objectivity in a number of ways. The overt partisanship of historians who had written propaganda in support of the war raised questions about their objectivity, while disputes among American historians over revisionist interpretations of the origins of the war made historians increasingly doubtful about whether they could ever agree on what constituted objective truth. More fundamentally, by undermining the optimism about progress that was behind their belief in objectivity, the war contributed to the increased questioning of this ideal during the 1920s and 1930s.[49]

Beard illustrated the way in which increasing doubts about progress, which were further fueled by the Depression, undermined faith in the ideal of objectivity. Like his predecessors, the scientific historians, Beard had assumed that an objective understanding of history – which for him meant a recognition of the importance of economic forces – would reveal the inevitable progress of humanity, and provide the historian with the tools to aid in that progress. Greater scientific knowledge and control over such forces was for Beard both a sign of and a means to progress. As Beard became increasingly uncertain about the inevitability of progress, he increasingly questioned both the possibility and desirability of objectivity. Beard's introduction to the ideas of

European thinkers such as Karl Mannheim, Karl Heussi, and Benedetto Croce added to these doubts about the possibility of objectivity, and he directly cited these thinkers to support his critique of objectivity. Like Becker, Beard did not question the existence of an objective reality external to the observer, or the possibility of falsehood and error. Nor did he repudiate scientific methods of studying history, arguing that only in this way could the historian gain "accurate knowledge of historical facts, personalities, situations, and movements." Sounding much like his predecessor Jameson, he also affirmed the social value of a scientific approach, declaring that it possessed "a value high in the hierarchy of values indispensable to the life of a democracy," for the "inquiring spirit of science, using the scientific method, is the chief safeguard against the tyranny of authority, bureaucracy, and brute power."[50]

What Beard objected to was the unqualified reliance by historians on the scientific method as an instrument of truth, and the failure to recognize that it would yield only an interpretation of history, not an objective account of the past. Because in his view it was impossible for historians to divest themselves of their biases and the influence of their social context, the scientific ideal of objectivity was completely wrongheaded in its assumption that historians could know history as it actually was by turning themselves into a "neutral mirror" of the past. For Beard, this assumption was itself a theory that was "one of the most sweeping dogmas in the recorded history of theories," which ignored "problems of mind with which philosophers and theologians have wrestled for centuries." Although he believed that complete objectivity was unattainable, historians would actually come closer to truth if they could "clarify the mind by admitting its cultural interests and patterns – interests and patterns that will control, or intrude upon, the selection and organization of historical materials."[51] Just as he did not completely abandon his hopes for an approximation of truth, Beard also did not completely give up on the possibility of progress, despite his growing pessimism. Indeed, Beard turned to historical relativism partly as a way to hold on to the hope that history could still serve as an instrument of social improvement while recognizing the limited and contingent character of that improvement. Rather than illuminating the objective reality of progress as Beard had once believed, the historian in his view had to play an active role in defining and creating that progress by recognizing how much he was the product of his time and tailoring his interpretation of the past to best serve the needs of that time. For Beard, since value judgments were implicit in every interpretation of history, the historian could promote progress by making history an instrument for shaping and improving social values, rather than trying to suppress the expression of those values.[52]

The New Historians thus laid the basis for the expansion of the scope of history, the belief in the social function of history, and the challenge to the belief in objectivity that would come with the rise of social history in the latter part of the twentieth century. Yet just as these later developments had earlier roots in the work of the New Historians, so too did the ideas of the New Historians have precedents in the work of their opponents, the scientific historians, who had combined their commitment to objectivity with a belief in the social value of history and a recognition of its subjective character. And, as Jameson demonstrated, even while embracing the Rankean ideal of objectivity, at least some scientific historians had already begun to question its political emphasis and to urge the need to include social history – an imperative that would take increasing hold of the profession after World War II.

# Chapter Five

## *Social History, Fragmentation, and the Revival of Narrative*

During the second half of the twentieth century, historians seemed to become ever more fractured over how to approach their subject. One of the most important sources of conflict after World War II was the growing importance of social history, as embodied by the Annales school in France and the "new" social history in the United States. Just as the rise of social history was the product of a variety of imperatives, critics of this approach varied widely in the reasons for their misgivings about social history. Efforts to remedy these problems through the revival of narrative and the cultural turn in historical scholarship only divided historians further, as the intersection of these developments with the rise of postmodernism turned debates over how to approach history into debates over the attainability of truth itself.

The differences between the French historian Fernand Braudel and the American historian Jesse Lemisch illustrated the diverse forms that social history took in this period and its different political implications. As the debate over Lemisch's approach revealed, the rise of social history was a highly divisive development, especially in the United States. Yet the controversy over Simon Schama's work, *Dead Certainties*, showed how the effort to address some of the criticisms of social history through the revival of narrative was equally divisive owing to the threat it posed to the belief in objective truth.

### FERNAND BRAUDEL AND THE ANNALES SCHOOL

One of the most important developments in the writing of history after World War II was the growing interest by both European and American historians in social history, that is, the history of ordinary people and everyday life. While historians on both sides of the Atlantic agreed, and even influenced each other in their desire to expand the scope of history to this realm, their interest in social history took different forms and was the product of different sources. Although interest in this topic extended to many different nations, ranging from the "history from below" of E. P. Thompson and other British Marxist historians to the German historian Hans Ulrich Wehler's "Historical Social Science," the Annales school in France and the new social history in the United States illustrated especially clearly the diversity of social history.[1] Where World War II was a turning point in the rise of the Annales school, the protest movements of the 1960s galvanized the new social history. And whereas the Annales historians disavowed any overt political purpose and indeed questioned the significance of politics altogether as a historical force, political concerns were very much central to the rise of the new social history.

The Annales school in France played an instrumental role in the rise of social history both in Europe and the United States. The Annales school dated back to 1929, when Marc Bloch and Lucien Febvre founded the journal from which the movement took its name, as part of their effort to challenge what they believed was the dominance of conventional narrative political history in France. Only after World War II did the Annales school emerge from its beginnings as a movement on the periphery of the French historical establishment to gain wide acceptance not only in France but in the international arena, becoming an important influence on the rise of social history in both Europe and the United States. The establishment of a research institute to promote interdisciplinary and collaborative research in social history both reflected and furthered the growing influence of the Annales school. Febvre laid the basis for the institutionalization of the Annales school in 1946 with the creation of the Sixth Section of the École Pratique des Hautes Études, which would become the École des Hautes Études en Sciences Sociales in 1972. With Febvre's death in 1956, Febvre's successor as both editor of the *Annales* journal and president of the Sixth Section, Fernand Braudel (1902–85), would become one of the most important figures in propagating the influence of the Annales school, and his prominence as one of the leading French historians of his time pointed to the ascendancy of this school in French historical studies.[2]

Although the Annales school did not embrace an overt political agenda, its founding members were very much shaped by the political context of World War II. Marc Bloch was killed by the Germans in 1944 for his participation in the French resistance, while Fernand Braudel wrote the first volume of his first book, a study of the Mediterranean region in the age of Philip II, from memory during his imprisonment in a German prisoner-of-war camp, and he himself noted the impact of this experience upon his conception of historical time.[3]

One of the most important innovations of the Annales school was its challenge to the conventional view of time as a unified, linear process. The Annales school instead emphasized the multiplicity of time. Braudel gave the best-known formulation of this view when he divided historical time into three levels, arguing that it was necessary for historians to examine all three levels to achieve what he called a *histoire totale* that comprehended the past in all its complexity. Identifying the short-term level with rapid change in the form of military and political events such as wars or revolutions, Braudel referred to history that focused on this level as *histoire événementielle*. Criticizing previous historians for giving too much attention to this level, Braudel considered such events the least important form of history. Comparing an event to "an explosion 'blaring out the news,'" Braudel remarked that "[c]ontemporary consciousness is blinded by its deceptive smoke, but its flash is brief and cannot be recalled." The intermediate level, or what Braudel called the history of conjunctures, covered more gradual change that took place over a longer span of time, such as economic or demographic changes. For Braudel, the most important level was what he called the *longue durée*, which extended over very long spans of time. On this level were structures where very little if any change took place at all. By structures, not only did he mean physical structures such as geography and the environment, but he also used the term more broadly to refer to deeply rooted patterns resistant to change, which could include habits of behavior or thought.[4]

Hence, rather than following a chronological linear narrative, he divided his study of the Mediterranean in the age of Philip II into three sections that corresponded to each of these levels of historical time. Beginning with what he considered the most important level, the *longue durée*, Braudel focused in the first section on the unchanging geographic structures that influenced the history of this region, looking at such topics as the impact of mountains on culture and the role of the sea itself in shaping the Mediterranean region. In the second section, he examined the history of conjunctures by looking for social and economic patterns of change, tracing the economic polarization that he believed characterized the Mediterranean region during the sixteenth and seventeenth centuries. Only in the third section did he turn to the political and military events that had been traditionally considered the most important to Philip II's reign. He minimized the importance of these events not only by leaving them to the end of his work, but also through the way he spoke of them. Repeatedly in this section, he brought up events and individuals such as Don Juan of Austria's victory at the Battle of Lepanto, only to emphasize their unimportance and to point to how they were the product of larger forces. While, then, Braudel did not deny a role for events altogether, his emphasis on the power of unchanging material and mental structures drastically reduced their importance as a historical force.[5] As he summed up his view of the relationship between events and larger forces, events were for him "surface disturbances, crests of foam that the tides of history carry on their strong backs."[6]

Paradoxically, this perspective was partly the product of Braudel's experience as a prisoner of war during World War II – the very kind of political event whose significance he belittled. Braudel explained how this experience contributed to his emphasis on the *longue durée* when he declared,

> I myself during a rather miserable period of captivity struggled hard to escape the chronicle of those difficult years (1940–1945). Refusing to recognize events and the time during which they occurred was a way of withdrawing to a sheltered vantage point from which one could view them at a distance, judge them more dispassionately, and believe in them a little. To move from a close-up view to a medium range and then a very distant perspective (the last if it exists must be that of the sages), then having reached that point, to stop, reconsider, and reconstruct the picture one sees, to order the revolving elements – all this is very tempting to the historian.

By focusing on larger structures and the *longue durée*, he was able to distance himself from the suffering inflicted by his immediate context and to see how unimportant that suffering was when placed in the broader framework of the unchanging structures that determined human history.[7] Accordingly, repeatedly using the metaphor of a prison to describe these structures, speaking, for example, of how even "mental habits too can be a long-term prison," Braudel made his own imprisonment appear less of a departure by suggesting that all human beings were prisoners in some sense of the long-term structures that constrained them.[8]

To understand the complex interplay between the *longue durée* and the other levels of historical time, which he believed were all inextricably linked to one another, and to achieve his ideal of a total history, Braudel urged historians to incorporate the methods and insights of social science into their work.[9] Through the use of economic theory, for example, he believed that historians could illuminate the gradual patterns of change that characterized the history of conjunctures. As critical as he was, then, of French scientific historians such as Charles Langlois and Charles Seignebos, he shared their view of history as a science, even using scientific terms such as "laboratory" to describe the work of historians. He differed, however, in defining science more broadly to emphasize how interconnected history was with other disciplines, giving history a lead role in what he termed "the sciences of man." The scientific character of history also required collaborative research that would enable historians to pool together and organize their resources in the most efficient way.[10] His concern with integrating all of these different levels of history into a larger whole and with looking broadly at large-scale structures also led him to expand the geographic scope of history beyond the nation and to downplay the importance of national boundaries – hence his work on the age of Philip II did not focus on a particular nation but examined the Mediterranean region as a whole.[11] Braudel went even further in crossing national borders in his next work, *Civilization and Capitalism* (1967–79), to examine the history of everyday life and material culture from a global perspective, arguing that such a perspective was necessary to understand the large-scale transformations that shaped the history of everyday life.[12]

## THE NEW LEFT AND THE "NEW" SOCIAL HISTORY IN THE UNITED STATES

While influenced by the Annales school, the rise of what has been termed the new social history in the United States also derived from other sources. Not as new as the label new social history proclaimed, this movement had roots in the efforts by the New Historians and their successors of the 1930s and 1940s to expand the scope of history beyond the traditional preoccupation with political elites. Thus, for example, showing the same interest in the dispossessed that would characterize the new social history, Angie Debo had long before published her studies of Native American history, *The Rise and Fall of the Choctaw Republic* (1935) and *And Still the Waters Run* (1940). W. E. B. Du Bois likewise challenged the prevailing view of Reconstruction during his time by pointing to the achievements of Reconstruction and emphasizing the role of African Americans themselves in these achievements with his *Black Reconstruction in America*, published in 1934.[13] Even while drawing on their early twentieth-century predecessors, the new social historians were at the same time reacting against the establishment of consensus history in the 1950s. So-called because of its emphasis on the unified and homogenous character of American history, consensus history – whose leading practitioners included Daniel Boorstin, Richard Hofstadter, and Louis Hartz – was itself not as unified as its name implied. While its practitioners agreed in minimizing the role of conflict in American history, they disagreed over whether this quality was cause for celebration or criticism. And so, even as the new social historians directly repudiated what they believed was the homogenized vision of American history given by the consensus historians, they were actually following the lead of some of the consensus historians in using history as a vehicle for social criticism.[14]

Their desire to use history for this purpose took on added urgency with the protest movements of the 1960s, which were another important force in the emergence of the new social history. For these historians, greater attention to groups that had been previously marginalized by the traditional emphasis on political and military history, such as women, African Americans, and Native Americans, would not only demonstrate the diversity and conflict that they believed characterized American history. In doing so, it would also further their political goals of promoting more equal treatment of these groups in the present. One of the pioneers in the advent of the new social history, Jesse Lemisch (1936–), revealed the New Left affiliations of the new social history and its political agenda in his famous call for American historians to write history "from the bottom up." While a number of American historians during this period came to be classified as "New Left historians" because of their leftist political sympathies, including among them Eugene Genovese, William Appleman

Williams, and Staughton Lynd, these historians varied widely in their relationship to the student protest movements that were associated with the rise of the New Left in the United States. A member of SDS (Students for a Democratic Society), who had participated both in protests against the Vietnam War and in the civil rights movement, Lemisch was one of the New Left historians with the most direct ties to the New Left student movement.[15]

Using the American Revolution to illustrate the need for a history of the "inarticulate," Lemisch criticized prior accounts of American history for focusing on the elites and portraying their perspective as representative of the people as a whole. For Lemisch, the problem with this tendency was not just that it was misleading and inaccurate; it also offered a version of history that benefited those in power by masking the injustices and structures of oppression that maintained their power. Thus, he declared that the study of the American Revolution from the bottom up would provide "a point of view which assumes that all men are created equal, and rational, and since they can think and reason they can make their own history. These assumptions are nothing more nor less than the democratic credo." Here, he suggested that a history of the inarticulate would not only reflect democratic values, but would also further them in the present by making ordinary Americans of his own time more aware of their oppression and empowering them to act against that oppression.[16] For Lemisch, such an approach was not just socially valuable but would also result in a more objective and truthful understanding of the past. Claiming that the neglect of the powerless by previous historians had "distorted" "past reality," Lemisch asserted that a "sympathy for the powerless brings us closer to objectivity." Thus Lemisch saw no conflict between his political purposes and a commitment to objective truth.[17]

Lemisch was even more clear about how he reconciled these two imperatives in an essay he presented to the 1969 meeting of the American Historical Association, "Present Mindedness Revisited: Anti-Radicalism as a Goal of American Historical Writing since

World War II," later published as *On Active Service in War and Peace: Politics and Ideology in the American History Profession* (1975). In this essay, Lemisch sought to refute criticisms that the political goals of radical historians like himself had distorted their accounts of the past with a biased and present-minded perspective. Lemisch defended the legitimacy of the work of radical historians by arguing that it was his opponents who had distorted history by using it to further their conservative political purposes, contrary to their claims to be neutral and objective. Therefore, radical historians were no more present minded than their opponents in using history for activist purposes. To the contrary, in providing a corrective to the distortions and the "unreal and unprincipled" politics of their conservative opponents, radical historians were actually contributing to a more real and true understanding of American history. Declaring, "It is the Left which has spoken … of real issues, of pain and suffering, and of a better world which has *not* been seen before," Lemisch saw no conflict between his political purposes and his commitment to objective truth because of his assumption that the political principles he embraced were more true to reality than those of his opponents. Thus, echoing Ranke, he concluded his essay with the proclamation, "And we are in the libraries, writing history, trying to cure it of your partisan and self-congratulatory fictions, trying to come a little closer to finding out how things actually were."[18]

Lemisch's essay provoked sharply polarized responses from the American historical profession, revealing how divisive his call for a history from the bottom up was among American historians. While the session where Lemisch presented the essay was one of the most highly attended at the AHA meeting, the response of one anonymous critic demonstrated how unwilling more established historians were to even entertain Lemisch's critique of the American historical profession, as this critic declared, "I don't know how you can tell them that he simply cannot do this, and that he certainly cannot do it in the pages of the *Journal*. He probably believes that he can, which says something about how far he and his ilk are estranged from civilization."[19] The attacks on Lemisch's call for a history from the bottom up came not just from established historians but from other radical historians. The most notable of these attacks came from Joan and Donald Scott, who criticized a pamphlet that Lemisch had published for the SDS in 1966, *Towards a Democratic History*, calling for a democratic approach to history which would show that "the common man has in fact had an ideology, that that ideology has been radical, and that conditions have been objectively bad enough so that a radical critique has been a sound one."[20] Criticizing Lemisch for romanticizing ordinary people "as glorious revolutionaries," the Scotts contended that the goal of a radical history should be to "provide us with a new way of looking at history" and "raise radical questions about all kinds of people," rather than focusing on the "common man" as Lemisch urged.[21]

   As this critique revealed, the new social historians varied widely among themselves in both their approach and their subject matter. While Lemisch sought to carry out his injunctions for a history from the bottom up by focusing on the working class in his study of sailors during the Revolutionary era, other proponents of the new social history directed their attention to recovering the experiences of other constituencies among the "inarticulate." Consequently, feminists wishing to demonstrate and challenge the oppression of women helped establish women's history as a field of study, while historians sympathetic to the civil rights movement contributed to a growing interest in African American history.[22] Not only did the new social historians vary in their political goals; they did not all share Lemisch's commitment to the political function of history. Thus, for example, John Demos and Philip Greven, who helped pioneer the new social history with their studies of colonial New England, did not write with an overt political agenda. Drawing on the theories and methods of social science to illuminate the history of everyday life, their works revealed another important attribute of the new social history – its desire to incorporate social science techniques into the study of history as a way to make up for the limited documentary evidence left behind by their subjects. While they differed, then, in their subject matter and political purposes, American social historians of this period shared with each other and their Annales counterparts a commitment to an interdisciplinary approach, looking variously to fields such as economics, psychology, and demography for historical insight.[23]

## THE "FRAGMENTATION" OF HISTORY: THE CULTURAL TURN AND THE RISE OF POSTMODERNISM

While the new social history began as an insurgent movement that saw itself as challenging professional orthodoxy about American history, it had become firmly entrenched by the 1980s as part of the mainstream of professional scholarship. The result was that once neglected or marginalized topics such as women's history or African American history had become mainstays in the profession. Yet the growing ascendancy of social history brought with it new problems and challenges, from both without and within. The emphasis on the conflict and diversity that charac-terized American history contributed to a growing sense of fragmentation, as social historians – in their desire to avoid the generalizations and homogenization that they believed charac-terized their predecessors – tended to focus narrowly on a particular group or segment of society, rather than providing a broad overview of American society as a whole.[24]

This sense of fragmentation only deepened with the turn to cultural history during the 1970s and 1980s, which itself arose partly as a remedy for the problems that resulted from the reliance on social science by social historians. While sharing the same concern with the history of ordinary people and everyday life, advocates of what has been termed the "cultural turn" in historical scholarship expressed growing doubts about the reliance of social history on the methods of social science. For these histo-rians, the problem with such methods was that they had focused too much on the material conditions and structures that shaped the lives of ordinary people, at the expense of their perceptions and individual experiences. Cultural historians did not reject the use of the social sciences altogether, but turned away from the emphasis on economics and looked instead to anthropology for insights that could illuminate the values and perceptions of ordinary individuals.[25] The influence of anthropology on cultural history was especially apparent in the emergence of microhistory, an approach that focused on a small community or locality, often using the story of a single ordinary individual or event to illuminate something larger about the culture. Among the most notable examples of microhistory have been Carlo Ginsburg's *The Cheese and the Worms* (1976), a study of a sixteenth-century Italian miller who was burned as a heretic, and Emmanuel Le Roy Ladurie's *Montaillou* (1975), a study of fourteenth-century peasants in a village in Languedoc.[26]

Influenced in particular by the work of cultural anthropologist Clifford Geertz, microhistorians like Robert Darnton in his *The Great Cat Massacre* (1984) applied Geertz's view of culture as a text that could only be understood by thick description to their analysis of specific events and individuals. Challenging anthropology's claims to science, Geertz portrayed the study of culture as an interpretive enterprise, likening culture to a text that had to be understood in terms of its own context. Because, in his view, cultural practices and beliefs were embedded in multiple layers of meaning, anthropologists could only understand these practices on their own terms by employing, to use his famous phrase, "thick description" that would convey all of those layers of meaning without imposing their own perspectives on their subjects. Therefore, following Geertz, microhistorians sought to understand a culture by using seemingly trivial and unimportant acts or signs as clues to its underlying assumptions rather than through larger generalizations based on a pattern of observations.[27] As the Italian historian Giovanni Levi, one of the leading practitioners of microhistory, has summed up Geertz's approach and its relevance for microhistory, "This approach succeeds in using microscopic analysis of the most minute events as a means of arriving at the most far-reaching conclusions."[28] Through microhistory, cultural historians sought to restore the regard for individual subjectivity that they believed had been obscured by social historians in their emphasis on large-scale social structures and processes. Yet in directing their attention to the local and individual – even smaller units of analysis than a social class or ethnic group – microhistorians have fueled fears about the fragmentation of history.[29]

The American historian Thomas Bender expressed those fears in an influential 1986 article for the *Journal of American History* calling for the "need for synthesis" in American history. While recognizing the value of the work done by recent social historians, Bender argued that because their scholarship "is devoted almost exclusively to the private or *gemeinschaftlich* worlds of trades, occupations, and professions; locality; sisterhood; race and ethnicity; and family," the result has been that "[w]hat we have gotten are the parts, all richly described. But since they are somehow assumed to be autonomous, we get no image of the whole, and no suggestions about how the parts might go together or even whether they are intended to go together."[30] The rise of cultural history had in his view further contributed to this sense of fragmentation in its emphasis on "interior meaning," making different groups appear to be "more and more self-contained," with the result that it had become increasingly difficult "to grasp their connection with larger social units."[31] In order to restore a sense of synthesis to American history, Bender urged the need for the study of public culture, which would examine the interplay and conflict among different social groups for power in the public realm. For Bender, such a synthesis was necessary for history to maintain its social value and relevance, since the fragmentation and specialization of history had increasingly alienated it from the larger public.[32] Bender's call for synthesis in turn provoked sharp debate among American historians. Challenging such calls,

Eric Monkkonen in a 1986 article for the *American Historical Review* pointed to "the dangers of synthesis." Arguing for the value of "what is unfortunately but commonly construed as fragmentation, narrowness, technicality, and low public appeal," Monkkonen reasoned that "[f]ocused work produces exciting breakthroughs and generates historical insights," while "synthesis opens the way to erroneous and vacuous statements about American character and culture."[33]

As the debate over Bender's calls for synthesis revealed, not only did the past appear increasingly fractured by the 1980s; historians responded to this sense of fracture by dividing even more sharply among themselves. The consolidation of social and cultural history as part of the profession thus provoked sharp opposition from critics who questioned not only the legitimacy and value of its subject matter but its underlying assumptions about truth and human nature. While critics of social history varied among themselves, the neoconservative historian Gertrude Himmelfarb, one of the most influential and vocal of these critics, voiced a central theme in their objections to social history, and revealed the conservative political leanings of the opposition to social history, when she called social history "history with the politics left out" in a 1984 article for *Harper's Weekly*. While recognizing a place for social history, Himmelfarb argued that historians of her time had gone too far in giving primacy to this topic at the expense of politics. The reason why it was so important for her to restore politics back to its rightful prominence in human history was that it was through participation in politics that human beings exercised their capacity for reason and demonstrated what differentiated them from other species. As Himmelfarb explained, in devaluing political history, social history undermined a regard for "reason itself: the reason embodied in the polity, in the constitutions and laws that permit them to order their affairs in a rational manner," as well as "the reason inherent in the historical enterprise itself, in the search for objective truth that always eludes the individual historian but that always (or so it was once thought) informs and inspires his work." Ultimately for Himmelfarb, social history threatened historical truth not only in providing a partial and incomplete view of the past that denied the importance of politics to human affairs, but in relying on speculation and theory to answer "questions of the past which the past did not ask itself, for which the evidence is sparse and unreliable."[34]

In her attack on social history for undermining the ideal of objective truth, Himmelfarb expressed more widespread fears about the status of this ideal that revealed yet another source of contention among historians – divisions over whether objective truth was an attainable or even desirable goal for historians. While such divisions were partly the product of the rise of social and cultural history, postmodernism also played an important role in these debates. These two developments were in fact closely related to one another. Thus, for example, cultural history and postmodernism both arose as part of what has been termed the linguistic turn in historical scholarship, which gave primacy to language in the construction of social reality. In the structuralist theory of Ferdinand de Saussure – a major influence on the linguistic turn – language was more than simply a reflection of social reality, but was itself an autonomous system with a structure of its own. Because language provided the structures through which people understood reality, it defined the very nature and meaning of that reality.[35]

Structuralist theory in turn laid the basis for postmodernism. Because postmodernism is a broad category that has been loosely used to group together a set of ideas and developments that did not form a coherent ideology, defining this term is difficult. Indeed, to try to impose coherence on postmodernism by giving it a fixed definition would go against the very repudiation of coherence and fixity that has characterized postmodernism in its many different guises; hence, even thinkers who have been identified with postmodernism have either disavowed this label for themselves or have been reluctant to define postmodernism as an ideology. For example, one advocate of postmodernism,

Keith Jenkins, declares that "postmodernity is not an ideology or position we can choose to subscribe to or not, postmodernity is precisely our condition: it is our historical fate to be living now." In explaining why he believed that postmodernity was a condition, not an ideology, Jenkins revealed how growing pessimism about the state of modern society and its capacity for progress contributed to the rise of postmodernism. In particular, Jenkins, like many other postmodern thinkers, challenged the modern belief in the power of reason and science – which had its roots in Enlightenment thought – to bring about human progress.[36]

Although the term was not widely used until the 1980s, the ideas associated with postmodernism had their origins in literary theory of the 1960s – especially that of the literary theorist Roland Barthes and the philosopher Jacques Derrida. While the influence of postmodernism extended to many different disciplines, and the forms it took varied by discipline, most relevant for the writing of history, postmodern thinkers went even further than structuralists did in privileging the role of language to deny the knowability and indeed the existence of objective reality altogether, claiming that history itself was nothing more than a text – a viewpoint encapsulated by Derrida's oft-quoted statement that "there is nothing outside the text." That is, according to postmodernists, historical accounts were simply literary constructions that did not refer to an outside reality, making history no different from fiction.[37] Hayden White offered one of the most influential and controversial formulations of this view with his argument that historical narratives are "verbal fictions, the contents of which are as much *invented* as *found* and the forms of which have more in common with their counterparts in literature than they have with those in the sciences."[38] It followed then for White that the only basis for differentiating between conflicting historical accounts was moral and aesthetic, not their correspondence to reality. Or for Michel Foucault, another theorist associated with postmodernism, because knowledge – including historical knowledge

– was an instrument of power, it was the relations of power within a society, not truthfulness, that determined which interpretation of the past would prevail.[39]

While postmodernist theory originated with thinkers from outside the United States, it had a greater influence on American than on European historians, provoking the sharpest debates in the United States. Paradoxically, although most historians agreed – at least on the level of practice – in repudiating the most extreme forms of postmodernism that denied the existence of objective reality altogether, postmodernism fueled conflicts among historians over the desirability and attainability of objective truth, intensifying divisions between social historians and their critics while at the same time creating other lines of division – and convergence – among historians.[40] Even though most of the new social historians of the 1960s and 1970s were as committed to objective truth as their opponents, their self-conscious use of history to further their political goals came to be seen by their critics as a threat to the ideal of objectivity. Not only did the conflicts that arose from their politicization of history call into question faith in the attainability of objective truth; their open avowal of their political purposes laid them open to charges of abandoning objectivity as an ideal altogether.[41] Consequently, conservative critics of social history like Himmelfarb associated the politicization and particularization of history by social historians with postmodern attacks on truth, even though social historians were themselves divided in their view of postmodernism. While some historians of women and gender – most notably among them Joan Scott – drew on postmodern theory for their analysis of gender as a social construct, other social historians sharply criticized postmodernism both for what they saw as its conservative political implications and its threat to truth.[42] For example, in 1984, Lawrence Stone, a pioneering figure in the emergence of social history, called on historians to come together in opposition to "the growing army of enemies of rationality," embodied by postmodernism, who denied "the possibility of accurate communication by the use of language, the force of logical deduction, and the very existence of truth and falsehood."[43]

## THE "REVIVAL OF NARRATIVE"

The revival of narrative brought together and revealed the complex relationship between all of these different developments, but in doing so became yet another source of contention among historians. A phrase first coined by Lawrence Stone in 1979 to refer to the renewed interest in a narrative mode of historical writing that had been forsaken by social historians in the 1950s and 1960s in favor of a more analytic approach, the revival of narrative also involved a broader reaction against the social science orientation of social historians and its underlying assumptions about the nature of the historical process. Namely, for Stone, the revival of narrative signified an affirmation of human agency against the deterministic tendencies of social history, with its emphasis on large-scale impersonal social forces, and the "end of the attempt to produce a coherent scientific explanation of change in the past."[44] Consequently, this trend came to encompass historians writing on a variety of topics from many different approaches. While many of the works that Stone cited as examples of the revival of narrative, such as Carlo Ginzburg's *The Cheese and the Worms* and Emmanuel Le Roy Ladurie's *Montaillou*, came from European historians, American historians such as John Demos also took part in this trend with his *The Unredeemed Captive* (1994) and Linda Gordon in her *The Great Arizona Orphan Abduction* (2001).

So many of the early contributions to the revival of narrative came from cultural historians writing microhistory because they saw narrative as a means of restoring the individuality and agency of their subjects. For Stone, narrative provided a useful vehicle for conveying the level of detail necessary for historians wishing to apply Geertz's model of thick description to their study of culture. Historians also embraced the revival of narrative as a remedy for some of the other problems that resulted from the rise of social history. Fearing that the increasingly specialized and fragmented character of history had alienated general audiences by making history seem too esoteric and inaccessible, historians turned to narrative as a way to re-engage general audiences in history. While, then, like their nineteenth-century Romantic predecessors, practitioners of the new narrative history were very much concerned with dramatizing history and bringing the past to life for their readers, they differed from their predecessors in their subject matter, giving much more attention to ordinary people and everyday life. In addition, like the Romantic historians of the nineteenth century, contemporary practitioners of the new narrative history emphasized the importance of using the imagination to make the past more vivid and dramatic for their readers, incorporating fictional techniques that gave their works a novelistic quality.[45]

Yet the revival of narrative also proved to be a divisive development among historians, since the willingness to blur the boundary between history and fiction provoked sharp criticism from historians who identified this approach with postmodern challenges to objective truth.[46] The response to Simon Schama's work *Dead Certainties* (1991) – one of the most influential and controversial examples of the new narrative history – revealed how anxieties about postmodernism shaped and contributed to the debate over the revival of narrative.[47] In this work, Schama sought to demonstrate the uncertainty of historical knowledge by presenting multiple perspectives on two events – the death of general James Wolfe at the siege of Québec, and the trial of John Webster for the murder of George Parkman. Often resorting to speculation and imagination to illuminate his historical subjects, Schama sought to engage his readers by adopting a narrative style similar to that of the novelist. What made his work so controversial was the blending of the fictional with factual that resulted from the style of writing, making it difficult for the reader to tell when he was drawing on the imagination. Thus he opened the work with a fictionalized account of the siege of Québec from the perspective of an ordinary soldier, without telling the reader that this section was fictionalized until the afterword. One of the sharpest criticisms of Schama's approach came from the historian Gordon Wood, who attacked Schama's "narrative experiment" for putting "the integrity of the discipline at risk," arguing that Schama's use of the imagination threatened the integrity of history through its challenge to truth. Declaring that the "conventions of objectivity and documentary proof" should "not to be abandoned without a fight either to postmodern skepticism or to Schama's playful experiments in narration," Wood concluded his review of Schama's work with the affirmation that, while recognizing the interpretive character of history, one "can still believe intelligibly and not naively in an objective truth about the past that can be observed and empirically verified."[48] Even though Schama had emphasized his belief in the distinction between fact and fiction, stating that he had only fictionalized where there were no facts available, Wood here associated his work with "postmodern skepticism" about the possibility of objective knowledge about the past, revealing how postmodernism had come to be used as a term of opprobrium even against historians who did not fully subscribe to its tenets.[49]

Yet while historians have not come together in the way that Stone urged, they did increasingly by the 1990s attempt to come to terms with the challenge posed by postmodernism, with the efforts of historians like Joyce Appleby, Margaret Jacob, Lynn Hunt, James Kloppenberg, and Thomas Haskell to establish a new basis for historical knowledge in response to the growing skepticism about the possibility of objective truth. Although they differed in the solutions they offered, these works shared a belief in the possibility of establishing a workable foundation for historical knowledge while recognizing the obstacles and limits to truth.[50] As Appleby, Hunt, and Jacob declared of their work, *Telling the Truth about History* (1994), their goal was to promote "a democratic practice of history" that "encourages skepticism about dominant views, but at the same time trusts in the reality of the past and its knowability."[51] Thus, far from betokening the end of the discipline as some historians feared, the sense of crisis created by the fragmentation of history and the rise of postmodernism has led historians to reflect more deeply on what defines history as a discipline and to clarify their methodological and epistemological assumptions.[52] If, then, efforts to create synthesis among historians have in some ways resulted in further fragmentation, the growing fragmentation of the discipline has in its turn contributed to renewed efforts by historians to define what they have in common and to find ways to integrate their scholarship. This desire to integrate the findings of the recent work in social and cultural history has also laid the basis for the rise of global history – the most important development in current historical scholarship and the subject of the next chapter.

# Chapter Six

## *History and Historiography in Global Perspective*

The most important recent development in professional historical scholarship has been the shift to a more global perspective, which emphasizes the importance of analyzing transnational connections between historical events and developments. Like the revival of narrative and the cultural turn, global history, or world history as it has also been termed, represented in some ways an effort to achieve the goals of social history while providing a remedy for some of its problems. In addition, as was the case with social history, the rise of global history has provoked sharp debate not only over its intellectual merits but over its political implications, reflecting contemporary concerns about the effects of globalization and nationalism.

Amid the many different forms and examples of global history, one way to illustrate its workings and implications is by showing how it has been applied to the history of historical writing. Two historians who lend themselves especially well to a global approach and illustrate the kinds of transnational connections that such an approach would entail are the Yoruba historian Samuel Johnson and the Chinese historian Hu Shi. Where Johnson sought to reconcile Western religious beliefs with an affirmation of his Yoruba identity, Hu Shi in contrast emphasized the compatibility between Western scientific ideals and Chinese scholarly tradition.

### THE RISE OF A GLOBAL APPROACH

Long before the current growth of interest in global history, historians had recognized, at least in theory, the need to consider the history of the world in broad terms. Thus, calls for a universal history came from historians as different as the bishop Jacques-Bénigne Bossuet in the seventeenth century and Johann Gatterer in the eighteenth century, while Voltaire placed his history of European culture in a broader context by beginning his essay on manners with Asian and Persian history. Nor did the rise of nationalistic history in the nineteenth century bring about a complete abandonment of this concern. Leopold von Ranke still urged the need for a universal history, while even so ardent a nationalist as George Bancroft recognized the importance of a transnational perspective by devoting extensive attention to the European context for American developments. What has distinguished the recent turn to global history has been, first, its commitment to recovering the history of regions outside Europe and the United States – namely Asia, Africa, and Latin America – without judging those regions according to Western cultural standards. In contrast, earlier exponents of so-called "universal" history either equated a universal history with a history of Europe, making only a limited effort to be universal in their coverage, or, when they did examine cultures outside of Europe, assessed those cultures in terms of European standards.[1] Second, rather than trying to give a comprehensive view of world history, global history has been defined by its concern with analyzing transnational connections between different countries and regions of the world. And so, while some works of global history have tried to provide a broad geographic coverage of their subject, others have centered more narrowly on events or developments within a particular geographic setting, while placing those developments in a transnational context.[2]

One of the most influential early pioneers in the advent of global history was the historian William McNeill. Focusing on the diffusion of technology and skills between different regions of the world, McNeill's *The Rise of the West: A History of the Human Community* (1963) provided other historians with a model for examining large-scale historical developments across a broad geographical expanse. By showing how such cross-cultural exchanges were themselves important forces of historical change,

McNeill's work contributed to the growth of scholarly interest in cross-cultural approaches to history.[3] As McNeill revealed, interest in global history had already begun to emerge by the 1960s and 1970s, but this approach would not fully come into its own until the 1990s. The founding of the *Journal of World History* in 1990, followed by the founding of the *Journal of Global History* in 2006, marked the growing prominence of global history in the historical profession.[4] As a relatively new development, global history is still very much in the process of defining itself as an approach. Hence, even the terminology used to speak of global history has been somewhat amorphous, since historians have referred to this trend as both global history and world history. While the two terms have sometimes been used interchangeably, global history has been more closely associated with globalization and has become increasingly prevalent as a term since 1990.[5]

The rise of global history has been the product of forces both inside and outside the historical profession. Taking its inspiration from both philosophy of history and social science theory, global history drew from philosophers of history such as Oswald Spengler and Arnold Toynbee its concern with analyzing history in terms of large-scale social units that cut across national lines and its interest in cross-cultural interactions, while turning to social science for theories and approaches that could provide an analytical framework for understanding these processes – the most notable of which was the world system analysis of Immanuel Wallerstein.[6] Revealing the importance of the rise of social history to the emergence of global history, the Annales historian Fernand Braudel, who was himself influenced by the world system approach, helped lay the basis for understanding history in terms of a global perspective in his concern with large-scale, long-term structures that spanned national boundaries, adopting a transnational approach in all his major works.[7] The rise of interest in global history was therefore in some ways simply an extension of the growing importance of social history in the historical profession, serving as a different means of achieving the goals of social history. Where social historians had previously sought to shift the focus of historical attention from the elites to ordinary people by examining marginalized or oppressed groups within a given society, many of the practitioners of global history have sought to further the same goal by looking at regions of the world that have been marginalized or oppressed by the West. In addition, by examining the transnational connections between these regions and the West, global history has also illuminated the intercultural forces shaping the lives of ordinary people in Europe and the United States. For example, the transatlantic character of the African slave trade has made the study of transnational connections between Africa and the Americas, and the ways in which developments in the two regions influenced each other, especially appealing to scholars of American slavery as a means of deepening their understanding of this institution and its effects.[8]

At the same time, scholars have also looked to global history as a remedy for the sense of fragmentation that came out of the rise of social history. The adoption of a global perspective has enabled historians to go beyond the local orientation that characterized so much of the scholarship on social and cultural history, while the emphasis on examining transnational connections has provided historians with a way to integrate the local with broader trends and synthesize the seemingly fragmented picture of the past that came with the explosion of scholarship on social and cultural history. Yet the turn to global history has given rise to new divisions among historians, as scholars have differed widely both over the forms it should take and the value and political implications of this approach. Illustrating the breadth and variety of topics encompassed by global history, the areas that have attracted the most attention from scholars of global history have been trade and other large-scale economic developments, biological processes such as disease and environmental change, cultural interactions and exchanges, imperialism and colonialism, and migrations and diasporas. The rise of global history has thus shed new light on topics that have long been studied by historians, such as imperialism, while at the same time stimulating interest in fields like environmental history that have emerged more recently.[9]

Even as global history has taken wider hold in the historical profession, it has provoked growing debate among historians over its political implications. By giving more attention to the history of areas outside the West and showing their influence on world history, many scholars of global history have sought to challenge the Eurocentrism they believe has dominated Western understandings of history since the nineteenth century. Eurocentrism for these scholars entailed a way of thinking that not only made Europeans and European Americans central to the historical process at the expense of other peoples, but privileged Western cultural standards as superior to those of other peoples.[10] Among those standards was the concept of the nation so central to European and American history from the nineteenth century onward. As part of their critique of Eurocentrism, some advocates of global history have also questioned the validity of nationalism and the nation state as both a unit of historical analysis and a mode of political organization. Global history has therefore served for some historians as a way of questioning the legitimacy of the modern nation state, providing them with a way to "rescue history from the nation," to use Prasenjit Duara's widely quoted phrase, and counter the cultural imperialism that they believe is embedded in the concept of the nation.[11]

The relationship between global history and nationalism has been among the most contentious issues surrounding the rise of global history, as critics have questioned whether global history has gone too far in repudiating the nation, arguing that such an approach risks losing sight of the real importance nation states and nationalism had as historical forces. Rather than rejecting a global approach altogether, scholars committed to retaining the nation as a category of historical analysis have advocated another variant of global history that would bring together global and national perspectives. Arguing that the nation "need not be thrown out with the global bathwater" as a framework for historians, the American historian Rosemarie Zagarri has been among those scholars who have questioned the assumption that national history and global history are mutually exclusive modes of analysis. To the contrary, according to Zagarri, the adoption of a global perspective could actually enhance an understanding of nationalism as a historical force by placing the development of nations in a broader transnational context.[12] The very title of Stefan Berger's *Writing the Nation: A Global Perspective* (2007) embodies this assumption of the compatibility between global and national history.

Yet another source of conflict over the implications of global history has been on the question of its relationship to globalization. The growing interest in global history has been partly a product of the rise of globalization from the 1990s to the present. As globalization has contributed to an increased awareness of the global interconnections linking together different regions of the world – whether through trade, the growing power of transnational corporations, or through networks of communication like the Internet – historians have taken this awareness and applied it to their understanding of the past.[13] Consequently, although not necessarily the intent of global history, some critics have feared the danger that global history could serve to legitimize and sanction globalization as the natural outcome of the historical process. For this reason, critics have cautioned that in privileging a global or transnational perspective as somehow more real or comprehensive than a national one, global history runs the risk of replacing the sanctification of the nation with the sanctification of a global viewpoint – a viewpoint that for some scholars is no less Eurocentric than a nationalistic one.[14] As one such critic Arif Dirlik has explained, "Where world history once underwrote the triumph of Western Civilization, it is now to be rewritten to bear witness to the triumph of globalization," in its failure to "suggest any critical awareness of the possibility that from perspectives other than those of its promoters, globalization may well appear to be a contemporary substitute for earlier paradigms of modernization – and even Westernization."[15]

On the other side, advocates of a global approach have argued that the broader perspective afforded by global history is important not just historically but socially in a globalized world where people of different regions are coming into increased contact with one another. Thus, for example, Jerry Bentley and Herbert Ziegler have described a global perspective as "a vision of history that is meaningful and appropriate for the interdependent world of contemporary times," making it "an essential tool for informed and responsible citizenship."[16] Likewise, the American historian Thomas Bender has urged the value of a global approach to American history on the basis that it would "better educate us and our children to the kind of cosmopolitanism that will make us better citizens of both the nation and the world," serving as a corrective to the "narrow parochialism" that grew out of nineteenth-century nationalism.[17]

According to Bender, another effect of expanding the geographical scope of history would be to create a greater awareness of how time itself is a historical construct that has been experienced and defined differently in different historical contexts.[18] The changes that have started to occur in the study of historiography as a result of the global turn in historical scholarship illustrate this historicization of time, as recent scholars of historiography have increasingly taken a global approach to their subject. The result has been to promote a greater awareness of the multiplicity of ways of representing the past, as these scholars have shown more interest in traditions of historical writing from outside Europe and the United States. And so, whereas earlier surveys of historiography focused on Europe and the United States, more recent surveys such as Daniel Woolf's *A Global History of History* and Georg Iggers' and Q. Edward Wang's *A Global History of Modern Historiography* have taken a global perspective on the subject. Or, taking a somewhat different approach have been the collections of essays published by such scholars as Stefan Berger, Eckhardt Fuchs, and Benedikt Stuchtey, which have tried to provide a transnational and comparative perspective on the historiography of particular regions or countries by bringing together essays about different areas of the world.[19]

## SAMUEL JOHNSON AND THE WRITING OF HISTORY IN AFRICA

One of the reasons why American and European historians had traditionally shown so little interest in the historiography of regions outside the West was the long-standing assumption that many of those regions lacked a sense of history, and hence had not produced any historical works that could constitute the basis for historiography. A society without a history was, in this way of thinking, also a society without a historiography. A region that that has been especially subject to this assumption is Africa. The German philosopher Hegel expressed the widely held view in his time of Africa as a "continent without history" when he declared in the 1830s that Africa "is no historical part of the World, it has no movement or development to exhibit … What we properly understand by Africa, is the Unhistorical, Underdeveloped Spirit."[20] The denial of a historical consciousness to Africa both reflected and furthered a belief in European superiority, as adherents of this view made a sense of history a function of civilization. Europeans could, in this way of thinking, point to Africa's lack of a historical consciousness as a sign of its uncivilized status, while using their own sense of history to affirm their claims to superiority as a civilized society. The denial of a history to Africa was also the product of the widespread tendency by European and American historians to define history as written history. By this definition, the oral tradition that Africans had long used to preserve their past did not count as real history.[21]

Although Africans relied heavily on oral tradition to preserve their history prior to the establishment of history as an academic discipline in Africa after World War II, they did also possess an earlier tradition of written history. Among the best-known contributors to this tradition was the Yoruba missionary Samuel Johnson (1846–1901), who was himself following the lead of other local amateur historians who had already begun to preserve and record African oral traditions in written form during the second half of the nineteenth century.[22] Born in Sierra Leone, Johnson was educated by Christian missionaries after moving to Nigeria, going on to become a teacher and missionary himself in Yorubaland, located in southwestern Nigeria. Believing that British colonial rule was necessary to bring an end to the destructive conflicts among the Yoruba, Johnson firmly supported British colonial authority, even serving as a diplomatic intermediary between local Yoruba leaders and the British. Yet Johnson's commitment to Christianity and his support for British colonial rule did not mean that he rejected his Yoruba heritage. On the contrary, Johnson revealed the complex intermingling of Western and Yoruba cultural influences in his history of the Yorubas, as he used his knowledge of Western culture to preserve Yoruba history and promote a stronger sense of Yoruba identity. Johnson completed his history in 1897, but as a result of his death in 1891 and the loss of his original manuscript by the publisher, his brother Obadiah had to reconstruct the history from his notes and drafts, publishing this version of the history in 1921.[23]

Offering a broad overview of Yoruba history that went back to the origins of the Yoruba people in the eleventh or twelfth century and extended to his own time, Johnson's work covered a wide range of topics and drew from a variety of sources, mixing together his own observations, which were largely based on his experiences as an intermediary between the British and the Yoruba, the eyewitness testimony of other participants in the events he described, written documents, and the oral traditions preserved by the "bards" of the Oyo court, one of the Yoruba kingdoms. As the first such work of its kind, Johnson's history would come to have a preeminent influence on the study of

Yoruba history and is still used by scholars today, even though they have questioned the accuracy of some of his analysis. What made his work so influential was his recording of Yoruba oral traditions and the material he provided on Yoruba history before the 1840s (when Christian missionaries first arrived in the area), for which there were limited written records.[24]

Believing that Yoruba history had been neglected at the expense of European history not just by Europeans but by the Yoruba themselves, Johnson expressed his desire to provide a corrective to this tendency in the preface to his history when he exclaimed, "Educated natives of Yoruba are well acquainted with the history of England and with that of Rome and Greece, but of the history of their own country they know nothing whatever! This reproach it is one of the author's objects to remove." For Johnson, it was all the more imperative to remedy this neglect and preserve Yoruba history because of his fear that it would otherwise be "lost in oblivion, especially as our old sires are dying out."[25] His concern with preserving Yoruba oral traditions before they died out revealed both his attachment to his Yoruba identity and his willingness to depart from European canons of historical writing, which denied the legitimacy of oral tradition as a historical source. By preserving those traditions in written form, Johnson at once demonstrated how he used the tools afforded by his Western education to affirm his sense of Yoruba identity and showed how his Western education influenced his definition of that identity. Simply by turning to writing as a vehicle for preserving Yoruba history, Johnson adhered to Western canons that gave primacy to the authority of the written over the oral and imposed a sense of coherence and unity on the oral traditions he recorded that they did not possess in their original forms.[26] And while he saw himself as preserving and promoting Yoruba national identity, his very notion of the Yoruba as a unified culture sharing a common descent was itself a product of European concepts of nation and race, since the Yoruba had not existed as a unified political entity before the colonial period.[27]

Johnson likewise revealed the complex interaction between Western and Yoruba influences in his treatment of religion, as his history both reflected and furthered his Christian beliefs. Frequently referring to God as a causal force in history, Johnson portrayed Yoruba history as following an inevitable path toward conversion to Christianity.[28] Johnson sought to reconcile his Christian beliefs with his Yoruba heritage by emphasizing the monotheistic character of traditional Yoruba religion. Thus, he suggested, in embracing Christianity, the Yoruba were not betraying their own religious traditions but were actually returning to them.[29] In this way, Johnson illustrates the kind of complicated cross-cultural interactions that have been such a central concern for scholars of global history.

## HU SHI AND SCIENTIFIC HISTORY IN CHINA

The Chinese historian Hu Shi (1891–1962) revealed the diverse character of these cross-cultural interactions as he sought to bring Western scientific history to China. After studying at Cornell and Columbia University in the United States, where he did his doctoral work and studied with the philosopher John Dewey, Hu Shi returned to China in 1917 to become a professor of philosophy at Peking University. A leading figure in the May 4/New Culture movement during the 1910s and 1920s, which sought to modernize China by embracing Western ideas and culture, Hu Shi wished to place the study of Chinese history on a more scientific basis by adopting Western scientific methods of historical writing. Drawing from John Dewey's philosophy of pragmatism, Hu Shi adapted Dewey's pragmatism to articulate an understanding of the scientific method which he believed had wide applicability beyond the realm of science. Defining the scientific method broadly to mean a "boldness in setting up hypotheses and a minuteness in seeking evidence," Hu Shi did not believe that this method was the exclusive preserve of any one culture.[30] Therefore, rather than seeing the adoption of Western scientific methods as a repudiation of Chinese culture, Hu Shi believed they had roots in the Chinese tradition of evidential learning. In their skepticism about the validity of ancient texts and their belief in the importance of subjecting these texts to rigorous source criticism, evidential scholars of the Qing Dynasty had in his view displayed a scientific spirit that aligned them with the ideals and methods of Western science.[31] Sounding much like Ranke in his praise for this tradition, Hu Shi declared,

> History saw the gradual development of a new spirit and a new method based on doubt and the resolution of doubt. The spirit was the moral courage to doubt even on questions touching sacred matters, and the insistence on the importance of an open mind and impartial and dispassionate search for truth. The method was the method of evidential thinking and evidential investigation.[32]

For Hu Shi, as for Ranke, the goal of scientific history was the pursuit of objective truth, which could only be achieved if the historian verified his claims through a critical analysis of his sources.

Not only did Hu Shi wish to apply scientific methods to the study of history in China; he believed that by doing so, Chinese scholars would uncover manifestations of the scientific spirit in their own tradition.[33] By showing how modern scientific practices were rooted in Chinese tradition, Hu Shi sought to make these practices seem less alien, and therefore more acceptable to his countrymen, while at the same time elevating the status of Chinese civilization and advancing its claims to equality with the West.[34] Viewing scientific history as a sign and instrument of Western power and advancement, Hu Shi hoped that China could enhance its own power and success in the eyes of the world by adopting this mode of historical writing, while fearing that the failure to do so would allow foreigners – in particular Japanese historians who had already begun to apply scientific techniques to the study of Chinese history – to overtake the writing of

Chinese history. And so, like his counterparts in the West, even as he urged the need for a more scientific and objective approach to Chinese history, Hu Shi furthered his nationalist purposes with that approach.[35]

Hu Shi sought to carry out his goal of reconstructing Chinese history on a scientific basis through the "National Studies" project that he began at Peking University during the 1920s, aided by his former student Gu Jiegang. Declaring that his purpose was to "[re]organize the national past and to recreate [its] civilization," Hu Shi believed that the National Studies project could further this goal by subjecting the Chinese literary tradition which formed the basis for Chinese history to a critical analysis that would sort out false from authentic sources. Hoping to promote a Chinese Renaissance, Hu Shi even likened his efforts to restore Chinese literary tradition and place it on a more secure basis to the work of Renaissance humanists in Europe. While the findings of the National Studies project provoked sharp controversy for their challenge to deeply held nationalist myths about ancient Chinese history, the approach this project advocated gained widespread influence among Chinese academic historians during the late 1920s and 1930s, both benefiting from and contributing to the professionalization of history in China.[36]

## CONCLUSION

In ending with the rise of global history, this book does not mean to suggest that it represents an end point to the development of historical writing. On the contrary, as current debates over global history reveal, global history is as much the product of its context as earlier developments in the history of historical writing have been, and is therefore subject to the same kind of contestation and change as those earlier developments. Thus, rather than an end point or culmination, the global turn represents simply another transformation in a long history of transformations in the writing of history.[37] And so, just like history itself, where, as the English historian Herbert Butterfield pointed out, the only constant is change, the history of historical writing has been characterized by a constant process of change and conflict.[38] What a study of historiography shows us, then, is that all history is in a sense revisionist history, thereby challenging the widely held view that revisionist history is by definition false history. And far from detracting from its legitimacy, the revisionist character of historical writing has been a source of its dynamism and significance, as historians have repeatedly had to rethink and rework not just their understanding of specific historical events but the parameters of the discipline itself, both in response to the critical scrutiny of other historians and to the political and social currents of their time.[39]

# Notes

*Notes to Introduction*

1   Carl Becker, "What Is Historiography?," *American Historical Review* 44 (1938): pp. 20–8; Lawrence D. Walker, "Qu' est-Ce Que L'histoire De L'historiographie?: The History of Historical Research and Writing Viewed as a Branch of the History of Science," *Storia della Storiografia* 2 (1982): 102; Daniel Woolf, *A Global History of History* (Cambridge: Cambridge University Press, 2011), pp. 4–5; D. R. Woolf, ed., *A Global Encyclopedia of Historical Writing* (New York: Garland Publishing, 1998), 1, p. xiii; Michael Bentley, *Companion to Historiography* (New York: Routledge, 1997), pp. xi–xiv.

2   G. R. Elton, "Review Essay: Clio Unbound," *History and Theory* 20 (1981): 92; Woolf, *Global History*, p. xix.

3   D. R. Woolf, "Disciplinary History and Historical Culture. A Critique of the History of History: The Case of Early Modern England," *Cromohs* 2 (1997): n3; Becker, p. 20.

4   Woolf, "Disciplinary History," pp. 2–4; Peter Novick, *That Noble Dream: The "Objectivity Question" and the American Historical Profession* (Cambridge: Cambridge University Press, 1988), pp. 12–13; Harvey Wish, *The American Historian: A Social-Intellectual History of the Writing of the American Past* (New York: Oxford University Press, 1960); Michael Kraus, *The Writing of American History* (Norman: University of Oklahoma Press, 1953); Harry Elmer Barnes, *A History of Historical Writing* (Norman: University of Oklahoma Press, 1937).

5   Ernst Breisach, *Historiography: Ancient, Medieval, & Modern* (Chicago, IL: University of Chicago Press, 1983); Georg G. Iggers and Q. Edward Wang, *A Global History of Modern Historiography* (Harlow: Pearson Longman, 2008).

*Notes to Chapter One: Art and Science in Renaissance and Early Modern Historical Writing*

1    Petrarch, "To Titus Livy," in Donald R. Kelley, ed., *Versions of History from Antiquity to the Enlightenment* (New Haven, CT: Yale University Press, 1991), p. 225.

2    Petrarch, "To Posterity," in Kelley, p. 221; Paula Findlen, "Historical Thought in the Renaissance," in Lloyd Kramer and Sarah Maza, ed., *A Companion to Western Historical Thought* (Oxford: Wiley-Blackwell, 2006), pp. 99–100; Peter Burke, *The Renaissance Sense of the Past* (London: Edward Arnold, 1969), pp. 21–5; Donald R. Kelley, *Faces of History: Historical Inquiry from Herodotus to Herder* (New Haven, CT: Yale University Press, 1998), pp. 130–3.

3    Daniel Woolf, *A Global History of History* (Cambridge: Cambridge University Press, 2011), p. 180; Burke, pp. 1–3, 6, 138–41; Findlen, in Kramer and Maza, p. 100.

4    Kelley, *Faces of History*, pp. 134–5.

5    Burke, pp. 39–49; Tzvetan Todorov, *The Conquest of America: The Question of the Other* (New York: Harper & Row, 1984).

6    Findlen, in Kramer and Maza, pp. 101, 105–7; Kelley, *Faces of History*, pp. 141–6.

7    Findlen, in Kramer and Maza, p. 106.

8    Burke, pp. 77–83.

9    Findlen, in Kramer and Maza, pp. 101–2.

10   Francesco Guicciardini, *History of Italy*, in Kelley, p. 299; Kelley, *Faces of History*, pp. 150–2; Woolf, *Global History*, p. 188.

11   Quoted in Woolf, *Global History*, p. 189; Kelley, *Versions of History*, pp. 284, 297; Kelley, *Faces of History*, pp. 146–50.

12   Findlen, in Kramer and Maza, p. 113; Kelley, pp. 188–200.

13   Findlen, pp. 114–15; Woolf, *Global History*, pp. 190–2, 195; Burke, pp. 21–38, 50–76; George Huppert, *The Idea of Perfect History: Historical Erudition and Historical Philosophy in Renaissance France* (Urbana: University of Illinois Press, 1970); Donald R. Kelley, *Foundations of Modern Historical Scholarship: Language, Law, and History in the French Renaissance* (New York: Columbia University Press, 1970).

14   Anthony Grafton, *What Was History?: The Art of History in Early Modern Europe* (New York: Cambridge University Press, 2007), pp. 1–33, 67–8; Kelley, *Faces of History*, pp. 189–97; Kelley, *Foundations*, pp. 129–41.

15  Grafton, pp. 31–2, 165–7.

16  Bodin, *Method for the Easy Comprehension of History*, in Kelley, pp. 380–1.

17  Bodin, in Kelley, p. 384.

18  Kelley, *Faces of History*, pp. 197–200.

19  Huppert, pp. 93–4.

20  Grafton, pp. 167–8; 96–7.

21  Quoted in Grafton, p. 169.

22  Quoted in Huppert, p. 97.

23  Grafton, pp. 169–73.

24  Grafton, p. 168; Huppert, p. 90.

25  Quoted in Huppert, pp. 98–9.

26  Huppert, pp. 96–100, 103; Grafton, pp. 168–79.

27  Steven Shapin, *The Scientific Revolution* (Chicago, IL: University of Chicago Press, 1996).

28  Shapin, pp. 87–93, 127–31; Fussner, pp. 253–64.

29  Francis Bacon, *De augmentis scientiarum*, in Kelley, p. 402; F. Smith Fussner, *The Historical Revolution: English Historical Writing and Thought, 1580–1640* (New York: Columbia University Press, 1962), pp. 253–64.

30  Bacon, in Kelley, p. 402; Brian Vickers, Introduction, Francis Bacon, *The History of the Reign of King Henry VII and Selected* Works, ed. Brian Vickers (New York: Cambridge University Press), pp. xv–xviii; Fussner, pp. 256–62.

31  Bacon, in Kelley, p. 405.

32  Bacon, in Kelley, p. 411; Shapin, p. 139; Fussner, p. 261.

33  Quoted in Kelley, *Faces of History*, p. 196; Fussner, pp. 256–61; Vickers, p. xxi.

34  Vickers, pp. xii–xv; Fussner, pp. 264–8.

35  Vickers, p. xiii; Arnold Momigliano, "Ancient History and the Antiquarian," *Studies in Historiography* (New York: Harper & Row, 1966), pp. 1–39; D. R. Woolf, "Erudition and the Idea of History in Renaissance England," *Renaissance Quarterly* 40 (spring 1987): pp. 14–28; J. G. A. Pocock, *Barbarism and Religion* (New York: Cambridge University Press, 1999) pp. 4–25; Philip Hicks, *Neoclassical History and English Culture: From Clarendon to Hume* (New York: St. Martin's Press, 1996), pp. 31–40.

36  Vickers, pp. xv–xxxi; Fussner, pp. 273–4

37  Fussner, pp. 275–6.

38  Arthur B. Ferguson, *Clio Unbound: Perception of the Social and Cultural Past in Renaissance England* (Durham, NC: Duke University Press, 1979), p. 118.

39  Woolf, "Erudition," pp. 34–6; Fussner, p. 277; Ferguson, p. 122.

40  Quoted in Woolf, "Erudition," p. 35.

41  Woolf, "Erudition," p. 35.

42  Quoted in Woolf, "Erudition," p. 36.

43  Fussner, pp. 286–8; 291–3; Ferguson, pp. 120–1; Woolf, "Erudition," p. 36.

44  Fussner, pp. 279–83; Ferguson, pp. 119–22.

45  Woolf, "Erudition," pp. 36–9.

46  Woolf, "Erudition," pp. 39–48.

47  David D. Van Tassel, *Recording America's Past: An Interpretation of the Development of Historical Studies in America, 1607–1884* (Chicago, IL: University of Chicago Press, 1960).

48  Kelley, *Faces of History*, pp. 156–61; Howard Mumford Jones, *O Strange New World* (New York: Viking Press, 1964); Peter Burke, "America and the Rewriting of World History," in Karen Ordahl Kupperman, ed., *America in European Consciousness, 1493–1750* (Chapel Hill: Published for the Institute of Early American History and Culture by the University of North Carolina Press, 1995), pp. 33–47; David Armitage, "The New World and British Historical Thought," in Kupperman, pp. 52–70.

49  Francis Murphy, Introduction, William Bradford, *Of Plymouth Plantation, 1620–1647* (New York: Modern Library, 1981), pp. vii–xv.

50  Bradford, pp. 4, 8.

51  Bradford, p. 66; Alan B. Howard, "Art and History in Bradford's *Of Plymouth Plantation*," *William & Mary Quarterly* 28, no. 2 (April 1971): pp. 243–6; Gay, *Loss of Mastery*, pp. 26–38.

52  Bradford, pp. 302–3.

53  Bradford, pp. 351–2; Howard, pp. 246–8; David Levin, "William Bradford: The Value of Puritan Historiography," *in Forms of Uncertainty: Essays in Historical Criticism* (Charlottesville: University of Virginia Press, 1992), pp. 20–3, 31–4.

54  Howard, pp. 246, 249–51, 260–1, 265–6; Levin, p. 20 .

55  Peter Gay, *A Loss of Mastery: The Puritan Historians in Colonial*

*America* (Berkeley: University Of California Press, 1959), pp. 49–52; Murphy, Introduction, pp. xvi–xviii; Levin, p. 29.
56 Quoted in Howard, pp. 260, 257–63; Levin, pp. 25–9.

*Notes to Chapter Two: Enlightenment and Philosophical History*

1 Dorinda Outram, *The Enlightenment* (New York: Cambridge University Press, 1995), pp. 1–13; J. G. A. Pocock, *Barbarism and Religion* (New York: Cambridge University Press, 1999), pp. 5–10.

2 Immanuel Kant, "What Is Enlightenment?," in Immanuel Kant, *On History*, ed. Lewis Beck (Indianapolis, IN: Bobbs-Merrill, 1963), p. 3.

3 Peter Gay, *The Enlightenment: An Interpretation* (New York: Knopf, 1966).

4 Outram, pp. 47–62; Margaret C. Jacob, *The Enlightenment: A Brief History with Documents* (Boston, MA: Bedford/St. Martin's Press, 2001), pp. 15–22; Gay, *Enlightenment*, 2, pp. 167–215, 319–95.

5 Jerry Z. Muller, *The Mind and the Market: Capitalism in Modern European Thought* (New York: Alfred A. Knopf, 2002), p. 20; Gay, *Enlightenment*, 1, pp. 127–203.

6 Gay, *Enlightenment*, 1, pp. 207–419; Outram, pp. 31–46.

7 Johnson Wright, "Historical Thought in the Era of the Enlightenment," in Lloyd Kramer and Sarah Maza, eds., *A Companion to Western Historical Thought* (Oxford: Wiley-Blackwell, 2006), pp. 123–4; R. G. Collingwood, *The Idea of History* (New York: Oxford University Press, 1956), pp. 76–85; Gay, *Enlightenment*, 1, pp. 31–71; 2, pp. 368–96.

8 George H. Nadel, "Philosophy of History before Historicism," *History and Theory*, 3 (1964): pp. 291–315; R. N. Stromberg, "History in the Eighteenth Century," *Journal of the History of Ideas* 12 (1951): pp. 302–3; Mark Salber Phillips, *Society and Sentiment: Genres of Historical Writing in Britain, 1740–1820* (Princeton, NJ: Princeton University Press, 2000), pp. 21–32; Pocock, *Barbarism and Religion*, pp. 8–10; Mark Salber Phillips, "Adam Smith and the History of Private Life: Social and Sentimental Narratives in Eighteenth-Century Historiography," in Donald Kelley and David Harris Sacks, eds., *The Historical Imagination in Early Modern Britain: History, Rhetoric, and Fiction* (New York: Cambridge University

Press, 1997), pp. 318–19; Philip Hicks, *Neoclassical History and English Culture: From Clarendon to Hume* (New York: St. Martin's Press, 1996), pp. 7–22.

9    Bernard Bailyn, *The Ideological Origins of the American Revolution* (Cambridge, MA: Harvard University Press, 1967); J. G. A. Pocock, *The Machiavellian Moment: Florentine Political Thought and the Atlantic Republican Tradition* (Princeton, NJ: Princeton University Press, 1975); Gordon Wood, *The Creation of the American Republic, 1776–1787* (New York: W. W. Norton, 1969); Lester Cohen, *The Revolutionary Histories: Contemporary Narratives of the American Revolution* (Ithaca, NY: Cornell University Press, 1980), pp. 161–211; Arthur Shaffer, *The Politics of History: Writing the History of the American Revolution, 1783–1815* (Chicago: Precedent Publishing, 1975), pp. 31–48, 96–102; Lester Cohen, "Explaining the Revolution: Ideology and Ethics in Mercy Otis Warren's Historical Theory," *William and Mary Quarterly* 37 (April 1980): pp. 200–18.

10   Wright, in Kramer and Maza, pp. 123–4; H. R. Trevor-Roper, "The Historical Philosophy of the Enlightenment," *Studies on Voltaire and the Eighteenth Century* 27 (1963): pp. 1667–87; Stromberg, pp. 302–3.

11   Kelley, *Fortunes of History*, pp. 35–6; Phillips, *Sentiment and Society*, pp. 41–59, 171; Karen O'Brien, *Narratives of Enlightenment: Cosmopolitan History from Voltaire to Gibbon* (Cambridge: Cambridge University Press, 1997), 9; Pocock, *Barbarism*, pp. 7–25; Philip Hicks, "Bolingbroke, Clarendon, and the Role of Classical Historian," *Eighteenth Century Studies*, 20 (1987): 470; Hicks, *Neoclassical History*, pp. 182–8.

12   Kelley, pp. 6–9; Arnold Momigliano, "Ancient History and the Antiquarian," *Studies in Historiography* (New York: Harper & Row, 1966), pp. 1–39; Georg Iggers, *New Directions in European Historiography*, rev. ed. (1975; Middletown, Conn.: Wesleyan University Press, 1984), pp. 12–13; Georg Iggers, *Historiography in the Twentieth Century: From Scientific Objectivity to the Postmodern Challenge* (Middletown, Conn.: Wesleyan University Press, 1997), p. 23; D. R. Woolf, "Erudition and the Idea of History in Renaissance England", *Renaissance Quarterly* 40 (spring 1987): pp. 11–48; Pocock, *Barbarism*, pp. 4–25; Hicks, *Neoclassical History*, pp. 31–40.

13 Herbert Butterfield, *Man on His Past* (Cambridge: Cambridge University Press, 1955), pp. 36–61; Iggers, *New Directions*, pp. 12–17.

14 David Armitage, "The New World and British Historical Thought from Richard Hakluyt to William Robertson," in Karen Ordahl Kupperman, ed., *America in European Consciousness, 1493–1750* (Chapel Hill: University of North Carolina Press, 1995), pp. 66–9; John Kenyon, *The History Men: The Historical Profession in England since the Renaissance*, rev. edn (1983; London: Weidenfeld & Nicolson, 1993), pp. 55–6, 64; Devoney Looser, *British Women Writers and the Writing of History, 1670–1820* (Baltimore: Johns Hopkins University Press, 2000), pp. 14–15; *The Autonomy of History: Truth and Method from Erasmus to Gibbon* (Chicago, IL: University of Chicago Press, 1999), p. 172; Okie, pp. vii, 4–11, 47–68; Joseph Levine, *Humanism and History: Origins of Modern English Historiography* (Ithaca: Cornell University Press, 1987), pp. 14–16, 105–6.

15 Voltaire, "Letter to Abbe Jean Baptiste Dubos," in Fritz Stern, ed., *The Varieties of History* (New York: World Publishing, 1956), p. 39.

16 Wright, in Kramer and Maza, p. 132.

17 Peter Gay, *Voltaire's Politics: The Poet as Realist* (Princeton, NJ: Princeton University Press, 1959).

18 O'Brien, pp. 21–7; Wright, in Kramer and Maza, p. 132.

19 J. H. Brumfitt, *Voltaire, Historian* (London: Oxford University Press, 1958), pp. 12–16; Wright, in Kramer and Maza, p. 133; O'Brien, pp. 28–30; Jerry Muller, *The Mind and the Market: Capitalism in Modern European Thought* (New York: Alfred A. Knopf, 2002), p. 45; Gay, *Voltaire's Politics*, pp. 144–238, 309–40.

20 Gay, *Voltaire's Politics*, pp. 110–14.

21 Voltaire, "Introduction: The Age of Louis XIV," in Stern, p. 40.

22 Voltaire, "Introduction," pp. 43–4; O'Brien, pp. 32–45.

23 O'Brien, pp. 48–51; Wright, in Kramer and Maza, p. 133.

24 O'Brien, p. 22; Wright, in Kramer and Maza, p. 133.

25 O'Brien, pp. 48–51; Brumfitt, pp. 68–70.

26 O'Brien, pp. 51–3; Wright, in Kramer and Maza, p. 134.

27 Nicholas Phillipson, "Scottish Enlightenment," in *Wealth and Virtue: The Shaping of Political Economy in the Scottish Enlightenment* ed. Istvan Hont and Michael Ignatieff (New York: Cambridge University Press, 1986), pp. 19–40; Phillipson, "Adam Smith as Civic Moralist," in Hont and Ignatieff, pp. 179–202; J. G. A. Pocock,

*Virtue, Commerce, and History: Essays on Political Thought and History,*
*Chiefly in the Eighteenth Century* (New York: Cambridge University
Press, 1985), pp. 50, 119–23, 252–3; Pocock, *Barbarism*, pp. 268–329;
and Pocock, "Cambridge Paradigms and Scotch Philosophers," in
Hont and Ignatieff, pp. 244–5.

28  O'Brien, *Narratives of Enlightenment*, pp. 132–6; Pocock, *Virtue,*
*Commerce, and History*, pp. 252–3; Pocock, *Barbarism*, pp. 309–29;
Ronald Meek, *Social Science and the Ignoble Savage* (Cambridge:
Cambridge University Press, 1976); Kelley, *Fortunes of History*,
pp. 81–6; Istvan Hont, "The Language of Sociability and
Commerce: Samuel Pufendorf and the Theoretical Foundations of
the 'Four-Stages Theory,'" in Anthony Pagden, ed., *The Languages*
*of Political Theory in Early Modern Europe* (Cambridge: Cambridge
University Press, pp. 227–99), pp. 253–76.

29  O'Brien, *Narratives of Enlightenment*, pp. 132–6; Pocock, *Virtue,*
*Commerce, and History*, pp. 48–50, pp. 114–23; Pocock, *Barbarism*,
pp. 309–29; Donald Kelley, *Fortunes of History: Historical Inquiry*
*from Herder to Huizinga* (New Haven, CT: Yale University Press,
2003), pp. 20–5, 81–6; Phillips, *Society and Sentiment*, pp. 15–18,
131–70; Laird Okie, *Augustan Historical Writing: Histories of*
*England in the English Enlightenment* (Lanham, MD: University
Press of America, 1991), pp. 4, 110, 117–18, 178–87; Peter Burke,
"Ranke the Reactionary," in *Leopold von Ranke and the Shaping of*
*the Historical Discipline*, ed. Georg G. Iggers and James M. Powell
(Syracuse, NY: Syracuse University Press, 1990), pp. 38–41.

30  Mary Poovey, *A History of the Modern Fact: Problems of Knowledge*
*in the Sciences of Wealth and Society* (Chicago, IL: University of
Chicago Press, 1998), pp. 214–49; Phillips, *Society and Sentiment*,
pp. 171–89.

31  O'Brien, pp. 93–100.

32  O'Brien, pp. 134–5

33  Quoted in O'Brien, p. 135.

34  Armitage, pp. 66–9.

35  O'Brien, pp. 136–41.

36  O'Brien, pp. 122–8; 141–8.

37  O'Brien, pp. 151–8.

38  Stewart Brown, "An 18th-Century Historian on the Amerindians:
Culture, Colonialism and Christianity in William Robertson's

History of America," *Studies in World Christianity* 2 (1996): pp. 204–22; O'Brien, pp. 156–61; George Dekker, *The American Historical Romance* (Cambridge: Cambridge University Press, 1987), pp. 73–98; Roy Harvel Pearce, *Savagism and Civilization: A Study of the Indian and the American Mind* (Berkeley: University of California Press, 1988), pp. 66–73, 82–100; Roxann Wheeler, *The Complexion of Race: Categories of Difference in Eighteenth-Century British Culture* (Philadelphia: University of Pennsylvania Press, 2000), pp. 35–6, 181–90; Berkhofer, pp. 38–49; Pocock, *Barbarism*, 4, pp. 157–226, 269–93.

39  Joseph Levine, "Strife in the Republic of Letters," in *The Autonomy of History: Truth and Method from Erasmus to Gibbon* (Chicago, IL: University of Chicago Press, 1999), pp. 122–6; Arnold Momigliano, "Gibbon's Contribution to Historical Method," in *Studies in Historiography* (New York: Harper & Row, 1966), pp. 40–55.

40  David Womersley, *The Transformation of the Decline and Fall of the Roman Empire* (New York: Cambridge University Press, 1988).

41  David Womersley, Introduction, Edward Gibbon, *The History of the Decline and Fall of the Roman Empire* (London: Penguin, 2000), pp. ix–xvii; J. W. Burrow, *Gibbon* (New York: Oxford University Press, 1985), pp. 4–15.

42  Quoted in Womersley, Introduction, p. xvi.

43  Gay, *Style in History*, p. 48.

44  Burrow, Gibbon, pp. 34–5; Womersley, Introduction, pp. xviii–xix.

45  Burrow, Gibbon, pp. 24–7; Gay, *Style in History*, pp. 52–3.

46  O'Brien, pp. 199–202; J. W. Burrow, *A History of Histories: Epics, Chronicles, Romances and Inquiries from Herodotus and Thucydides to the Twentieth Century* (New York: Knopf, 2008), pp. 339–40.

47  Gibbon, p. 18.

48  Gibbon, p. 11; Womersley, Introduction, pp. xxviii–xxix.

49  Gay, *Style in History*, p. 41.

50  Burrow, *History of Histories*, p. 335.

51  Gibbon, p. 62.

52  Burrow, *History of Histories*, pp. 336–8.

53  Gibbon, pp. 437–8.

54  O'Brien, pp. 1–2, 172–4, 199–200; Burrow, *History of Histories*, pp. 342–3; Gay, *Style in History*, p. 50.

55  Burrow, *History of Histories*, p. 337; David Wootton, "Narrative,

Irony, and Faith in Gibbon's Decline and Fall," *History & Theory* 33, no. 4 (December 1994): p. 95; O'Brien, p. 169.

56  Gay, *Style in History*, pp. 40–56.

57  Paul Turnbull, "The 'Supposed Infidelity' of Edward Gibbon," *Historical Journal* 25, no. 1 (March 1982): pp. 23–4.

58  Burrow, *History of Histories*, p. 338.

59  Wootton, pp. 89–100.

60  Gibbon, p. 122; Wootton, pp. 91–2.

61  Wootton, pp. 96–7.

62  Shaffer, *Politics of History*, pp. 1–10, 123–31; Harvey Wish, *The American Historian: A Social-Intellectual History of the Writing of the American Past* (New York: Oxford University Press, 1960), pp. 39–41.

63  Shaffer, *Politics of History*, esp. pp. 9–29; David D. Van Tassel, *Recording America's Past: An Interpretation of the Development of Historical Studies in America, 1607–1884* (Chicago, IL: University of Chicago Press, 1960), pp. 31–59; Peter Messer, *Stories of Independence: Identity, Ideology, and Independence in Eighteenth-Century America* (DeKalb: Northern Illinois University Press, 2005), pp. 3–13, 105–69.

64  Lester Cohen, *The Revolutionary Histories: Contemporary Narratives of the American Revolution* (Ithaca, NY: Cornell University Press, 1980), pp. 161–211; Shaffer, *Politics of History*, pp. 31–48, 96–102; Messer, pp. 3–13, 105–38.

65  Rosemarie Zagarri, *A Woman's Dilemma: Mercy Otis Warren and the American Revolution* (Wheeling, IL: Harlan Davidson, 1995).

66  Ruth H. Bloch, "The Gendered Meanings of Virtue in Revolutionary America," *Signs: Journal of Women in Culture and Society* 13 (1987): pp. 37–58; Linda Kerber, *Women of the Republic: Intellect and Ideology in Revolutionary America* (New York: W. W. Norton, 1980), pp. 15–32; Linda Kerber, "'History Can Do It No Justice': Women and the Reinterpretation of the American Revolution," in Kerber, *Toward an Intellectual History of Women* (Chapel Hill: University of North Carolina Press, 1997), pp. 87–92; Kerber, "The Republican Ideology of the Revolutionary Generation," in *Toward an Intellectual History of Women*, pp. 131–56; D. R. Woolf, "A Feminine Past?: Gender, Genre, and Historical Knowledge in England, 1500–1800," *American Historical Review* 102 (June 1997): pp. 645–79; Phillips, *Society and*

*Sentiment*, pp. 103–4, 114; Bonnie Smith, *The Gender of History: Men, Women, and Historical Practice* (Cambridge, MA: Harvard University Press, 1998).

67 Devoney Looser, *British Women Writers and the Writing of History, 1670–1820* (Baltimore, MD: Johns Hopkins University Press, 2000).

68 Mercy Otis Warren, *History of the Rise, Progress and Termination of the American Revolution*, ed. Lester Cohen (1805; Indianapolis, IN: Liberty Classics, 1988), 1, pp. xli–xlii; Nina Baym, "Mercy Otis Warren's Gendered Melodrama of Revolution," *South Atlantic Quarterly* 90 (summer 1991): pp. 531–53; Baym, *American Women Writers*, 31.

69 Warren, p. xlii; Kerber, *Women of the Republic*; Peter Messer, "Writing Women into History," *Studies in Eighteenth-Century Culture* 28 (1999): pp. 351–6; Messer, *Stories of Independence*, pp. 133–5; Zagarri, pp. 140–7.

70 Warren, 1, pp. 3, 5; Lester Cohen, "Explaining the Revolution: Ideology and Ethics in Mercy Otis Warren's Historical Theory," *William and Mary Quarterly* 37 (April 1980): pp. 200–18.

71 Warren, 1, p. 4.

72 Cohen, *Revolutionary Histories* (Ithaca, NY: Cornell University Press, 1980), pp. 161–211; Cohen, "Explaining the Revolution: Ideology and Ethics in Mercy Otis Warren's Historical Theory," *William and Mary Quarterly* 37 (April 1980): pp. 200–18; Shaffer, *Politics of History*, pp. 31–48, 96–102.

73 Warren, 2, p. 629.

74 Warren, 2, p. 651; Zagarri, pp. 100–4.

75 Warren, 1, pp. 284–5.

76 Messer, *Stories of Independence*, pp. 110, 114–17, 124–9; Baym, pp. 531–50.

77 Warren, 2, p. 698; Cohen, *Revolutionary Histories*, pp. 57–113; Shaffer, *Politics of History*, pp. 59–63.

*Notes to Chapter Three: Romantic and Critical History*

1 Theodore Ziolkowski, *Clio the Romantic Muse: Historicizing the Faculties in Germany* (Ithaca, NY: Cornell University Press, 2004).

2   Georg Iggers and Q. Edward Wang, *A Global History of Modern Historiography* (Harlow: Pearson Longman, 2008), pp. 69–71.

3   Warren Breckman, *European Romanticism: A Brief History with Documents* (Boston, MA: Bedford/St. Martins Press, 2008), pp. 1–22; Hugh Honour, *Romanticism* (New York: Harper & Row, 1979), pp. 21–118.

4   M. H. Abrams, *The Mirror and the Lamp: Romantic Theory and the Critical Tradition* (New York: Oxford University Press, 1953), pp. 8–14, 21–6, 30–69, 47–69, 298–326.

5   Francis Bowen to John Gorham Palfrey, November 20, 1857, Palfrey Family Papers, Houghton Library, Harvard University; David Levin, *History as Romantic Art: Bancroft, Prescott, Motley, and Parkman* (Stanford, CA: Stanford University Press, 1959), pp. 3–23; George Callcott, *History in the United States, 1800–1860: Its Practice and Purpose* (Baltimore, MD: Johns Hopkins University Press, 1970), pp. 139–50; Mark Phillips, "Macaulay, Scott, and the Literary Challenge to Historiography," *Journal of the History of Ideas* 50 (1989): pp. 122–4; Eileen Cheng, *The Plain and Noble Garb of Truth: Nationalism & Impartiality in American Historical Writing, 1784–1860* (Athens, Ga.: University of Georgia Press, 2008), pp. 66–7.

6   Phillips, "Macaulay, Scott, and the Literary Challenge to Historiography," p. 131.

7   Honour, 156–216; Stephen Bann, *Romanticism and the Rise of History* (New York: Twayne Publishers, 1995), pp. 3–16.

8   Iggers and Wang, *Global History*, pp. 70–1; Honour, pp. 217–44; Breckman, pp. 31–7.

9   Thomas Baker, "National History in the Age of Michelet, Macaulay, and Bancroft," in Kramer and Maza, pp. 185–6; Iggers and Wang, *Global History*, pp. 71–2; Stefan Berger with Mark Donovan and Kevin Passmore, "Apologias for the Nation State in Western Europe since 1800," in Stefan Berger, Mark Donovan, and Kevin Passmore, *Writing National Histories: Western Europe since 1800* (London: Routledge, 1999), pp. 3–13.

10   Gordon Wright, Introduction, Jules Michelet, *History of the French Revolution*, ed. Gordon Wright (Chicago, IL: University of Chicago Press, 1967), pp. ix–xii; Baker, p. 192.

11   Jules Michelet, *The People*, in Stern, p. 117; Lionel Gossman, "Michelet and the French Revolution," in James A. W. Heffernan,

ed., *Representing the French Revolution: Literature, Historiography, and Art* (Hanover, NH: Dartmouth College: University Press of New England, 1992), pp. 83–8, 98–100.

12  Jules Michelet, *History of the French Revolution*, p. 3; Gossman, pp. 96–100.

13  Lionel Gossman, "Michelet and the French Revolution," pp. 88–105.

14  Thomas Macaulay, "History," in Stern, p. 86; J. P. Kenyon, *The History Men: The Historical Profession in England Since the Renaissance* (Pittsburgh, PA: University of Pittsburgh Press; 1984), pp. 71–9.

15  Thomas Babington Macaulay, *The History of England*, ed. Hugh Trevor-Roper (New York: Penguin Books, 1979), p. 52.

16  Macaulay, *History of England*, p. 295; Kenyon, pp. 84–6; Burrow, *History of Histories*, pp. 346–8; J. W. Burrow, *A Liberal Descent: Victorian Historians and the English Past* (New York: Cambridge University Press, 1983), pp. 87–93.

17  Herbert Butterfield, *Man on His Past* (Cambridge: Cambridge University Press, 1955), pp. 36–61; Iggers, *New Directions*, pp. 12–17.

18  George Gooch, *History and Historians in the Nineteenth Century* (New York: P. Smith, 1959), pp. 14–23; Kelley, pp. 114–24; James Westfall Thompson, *A History of Historical Writing* (New York: Macmillan, 1942), pp. 153–7.

19  Georg Iggers, Introduction, in Leopold von Ranke, *The Theory and Practice of History*, ed. Iggers and Konrad von Moltke (Indianapolis, IN: Bobbs-Merrill, 1973), pp. 3–7.

20  Iggers, *New Directions*, p. 17; Iggers, Introduction, 7; Kelley, pp. 132–40; Gooch, pp. 72–97; Thompson, 2, pp. 168–86; Leonard Krieger, *Ranke: The Meaning of History* (Chicago, IL: University of Chicago Press, 1977), pp. 4–7.

21  Iggers, *New Directions*, pp. 17–24; Iggers, *Historiography*, pp. 24–6.

22  Krieger, pp. 7–8.

23  Gay, *Style in History*, pp. 59–67.

24  Quoted in Krieger, p. 105.

25  Krieger, pp. 3–4.

26  Leopold von Ranke, "A Fragment from the 1830s," in Stern, p. 59; Krieger, pp. 17–18.

27  Iggers, Introduction, pp. 12–13; Gay, *Style in History*, pp. 85–6; Dorothy Ross, *The Origins of American Social Science* (Cambridge:

Cambridge University Press, 1991), pp. xv, 3–6; Hayden White, "On History and Historicisms," Introduction, in *From History to Sociology; the Transition in German Historical Thinking*, by Carlo Antoni (Detroit: Wayne State University Press, 1959), pp. xv–xxviii ; Dwight E. Lee and Robert N. Beck, "The Meaning Of 'Historicism'," *American Historical Review* 59 (1954), pp. 568–77; Georg Iggers, "Historicism," in *Dictionary of the History of Ideas* (New York: Scribner, 1973), 2, pp. 456–64; Georg Iggers, "Historicism: The History and Meaning of the Term," *Journal of the History of Ideas* 56 (1995): pp. 129–52, 142–51.

28  Gay, *Style in History*, pp. 85–6.

29  Ranke, quoted in Peter Novick, *That Noble Dream: The "Objectivity Question" and the American Historical Profession* (Cambridge: Cambridge University Press, 1988), p. 27; Novick, pp. 26–31; Iggers, "Image of Ranke," pp. 17–40; Iggers, *The German Conception of History: The National Tradition of Historical Thought from Herder to the Present* (1968; rev. edn, Middletown, CT: Wesleyan University Press, 1983), pp. 63–89.

30  Iggers, Introduction, pp. xix–xx; Novick, p. 28.

31  Ranke, quoted in Novick, p. 28.

32  Iggers, *German Conception of History*, pp. 76–80.

33  Iggers, *Historiography*, p. 26.

34  Ranke, "Fragment from the 1830s," in Stern, p. 59; Iggers, Introduction, pp. 17–20; Iggers, *New Directions*, pp. 20–1.

35  Iggers, Introduction, pp. 10–13; Iggers, *German Conception*, pp. 70–6, 84–6; Iggers, *Historiography*, p. 26.

36  Iggers, Introduction, p. 4; Iggers, pp. 85–6; Krieger, p. 300.

37  Ranke, "Fragment from the 1830s," Stern, p. 60; Iggers, *New Directions*, pp. 22–4; Iggers, *German Conception*, pp. 81–4; Harry Liebersohn, "German from Ranke to Weber: The Primacy of Politics," in Kramer and Maza, pp. 168–70.

38  Iggers, "Introduction," p. 11.

39  Krieger, pp. 246–8, 346; Liebersohn, pp. 167–71; Iggers, *German Conception*, pp. 86–9.

40  Harlow W. Sheidley, *Sectional Nationalism : Massachusetts Conservative Leaders and the Transformation of America, 1815–1836* (Boston, MA: Northeastern University Press, 1998), pp. 118–47; Levin, pp. 3–23.

41  Quoted in Russel Nye, *George Bancroft: Brahmin Rebel* (New York: Knopf, 1944), p. 106.

42 Lilian Handlin, *George Bancroft: The Intellectual as Democrat* (New York: Harper & Row 1984), pp. 115–33; Nye, *George Bancroft: Brahmin Rebel*, pp. 94–105; Robert Canary, *George Bancroft* (New York: Twayne, 1974); Wish, pp. 71–86; Dorothy Ross, "Historical Consciousness in Nineteenth-Century America," *American Historical Review* 89 (October 1984): pp. 909–28; Kraus, pp. 97–108; Sacvan Bercovitch, *The Rites of Assent* (New York: Routledge, 1993), pp. 173–89; David Noble, *Historians against History: The Frontier Thesis and the National Covenant in American Historical Writing Since 1830* (Minneapolis: University of Minnesota Press, 1965), pp. 18–36; Levin, *History as Romantic Art.*

43 Bercovitch, pp. 173–89; Ross, "Historical Consciousness," pp. 915–20; Noble, pp. 18–36.

44 Handlin, pp. 115–33; Nye, *George Bancroft: Brahmin Rebel*, pp. 94–105; Robert Canary, *George Bancroft* (New York: Twayne, 1974); Wish, pp. 71–86; Ross, "Historical Consciousness," pp. 909–28; Kraus, pp. 97–108.

45 George Bancroft, *A History of the United States, from the Discovery of the American Continent to the Present Time* (Boston, MA: Charles Bowen, 1858), 7, p. 23.

46 Ross, "Historical Consciousness," pp. 915–19; Noble, pp. 18–36; Bercovitch, pp. 174–9; Ross, *Origins of American Social Science*, pp. 22–50.

47 Richard C. Vitzthum, *The American Compromise: Theme and Method in the Histories of Bancroft, Parkman, and Adams* (Norman: University of Oklahoma Press, 1974), pp. 15–20; John W. Rathbun, "George Bancroft on Man and History," *Transactions of the Wisconsin Academy of Sciences, Arts and Letters*, 43 (1954): pp. 68–73; Noble, pp. 22–31.

48 Bancroft, 1, p. 500.

49 Noble, pp. 22–4.

50 Sheidley, pp. 122–227; Vitzthum, pp. 15–17; Bercovitch, pp. 181–4.

51 Noble, pp. 20–7, 30–4; Nye, *George Bancroft: Brahmin Rebel*, pp. 99–103; Bercovitch, pp. 175–84; Ross, "Historical Consciousness," pp. 912–13, 917–19; Merrill Lewis, "Organic Metaphor and Edenic Myth in George Bancroft's *History of the United States*," *Journal of the History of Ideas* 26 (1965): pp. 587–92.

52 Quoted in George Bancroft to J. C. Bancroft Davis, December 27,

1867, in Mark DeWolfe Howe, *Life and Letters of George Bancroft* (New York: Scribner's, 1908), 2, p. 183; Handlin, pp. 295–6; Georg Iggers, "The Image of Ranke in American and German Historical Thought," *History and Theory* 2 (1962): p. 19; Wish, pp. 70–87; Nye, *Brahmin Rebel*, pp. 98–101; Nye, *George Bancroft*, pp. 110–27; Rathbun, p. 54; Cheng, pp. 162–9.

53 Vitzthum, pp. 33–6; Handlin, p. 295.

54 Bancroft, *A History of the United States* (Boston, MA: Little Brown & Co., 1860), 8, p. 118; Handlin, pp. 126–7, 295–6, 341–2.

55 Handlin, pp. 65–6, 100–1; Nye, pp. 32–58; Wish, pp. 71–5; Rathbun, pp. 51–6, 62–6.

56 George Bancroft, *A History of the United States, from the Discovery of the American Continent to the Present Time* (Boston, MA: Charles Bowen, 1834), 1, p. v; Cheng, pp. 149–50.

57 Vitzthum, pp. 45, 65.

58 Cheng, pp. 150–1.

59 Vitzthum, pp. 48–51, 73–4; Peter Hoffer, *Past Imperfect* (New York: Public Affairs, 2004), p. 22; Watt Stewart, "George Bancroft," in *The Marcus W. Jernegan Essays in American Historiography*, ed. William T. Hutchinson (Chicago, IL: University of Chicago Press, 1937), pp. 20–2.

60 Bancroft, 1, p. 59n.

61 Lawrence Simon, Introduction, Karl Marx, *Selected Writings*, ed. Lawrence Simon (Indianapolis, IN: Hackett, 1994), pp. xi–xv.

62 Adamson, in Kramer and Maza, pp. 206–9; Simon, Introduction, in Simon, ed., pp. xvii–xxiii.

63 Karl Marx and Friedrich Engels, *The German Ideology*, in Stern, p. 149.

64 Simon, Introduction, in Simon, ed., pp. xv, pp. 157–8.

65 Karl Marx and Friedrich Engels, *Communist Manifesto*, in Simon, ed., pp. 164–5; Simon, Introduction, in Simon, ed., pp. xxiv–xxv.

66 Marx and Engels, *Communist Manifesto*, in Simon, p. 167.

67 Marx, *Communist Manifesto*, in Simon, p. 169; Simon, Introduction, in Simon, pp. xxviii–xxix.

68 Marx and Engels, *Communist Manifesto*, in Simon, p. 176; Simon, Introduction, pp. xxx–xxxii.

69 John Toews, Introduction, Karl Marx, *The Communist Manifesto: With Related Documents*, ed. John Toews (Boston, MA: Bedford/St. Martin's Press, 1999), p. 18.

70  Karl Marx, *Eighteenth Brumaire of Louis Bonaparte*, in Simon, ed., p. 188; Toews, pp. 54–7; Walter Adamson, "Marxism and Historical Thought," in Kramer and Maza, pp. 209–10; Krieger, pp. 401–3.

71  Peter Gay, Introduction, in Jacob Burckhardt, *The Civilization of the Renaissance in Italy* (New York: Modern Library, 2002), pp. xiv–xviii; Hajo Holborn, Afterword, in Burckhardt, *Civilization*, pp. 391–3; Burrow, *History of Histories*, pp. 389–91.

72  Quoted in Gay, Introduction, p. xv; Gay, *Style in History*, pp. 176–8; Holborn, pp. 391–2.

73  Gay, Introduction, p. xv; Burckhardt, p. 17; Gay, *Style in History*, pp. 146–50.

74  Burckhardt, pp. 318–19; Gay, *Style in History*, pp. 156–65.

75  Burckhardt, p. 96.

76  John Clive, "Looking over a Four Leaf Clover: A Quartet of 19th Century Historians," *Not by Fact Alone: Essays on the Writing and Reading of History* (New York: Alfred A. Knopf, 1989), p. 178.


*Notes to Chapter Four: Scientific History and Its Challengers*

1  W. Stull Holt, "The Idea of Scientific History in America," *Journal of the History of Ideas* 1 (1940): pp. 352–62; Iggers, *New Directions*, pp. 17–26, 47–8; Iggers, *Historiography*, pp. 25–30; Iggers, *Global History*, pp. 119–25; Woolf, *Global History*, p. 373; Burrow, *History of Histories*, pp. 425–8; Burke, "Ranke the Reactionary," pp. 41–3.

2  John Higham, *History* (Englewood Cliffs, NJ: Prentice Hall, 1965), pp. 92–103; Holt, pp. 52–62; Michael Kraus and David Joyce, *The Writing of American History*, rev. edn (Norman: University of Oklahoma Press, 1985), pp. 136–51; Peter Novick, *That Noble Dream: The "Objectivity Question" and the American Historical Profession* (Cambridge: Cambridge University Press, 1988), pp. 47–60; Iggers, *New Directions*, pp. 23–6; Iggers, *Historiography*, pp. 26–8; Burrow, *History of Histories*, pp. 425–8.

3  Iggers and Wang, *Global History*, pp. 128–30; Iggers, *Historiography*, pp. 23–4; Woolf, *Global History*, pp. 373–4; Burrow, *History of Histories*, pp. 426–7; Higham, pp. 4–25; Novick, pp. 47–50.

4  Burrow, *History of Histories*, p. 427; Woolf, *Global History*, pp. 374–6; Iggers and Wang, *Global History*, p. 130.

5   "Prefatory Note: *The English Historical Review*," in Stern, p. 176.
6   Iggers, *Historiography*, p. 28; Iggers and Wang, *Global History*, pp. 130–1.
7   "Prefatory Note," in Stern, p. 176.
8   "Preface: *Revue historique*," in Stern, pp. 173–4; Iggers, *New Directions*, p. 48.
9   Morey D. Rothberg, "'To Set a Standard of Workmanship and Compel Men to Conform to It': John Franklin Jameson as Editor of the American Historical Review," *American Historical Review* 89 (1984), pp. 957–75; Novick, pp. 52, 55–6; Higham, pp. 20–5, 101; Bert James Loewenberg, *American History in American Thought: Christopher Columbus to Henry Adams* (New York: Simon and Schuster, 1972), pp. 400–8; Novick, pp. 3–7; W. Stull Holt, "The Idea of Scientific History in America," *Journal of the History of Ideas* 1 (1940): pp. 352–62; Georg Iggers, "The Image of Ranke in American and German Historical Thought," *History and Theory* 2 (1962): pp. 17–27; Cushing Strout, *The Pragmatic Revolt in American History: Carl Becker and Charles Beard* (New Haven, CT: Yale University Press, 1958), pp. 13–29; Elizabeth Clark, *History, Theory, Text* (Cambridge: Harvard University Press, 2004), pp. 13–17; Ian Tyrrell, *The Absent Marx: Class Analysis and Liberal History in Twentieth Century America* (Westport, CT: Greenwood Press, 1986), pp. 16–18; Susan L. Mizruchi, *The Power of Historical Knowledge: Narrating the Past in Hawthorne, James, and Dreiser* (Princeton, NJ: Princeton University Press, 1988), pp. 56–70.
10  John Franklin Jameson, *The History of Historical Writing in America* (Boston, MA: Houghton, Mifflin, 1891) <http://www.eliohs.unifi.it/testi/800/jameson/jameson.html> (May 18, 2006), p. 71.
11  Jameson, *History*, p. 144; Eileen Cheng, "Exceptional History? The Origins of *Historiography* in the United States," *History and Theory* p. 47 (May 2008): pp. 200–12.
12  Jameson, *History*, p. 138.
13  Cheng, pp. 208–12; Ernst Breisach, *American Progressive History: An Experiment in Modernization* (Chicago, IL: University of Chicago Press, 1993), pp. 15–20.
14  Iggers, *Historiography*, p. 28.
15  Jameson, *History*, pp. 147, 145, 144; Rothberg, "To Set a Standard of Workmanship," pp. 961–3, 970–5; Morey Rothberg, Introduction,

in Morey Rothberg and Jacqueline Goggin, eds, *John Franklin Jameson and the Development of Humanistic Scholarship in America, Vol. 1: Selected Essays* (Athens: University of Georgia Press, 1993), pp. xxxvi–xl; Ian Tyrrell, "Making Nations/Making States: American Historians in the Context of Empire," *Journal of American History* 86 (December1999): pp. 1021–9.

16  Jameson, *History*, p. 141.

17  Ellen Fitzpatrick, *History's Memory: Writing America's Past, 1880–1980* (Cambridge, MA: Harvard University Press, 2002), pp. 18–27; Rothberg, Introduction, pp. xxix–xxxvi; Tyrrell, "American Historians in the Context of Empire," pp. 1030–1; Ross, *Origins of American Social Science*, pp. 267–70.

18  Dorothy Ross, "Historical Consciousness," pp. 912–13; Ross, *Origins of American Social Science*, pp. 25–30; Noble, *Historians against History*, pp. 1–55; Lewis, *American Adam*; Somkin, pp. 55–90; Tyrrell, "American Historians in the Context of Empire," pp. 1028, 1036; Fitzpatrick, pp. 27–8; Cheng, pp. 209–10.

19  Ian Tyrell, *Historians in Public: The Practice of American History, 1890–1970* (Chicago, IL: University of Chicago Press, 2005), pp. 44–61; Deborah L. Haines, "Scientific History as a Teaching Method: The Formative Years," *Journal of American History* 63 (1977): pp. 907, 901–8, 911–12; Dorothy Ross, "On the Misunderstanding of Ranke and the Origins of the Historical Profession in America," in *Leopold von Ranke and the Shaping of the Historical Discipline*, ed. Georg G. Iggers and James M. Powell (Syracuse, NY: Syracuse University Press, 1990), pp. 156–60; John Higham, "Herbert Baxter Adams and the Study of Local History," *American Historical Review* 89 (1984): pp. 1225–39; Higham, *History*, pp. 73–82; Joan Shelley Rubin, *The Making of Middlebrow Culture* (Chapel Hill: University of North Carolina Press, 1992).

20  J. Franklin Jameson, "The Future Uses of History," *American Historical Review* 65 (1959): 62.

21  Doris S. Goldstein, "J. B. Bury's Philosophy of History: A Reappraisal," *American Historical Review* 82, no. 4 (October 1977): pp. 896–7.

22  J. B. Bury, "The Science of History," in Stern, pp. 210, 212; Goldstein, pp. 917–18, 897.

23  Bury, in Stern, p. 215.

24 Goldstein, pp. 904, 912–14.

25 Bury, in Stern, pp. 218–19.

26 Bury, in Stern, p. 219; Goldstein, pp. 914–15.

27 Bury, in Stern, p. 223.

28 Bury, in Stern, pp. 219–20; Goldstein, pp. 904–6.

29 Quoted in Goldstein, p. 906.

30 Goldstein, pp. 906, 918–19; Iggers, *Historiography*, pp. 31–4; Woolf, *Global History*, pp. 463–4.

31 Strout, *Pragmatic Revolt*, pp. 21–9; Higham, pp. 104–16; Charles Crowe, "The Emergence of Progressive History," *Journal of the History of Ideas* p. 27 (1966): pp. 109–24; Breisach, *American Progressive History*; Tyrrell, *Absent Marx*, pp. 16–22; Tyrrell, *Historians in Public*, pp. 25–30; Novick, pp. 86–108; Ross, "On the Misunderstanding of Ranke," p. 169; Higham, pp. 104–16.

32 Morton White, *Social Thought in America: The Revolt against Formalism* (1947; New York: Oxford University Press, 1976), pp. 3–31, 47–58; Haskell, pp. 14–17, 24–47.

33 Quoted in Stern, pp. 256–7.

34 Strout, *Pragmatic Revolt*, pp. 9, 26–8, 38–9, 44–5; Novick, pp. 152–4.

35 Novick, p. 92.

36 Richard Hofstadter, *The Progressive Historians* (New York: Vintage Books, 1970), pp. 41–2, 181–6.

37 Hofstadter, pp. 167–81.

38 Forrest McDonald, Introduction, in Charles Austin Beard, *An Economic Interpretation of the Constitution of the United States* (1935; New York: Free Press, 1986), pp. xviii–xxiii.

39 McDonald, Introduction, p. xiv; Hofstadter, pp. 200–6, 214–20, 243–5; Beard, *Economic Interpretation*, p. liii.

40 McDonald, Introduction, pp. x–xiv; Hofstadter, pp. 190–206.

41 Beard, *Economic Interpretation*, pp. 7, 15, xlvii–xlviii, liii; Hofstadter, pp. 214–18.

42 Beard, *Economic Interpretation*, pp. xliii–xlix; McDonald, Introduction, p. xii; Hofstadter, p. 280.

43 Beard, *Economic Interpretation*, pp. xliii–xlvi; Hofstadter, pp. 227–328, 304–14; Higham, pp. 124–31; Tyrell, *Absent Marx*, pp. 18–23; Novick, pp. 252–60; Strout, *Pragmatic Revolt*, pp. 50–61.

44 Milton M. Klein, "Everyman His Own Historian: Carl Becker as Historiographer," *History Teacher* p. 19 (1985): pp. 101–9, 103;

Charlotte Watkins Smith, *Carl Becker: On History & the Climate of Opinion* (Ithaca, NY: Cornell University Press, 1956), pp. 97–9; Strout, pp. 26–49, 83–5; Burleigh Taylor Wilkins, *Carl Becker: A Biographical Study in American Intellectual History* (Cambridge, Mass.: M. I. T. Press, 1961), p. 189; Tyrrell, pp. 36–8; Higham, pp. 120–3; Breisach, *American Progressive History*, pp. 53–4; Novick, pp. 105–7; J. H. Hexter, *On Historians: Reappraisals of Some of the Makers of Modern History* (Cambridge, MA: Harvard University Press, 1979), pp. 16–20.

45 Smith, pp. 51–77; Strout, pp. 33–55.

46 Novick, pp. 167, 263, Smith, pp. 87–101, 104–12, 121–3; James Kloppenberg, "Objectivity and Historicism: A Century of American Historical Writing," *American Historical Review* 94 (1989): pp. 1018–20.

47 Charles Beard, "That Noble Dream," in Fritz Stern, ed., *The Varieties of History* (New York: Vintage, 1973), pp. 317–18.

48 Novick, pp. 111–32; Warren I. Cohen, *The American Revisionists; the Lessons of Intervention in World War I* (Chicago, IL: University of Chicago Press, 1967), pp. 14–20, 41–3.

49 Novick, pp. 206–24.

50 Charles Beard, "Written History as an Act of Faith," *American Historical Review,* 39 (Jan. 1934): 226–7; Hofstadter, pp. 304–15; Higham, pp. 123–6.

51 Beard, "That Noble Dream," in Stern, pp. 324, 317, 328.

52 Hofstadter, pp. 314–15; Higham, pp. 126–8; Novick, pp. 253–8.

*Notes to Chapter Five: Social History, Fragmentation, and the Revival of Narrative*

1 Iggers, *Historiography*, pp. 65–77, 87–94; Iggers and Wang, *Global History*, pp. 251–70.

2 Iggers, *Historiography*, pp. 51–64; Iggers and Wang, *Global History*, pp. 256–8; Hexter, pp. 64–7.

3 Iggers, *New Directions*, pp. 56–7; Iggers, *Historiography*, p. 54; Hexter, pp. 103–4.

4 Fernand Braudel, "History and the Social Sciences: The Long Term," in Stern, p. 407; Iggers, *New Directions*, pp. 58–9; Iggers,

*Historiography*, pp. 51, 56–7; Iggers and Wang, *Global History*, p. 258; Hexter, pp. 64–103.

5   Burke, pp. 34–6; Iggers, *New Directions*, p. 59; Iggers and Wang, *Global History*, pp. 258–9; Hexter, pp. 108–34.

6   Quoted in Peter Burke, *The French Historical Revolution: The Annales School, 1929–89* (Stanford, CA: Stanford University Press, 1990), p. 35.

7   Braudel, in Stern, p. 424; Hexter, pp. 104–5; Gertrude Himmelfarb, *The New History and The Old* (Cambridge, MA: Harvard University Press, 1987), pp. 10–11.

8   Braudel, in Stern, p. 411; Burke, p. 40.

9   Braudel, in Stern, pp. 419–29.

10   Hexter, pp. 88–92; Iggers, *Historiography*, pp. 59–60; Iggers and Wang, *Global History*, p. 259.

11   Burke, p. 42.

12   Burke, pp. 45–6.

13   Fitzpatrick, pp. 92–3, 124–40.

14   John Higham, "The Cult of 'American Consensus' : Homogenizing Our History," *Commentary* 27 (February 1959): pp. 93–100; Elaine Tyler May, " 'The Radical Roots of American Studies': Presidential Address to the American Studies Association, November 9, 1995," *American Quarterly* 48, (June 1996): pp. 179–200; Linda K. Kerber, "Diversity and the Transformation of American Studies," *American Quarterly* 41 (September 1989): pp. 415–31; Fitzpatrick, pp. 188–238.

15   Novick, pp. 417–22; Jonathan M. Wiener, "Radical Historians and the Crisis in American History, 1959–1980," *Journal of American History* p. 76, no. 2 (1989): pp. 405–24; Iggers and Wang, *Global History*, pp. 255–6.

16   Jesse Lemisch, "The American Revolution From the Bottom Up," in Barton J. Bernstein, ed., *Towards a New Past: Dissenting Essays in American History* (New York: Vintage Books, 1969), p. 29; Wiener, pp. 413, 421–4.

17   Lemisch, "American Revolution," p. 6.

18   Jesse Lemisch, *On Active Service in War and Peace: Politics and Ideology in the American Historical Profession* (Toronto: New Hogtown Press, 1975), p. 117; Novick, pp. 423–6, 436–7; Wiener, p. 422.

19   Thomas Schofield, Introduction, in Lemisch, *On Active Service*, p. 5; Wiener, pp. 423–4; Novick, pp. 436–7.

20  Quoted in Wiener, p. 421.

21  Quoted in Wiener, p. 421.

22  Novick, pp. 469–510; Wiener, pp. 424–7.

23  Iggers, *Historiography*, pp. 41–7, 51–64; Iggers, pp. 251–62; Burrow, *History of Histories*, pp. 454–5.

24  Wiener, pp. 427–34; Novick, pp. 415–45, 457–521; Thomas Bender, "Wholes and Parts: The Need for Synthesis in American History," *Journal of American History* p. 73, no. 1 (June 1, 1986): 128–9; Joyce Appleby, Lynn Hunt, and Margaret Jacob, *Telling the Truth about History* (New York: Norton, 1994), pp. 152–9; Richard J. Evans, *In Defense of History* (New York: W. W. Norton, 1999), pp. 145–52.

25  Iggers, *Historiography*, pp. 101–4; Iggers and Wang, *Global History*, pp. 270–5; Appleby et al., pp. 217–23.

26  Burrow, *History of Histories*, pp. 476–7; Iggers, pp. 104–17; David Bell, "Total History and Microhistory," in Kramer and Maza, pp. 266–73.

27  Clark, pp. 145–55; Adam Budd, ed., *The Modern Historiography Reader: Western Sources* (New York: Routledge, 2009), pp. 421–4; Iggers and Wang, *Global History*, pp. 275–7; Iggers, *Historiography*, pp. 108–9, 123–6.

28  Giovanni Levi, "On Microhistory," in Peter Burke, ed. *New Perspectives on Historical Writing* (University Park, PA: Pennsylvania State University Press, 1992), pp. 98–100.

29  Bender, "Wholes and Parts," pp. 129–30.

30  Bender, "Wholes and Parts," p. 127.

31  Bender, Wholes and Parts, p. 129.

32  Bender, "Wholes and Parts," pp. 135–6.

33  Eric H. Monkkonen, "The Dangers of Synthesis," *American Historical Review* 91, no. 5 (December 1986): 1149, 1152.

34  Himmelfarb, "History with the Politics Left Out," in Himmelfarb, *The New History and the Old*, pp. 21–2; Novick, pp. 609–10, 463–4; Appleby et al., pp. 146–59, 198–200.

35  Iggers and Wang, *Global History*, pp. 302–3; Iggers, *Historiography*, pp. 120–1.

36  Keith Jenkins, *The Postmodern History Reader* (New York: Routledge, 1997), p. 3; Iggers and Wang, *Global History*, pp. 301–2; Gertrude Himmelfarb, "Postmodernist History," in Elizabeth Fox-Genovese and Elisabeth Lasch-Quinn, eds, *Reconstructing History: The*

*Emergence of a New Historical Society* (New York: Routledge, 1999), pp. 71–2.

37  Iggers and Wang, *Global History*, pp. 303–4; Iggers, *Historiography*, pp. 9–13, 118–22; Appleby et al., pp. 199–217; Evans, pp. 80–7.

38  Hayden White, "The Historical Text as Literary Artifact," in Hayden White, *Tropics of Discourse: Essays in Cultural Criticism* (Baltimore, MD: Johns Hopkins University Press, 1978), p. 82.

39  Novick, pp. 599–607; Evans, pp. 168–9.

40  Iggers, *Historiography*, pp. 11–16.

41  Novick, pp. 422–45, 469–510; Appleby et al., pp. 198–200; Evans, pp. 169–71.

42  Himmelfarb, "Postmodernist History," pp. 83–5; Novick, pp. 462–5, 565–7, 598, 609–10; Evans, pp. 165–92; Iggers and Wang, *Global History*, p. 306; Iggers, *Historiography*, pp. 131–2.

43  Novick, p. 610.

44  Lawrence Stone, "The Revival of Narrative: Reflections on a New Old History," *Past and Present*, p. 85 (November 1979): p. 19.

45  Stone, pp. 8–15, 19; Novick, pp. 622–55; Clark, pp. 93–5; Iggers, *Historiography*, pp. 97–8.

46  Novick, pp. 622–55; Clark, pp. 93–5; Iggers, *Historiography*, pp. 97–8.

47  Simon Schama, *Dead Certainties* (New York: Knopf, 1991).

48  Gordon Wood, "Novel History," *New York Review of Books* June 27, 1991: 15–16.

49  Schama, p. 322.

50  Appleby et al., *Telling the Truth about History*; Kloppenberg, "Objectivity and Historicism," pp. 1011–30; Haskell, "Objectivity is Not Neutrality"; Evans, *In Defense of History*; Gaddis, *The Landscape of History*; Novick, pp. 625–8.

51  Appleby et al., p. 11.

52  Evans, pp. 152–6.

*Notes to Chapter Six: History and Historiography in Global Perspective*

1  Eckhardt Fuchs, "Provincializing Europe," in Eckhardt Fuchs and Benedikt Stuchtey, *Across Cultural Borders: Historiography in Global Perspective* (Lanham, MD: Rowman & Littlefield, 2002), p. 4; Andreas Eckert, "Historiography on a 'Continent

without History': Anglophone West Africa, 1880s–1940s," in Fuchs and Stuchtey, *Across Cultural Borders*, p. 100; Jerry H. Bentley, *Shapes of World History in Twentieth-Century Scholarship* (Washington, DC: American Historical Association, 1996), http://www.historians.org/pubs/free/BENTLEY.HTM, (accessed June 2011); Jerry Bentley, "The New World History," in Kramer and Maza, p. 394.

2   Bentley, "The New World History," in Kramer and Maza, p. 393.

3   Bentley, *Shapes*; Iggers and Wang, *Global History*, pp. 387–8.

4   Patrick Manning, *Navigating World History: Historians Create a Global Past* (New York, Palgrave Macmillan, 2003), pp. 77–105; Bentley, *Shapes*.

5   Iggers and Wang, *Global History*, pp. 388–9.

6   Bentley, *Shapes*.

7   Bentley, *Shapes*; Lutz Raphael, "The Idea and Practice of World Historiography in France: The Annales Legacy," in Stuchtey and Fuchs, *Writing World History*, pp. 155–71.

8   Manning, pp. 4–6; Bentley, "New World History," in Kramer and Maza, pp. 408–9.

9   Bentley, "New World History," in Kramer and Maza, pp. 400–9; Bentley, *Shapes*.

10  Bentley, "New World History," in Kramer and Maza, pp. 393–4.

11  Rosemarie Zagarri, "The Significance of the 'Global Turn' for the Early American Republic: Globalization in the Age of Nation-Building," *Journal of the Early Republic* 31 (spring 2011): pp. 6–7.

12  Zagarri, pp. 6–9; Johann N. Neem, "American History in a Global Age," *History and Theory* 50 (February 2011): pp. 41–70.

13  Zagarri, p. 3.

14  Arif Dirlik, "Confounding Metaphors, Inventions of the World: What Is World History for?," in Stuchtey and Fuchs, *Writing World History*, pp. 91–133; Brian Connolly, "Intimate Atlantics," *Common-Place: The Interactive Journal of Early American Life* 11, no. 2 (January 2011): p. 3.

15  Dirlik, p. 95.

16  Quoted in Dirlik, p. 94.

17  Thomas Bender, *A Nation Among Nations: America's Place in World History* (New York: Hill & Wang, 2006), pp. 10, 3.

18  Thomas Bender, "Historians, the Nation and the Plenitude of

Narratives," in Thomas Bender, *Rethinking American History in a Global Age* (Berkeley: University of California Press, 2002), pp. 8–9.

19  Eckhardt Fuchs and Benedikt Stuchtey, *Across Cultural Borders: Historiography in Global Perspective* (Lanham, MD: Rowman & Littlefield, 2002); Benedikt Stuchtey and Eckhardt Fuchs, *Writing World History, 1800–2000* (London: German Historical Institute, 2003); Stefan Berger, *Writing the Nation: A Global Perspective*. (Basingstoke: Palgrave Macmillan, 2007).

20  Quoted in Eckert, p. 100.

21  Eckert, pp. 100–1.

22  Robin Law, "How Truly Traditional is our Traditional History? The Case of Samuel Johnson and the Recording of Yoruba Oral Tradition," *History in Africa: A Journal of Method* 11 (1984): pp. 198–9; Eckert, in Fuchs and Stuchtey, *Across Cultural Borders*, pp. 101–2, 108–9.

23  Eckert, in Fuchs and Stuchtey, *Across Cultural Borders*, pp. 107–10; Law, pp. 195–6; Paul R. Spickard, *World History by the World's Historians* (Boston, MA: McGraw-Hill, 1998), pp. 373–4.

24  Law, pp. 196–7.

25  Quoted in Eckert, p. 110.

26  Law, pp. 197–8.

27  Eckert, pp. 110–11.

28  Law, p. 197.

29  Eckert, p. 111.

30  Q. Edward Wang, *Inventing China Through History: The May Fourth Approach to Historiography* (Albany, NY: State University of New York Press, 2001), pp. 55–6.

31  Wang, *Inventing China*, pp. 18, 58; Q. Edward Wang, "Cross-Cultural Developments of Modern Historiography," in Q. Edward Wang and Franz L. Fillafer, *The Many Faces of Clio: Cross-Cultural Approaches to Historiography* (New York: Berghahn Books, 2007), p. 193.

32  Quoted in Wang, *Inventing China*, p. 51.

33  Wang, *Inventing China*, p. 63.

34  Q. Edward Wang, "Between Myth and History: The Construction of a National Past in Modern East Asia," in Berger, p. 141.

35  Wang, *Inventing China*, pp. 4–5; Wang, "Between Myth and History," p. 140; Iggers and Wang, *Global History*, p. 216.

36  Wang, "Between Myth and History," pp. 139–41; Iggers and Wang, *Global History*, pp. 214–15; Wang, *Inventing China*, pp. 63–6; Wang, "German Historicism and Scientific History in China, 1900–1940," in Fuchs and Stuchtey, *Across Cultural Borders*, pp. 146–7.

37  Woolf, *Global History*, p. 506.

38  Herbert Butterfield, *The Whig Interpretation of History* (New York: Norton, 1965), p. 58.

39  James McPherson, "Revisionist Historians," *Perspectives* (September 2003), pp. 5–6.

# Appendix

A selected list of important American and European historians from the Renaissance to the twentieth century[1]

| Name | Birth and Death Dates | Selected Titles of Main Historical Work(s) | Nationality |
|---|---|---|---|
| **14th–16th-Century Historians** | | | |
| Bodin, Jean | 1529/30–96 | *Methodus ad facile historiarum cognitionem.* 1566 | French |
| Bruni, Leonardo | 1370–1444 | *Histories of the Florentine People* | Italian |
| Camden, William | 1551–1623 | *Britannia.* 1586 | English |
| Foxe, John | 1517–77 | *Commentarii Rerum in Ecclesia Gestarum.* 1554 | English |
| Guicciardini, Francesco | 1483–1540 | *Storia d' Italia.* 1579 | Italian |
| Hotman, François | 1524–90 | *Francogallia.* 1573 | French |
| La Popelinière, Henri Lancelot Voisin | 1541–1608 | *Histoire des histoires.* 1599 | French |
| Leland, John | 1506–52 | *Itinerary.* 1710–12 | English |

| Name | Birth and Death Dates | Selected Titles of Main Historical Work(s) | Nationality |
|---|---|---|---|
| Machiavelli, Niccolo | 1469–1527 | *The Prince*. 1516 *The Discourses*. 1513–21 | Italian |
| Pasquier, Etienne | 1529–1615 | *Le Reserches de la France*. 1643 | French |
| Petrarch | 1304–74 | *De viris illustribus*. 1829–34 | Italian |
| Raleigh, Walter | 1554–1618 | *The Discoverie of the Large … Empyre of Guiana*. 1596 | English |
| Sleidan, Johann | 1506–56 | *Zwei Reden an Kaiser und Reich*. 1544 | German |
| Thou, Jacques-Auguste de | 1553–1617 | *Historiarum sui temporis*. 1603 | French |
| Valla, Lorenzo | *c.* 1407–57 | *De falso credito et ementita Constantini donation*. 1570 | Italian |
| Vergil, Polydore | *c.* 1470–1555 | *Anglica historia*. 1534 | Italian |
| **17th-Century Historians** | | | |
| Bacon, Francis | 1561–1626 | *The History of Henry VII*. 1622 | English |
| Bayle, Pierre | 1647–1706 | *Dictionnaire historique et critique*. 1695–7 | French |

| Name | Birth and Death Dates | Selected Titles of Main Historical Work(s) | Nationality |
|------|------|------|------|
| Bossuet, Jacques | 1627–1704 | *Discourse on Universal History.* 1681 | French |
| Bradford, William | 1590–1657 | *History of Plymouth Plantation.* 1856 | English |
| Burnet, Gilbert | 1643–1715 | *History of the Reformation in England.* 1679 | Scottish |
| Clarendon, Edward Hyde | 1609–74 | *The History of the Rebellion and Civil War in England.* 1702–4 | English |
| Hobbes, Thomas | 1588–1679 | *Behemoth.* 1679 | English |
| Mabillon, Jean | 1632–1707 | *De re diplomatic libri.* 1681 | French |
| Mather, Cotton | 1663–1728 | *Magnalia Christi Americana.* 1702 | American |
| Selden, John | 1584–1654 | *Historie of Tithes.* 1618 | English |
| Smith, John | 1580–1631 | *The Generall Historie of Virginia, New England, and the Summer Isles.* 1624 | English |

| Name | Birth and Death Dates | Selected Titles of Main Historical Work(s) | Nationality |
|---|---|---|---|
| Winthrop, John | 1588–1649 | *A Journal of the Transactions and Occurrences in the Settlement of Massachusetts and the Other New-England Colonies.* 1790 | English |
| **18th-Century Historians** | | | |
| Adair, James | *c.* 1709 – *c.* 1783 | *History of the American Indians.* 1775 | Irish (parentage uncertain) |
| Adams, Hannah | 1755–1831 | *Summary History of New England.* 1799 | American |
| Allen, Ira | 1751–1814 | *Natural and Political History of the State of Vermont.* 1789 | American |
| Belknap, Jeremy | 1744–98 | *History of New Hampshire*, 3 vols. 1785, 1791, 1792 | American |
| Beverley, Robert | 1667/8–1722 | *History and Present State of Virginia.* 1705 | American |
| Bolingbroke, Henry St. John | 1678–1751 | *Remarks on the History of England.* 1730–1 | English |

| Name | Birth and Death Dates | Selected Titles of Main Historical Work(s) | Nationality |
|---|---|---|---|
| Byrd, William II | 1674–1744 | *History of the Dividing Line Betwixt Virginia and North Carolina.* 1741 | American |
| Chalmers, George | Bap. 1742–1825 | *Introduction to the History of the Revolt of the American Colonies.* 1845 *Political Annals of the United Colonies.* 1780 | Scottish |
| Colden, Cadwallader | 1689–1776 | *History of the Five Indian Nations,* 2 vols. 1727, 1747 | Born in Ireland to Scottish parents |
| Condorcet, Jean Antoine Nicolas de Caritat | 1743–94 | *Esquisse d' un tableau historique des progrès de l' esprit humain.* 1795 | French |
| Douglass, William | 1681–1752 | *Summary, Historical and Political … of the British Settlements in North America.* 1755 | Scottish |

| Name | Birth and Death Dates | Selected Titles of Main Historical Work(s) | Nationality |
|---|---|---|---|
| Ferguson, Adam | 1723–1816 | *An Essay on the History of Civil Society. 1767* | Scottish |
| Galloway, Joseph | c. 1731–1803 | *Historical and Political Reflections on the Rise and Progress of the American Rebellion. 1780* | American |
| Giannone, Pietro | 1676–1748 | *A Civil History of the Kingdom of Naples. 1723* | Italian |
| Gibbon, Edward | 1737–94 | *The Decline and Fall of the Roman Empire. 1776–88* | English |
| Gordon, William | 1727/8–1807 | *History of the Rise, Progress, and Establishment of the United States. 1788* | English |
| Hewatt, Alexander | 1740?–1824 | *Historical Account of the Rise and Progress of the Colonies of South Carolina and Georgia. 1779* | Scottish |

| Name | Birth and Death Dates | Selected Titles of Main Historical Work(s) | Nationality |
|---|---|---|---|
| Hume, David | 1711–76 | *The History of England from the Invasion of Julius Caesar to the Revolution in 1688.* 1754–62 | Scottish |
| Hutchinson, Thomas | 1711–80 | *History of the Colony and Province of Massachusetts Bay,* 3 vols. 1764, 1767, 1828 | American |
| Jefferson, Thomas | 1743–1826 | *Notes on the State of Virginia.* 1784 | American |
| Lawson, John | d. 1711 | *New Voyage to Carolina Containing an Exact Description and Natural History of that Country.* 1709 | English |
| Morse, Jedidiah | 1761–1826 | *American Geography.* 1789 *History of the Americas in Two Books.* 1790 | American |
| Neal, Daniel | 1678–1743 | *History of New England.* 1720 | English |

| Name | Birth and Death Dates | Selected Titles of Main Historical Work(s) | Nationality |
|------|----------------------|-------------------------------------------|-------------|
| Peters, Samuel | 1735–1826 | *General History of Connecticut.* 1781 | American |
| Prince, Thomas | 1687–1785 | *Chronological History of New England,* 2 vols. 1736, 1755 | American |
| Proud, Robert | 1728–1813 | *History of Pennsylvania.* 1797 | English |
| Ramsay, David | 1749–1815 | *History of the Revolution of South Carolina.* 1785 *History of the American Revolution.* 1789 *History of South Carolina.* 1809 *History of the United States,* 3 vols. 1816–17 | American |
| Randolph, Edmund | 1753–1813 | *History of Virginia.* 1970 | American |
| Raynal, Guillaume Thomas François | 1713–96 | *Histoire philosophique des deux Indes.* 1770 | French |

| Name | Birth and Death Dates | Selected Titles of Main Historical Work(s) | Nationality |
|------|------|------|------|
| Robertson, William | 1721–93 | *History of Scotland.* 1759 *History of the Reign of the Emperor Charles V.* 1769 *History of America.* 1777 | Scottish |
| Schlozer, August Ludwig | 1735–1809 | *General Laws of States and Constitutions.* 1793 | German |
| Smith, William, Jr. | 1728–93 | *History of the Province of New York,* 2 vols. 1752, 1824 | American |
| Stith, William | 1707–55 | *History of the First Discovery and Settlement of Virginia.* 1747 | American |
| Vico, Giambattista | 1668–1744 | *De nostri temporis studiorum ratione.* 1709 | Italian |
| Voltaire François Marie Arouet | 1694–1778 | *History of Charles XII.* 1731 *The Age of Louis XIV.* 1751 *Essay on Manners and the Spirit of Nations.* 1754 | French |

| Name | Birth and Death Dates | Selected Titles of Main Historical Work(s) | Nationality |
|---|---|---|---|
| Weems, Mason Locke | 1759–1825 | *A History of the Life and Death, Virtues, and Exploits of General George Washington.* 1800 | American |
| Wolf, F. A. | 1759–1824 | *Prolegomena to Homer.* 1795 | German |
| **19th-Century Historians** | | | |
| Acton, Lord | 1834–1902 | *Lectures on Modern History.* 1906 | English |
| Adams, Henry | 1838–1918 | *History of the United States during the Jefferson and Madison Administrations.* 1889–90 | American |
| Adams, Herbert Baxter | 1850–1901 | *The German Origin of New England Towns.* 1882 | American |
| Bancroft, George | 1800–91 | *History of the United States from the Discovery of the American Continent to the Present Time*, 10 vols. 1834–75 | American |

| Name | Birth and Death Dates | Selected Titles of Main Historical Work(s) | Nationality |
|---|---|---|---|
| Blanc, Louis | 1811–82 | *Organisation de travail.* 1840 | French |
| Buckle, Henry | 1821–62 | *The History of Civilization in England.* 1857–61 | English |
| Burckhardt, Jacob | 1818–97 | *The Civilization of the Renaissance in Italy.* 1860 | German |
| Burk, John Daly | 1776?–1808 | *History of Virginia from its First Settlement to the Commencement of the Revolution,* 3 vols. 1804–5 | Irish |
| Carlyle, Thomas | 1795–1881 | *The French Revolution.* 1837 | Scottish |
| Droysen, Johann Gustav | 1808–84 | *Geschichte der Hellenismus.* 1836–43 | German |
| Dunlap, William | 1766–1839 | *A History of the American Theater.* 1832 *History of the Rise and Progress of the Arts of Design in the United States.* 1834 | American |

| Name | Birth and Death Dates | Selected Titles of Main Historical Work(s) | Nationality |
|---|---|---|---|
| Ellet, Elizabeth F. | 1818?–77 | *The Women of the American Revolution*, 3 vols. 1848–50 | American |
| Engels, Friedrich | 1823–95 | *The Condition of the Working Class in England.* 1845 | German |
| Force, Peter | 1790–1868 | *Tracts and Other Papers Relating Principally to the Origin, Settlement, and Progress of the Colonies in North America, From the Discovery to the Country to the Year 1776*, 4 vols. 1836, 1838, 1844, 1846 *American Archives*, 9 vols. 1837–53 | American |
| Freeman, Edward Augustus | 1823–92 | *The Norman Conquest of England.* 1867–79 | English |

| Name | Birth and Death Dates | Selected Titles of Main Historical Work(s) | Nationality |
|---|---|---|---|
| Froude, James Anthony | 1818–94 | *The History of England from the Fall of Wolsey to the Defeat of the Spanish Armada.* 1856–70 | English |
| Fustel de Coulanges, N. D. | 1830–89 | *La cité antique.* 1864 | French |
| Gardiner, Samuel Rawson | 1829–1902 | *History of England from the Accession of James I to the Outbreak of the Civil War.* 1863–84 | English |
| Gayarré, Charles E. A. | 1805–95 | *History of Louisiana,* 4 vols. 1854–66 | American |
| Green, John Richard | 1837–83 | *The Conquest of England.* 1883 | English |
| Greenhow, Robert | 1800–54 | *The History of Oregon and California.* 1844 | American |
| Guizot, François | 1787–1874 | *Histoire des origins du gouvernement répresentatif en Europe.* 1821–2 | French |

| Name | Birth and Death Dates | Selected Titles of Main Historical Work(s) | Nationality |
|---|---|---|---|
| Hallam, Henry | 1777–1859 | *The Constitutional History of England.* 1827 | English |
| Hart, Albert Bushnell | 1854–1943 | *Practical Essays on American Government.* 1893 | American |
| Headley, Joel T. | 1813–97 | *Washington and His Generals,* 2 vols. 1847 *The Great Riots of New York, 1712–1873.* 1873 | American |
| Hildreth, Richard | 1807–65 | *The History of the United States of America,* 6 vols. 1856–60 | American |
| Holmes, Abiel | 1763–1837 | *American Annals: Or a Chronological History of America.* 1805 | American |
| Irving, Washington | 1783–1859 | *A History of New York,* 2 vols. 1809 *Life of George Washington,* 5 vols. 1855–9 | American |

| Name | Birth and Death Dates | Selected Titles of Main Historical Work(s) | Nationality |
|---|---|---|---|
| Jameson, J. Franklin | 1859–1937 | *The History of Historical Writing in America.* 1891 *The American Revolution Considered as a Social Movement.* 1926 | American |
| Lamprecht, Karl | 1856–1915 | *Selected Writings on Economic and Cultural History and on the Theory of Historiography.* 1974 | German |
| Langlois, Charles-Victor | 1863–1929 | *Introduction to the Study of History.* 1898 | French |
| Lecky, William | 1838–1903 | *Leaders of Public Opinion in Ireland.* 1861 | English |
| Lingard, John | 1771–1851 | *The Antiquities of the Anglo-Saxon Church.* 1806 | English |
| Lossing, Benson J. | 1813–91 | *The Pictorial Field-Book of the Revolution,* 30 parts. 1850–2 | American |

| Name | Birth and Death Dates | Selected Titles of Main Historical Work(s) | Nationality |
|------|-----------------------|--------------------------------------------|-------------|
| Macaulay, Thomas | 1800–59 | *History of England from the Accession of James II.* 1848–55 | English |
| Marshall, John | 1755–1835 | *Life of George Washington,* 5 vols. 1804–5 | American |
| Marx, Karl | 1818–83 | *The German Ideology.* 1845–6 | German |
| Michelet, Jules | 1798–1874 | *Histoire de France.* 1855–67 | French |
| Mommsen, Theodor | 1817–1903 | *Romische geschichte.* 1856 | German |
| Monod, Gabriel | 1844–1912 | *Études critiques sur les sources de l' histoire mécrov-ingienne.* 1872–85 | French |
| Motley, John Lothrop | 1814–77 | *The Rise of the Dutch Republic: A History,* 3 vols. 1856 *Causes of the Civil War in America.* 1861 | American |
| Niebuhr, Barthold Georg | 1776–1831 | *The History of Rome.* 1811–12 | Danish |

| Name | Birth and Death Dates | Selected Titles of Main Historical Work(s) | Nationality |
|------|------------------------|---------------------------------------------|-------------|
| Palfrey, John G. | 1796–1881 | *History of New England*, 5 vols. 1858–90 | American |
| Parkman, Francis | 1823–93 | *Montcalm and Wolfe*, 2 vols. 1884 | American |
| Pitkin, Thomas | 1766–1847 | *A Political and Civil History of the United States of America*, 2 vols. 1828 | American |
| Prescott, William Hickling | 1796–1859 | *History of the Conquest of Mexico*, 3 vols. 1843 | American |
| Randall, Henry S. | 1811–76 | *The Life of Thomas Jefferson*, 3 vols. 1858 | American |
| Ranke, Leopold von | 1795–1886 | *Histories of the Latin and Germanic Nations from 1494 to 1514.* 1824 | German |
| Savage, James | 1748–1873 | *A Genealogical Dictionary of the First Settlers of New England*, 4 vols. 1860–2 | American |

| Name | Birth and Death Dates | Selected Titles of Main Historical Work(s) | Nationality |
|---|---|---|---|
| Savigny, Friedrich Karl von | 1779–1861 | *The Ius Possessionis of the Civil Law.* 1803 | German |
| Seeley, J. R. | 1834–95 | *The Expansion of England.* 1883 | English |
| Seignobos, Charles | 1854–1942 | *Introduction to the Study of History.* 1898 | French |
| Simms, William Gilmore | 1806–70 | *The History of South Carolina.* 1840 | American |
| Sismondi, Jean Charles Léonard Simonde de | 1773–1842 | *Histoire des républiques italiennes du moyen age.* 1807–18 | Swiss |
| Sparks, Jared | 1789–1866 | *The Writings of George Washington,* 12 vols. 1834–7 | American |
| Stubbs, William | 1829–1901 | *The Constitutional History of Medieval England in Its Origin and Development.* 1873–8 | English |
| Sybel, Heinrich von | 1817–95 | *Geschichte der Revolutionszeit von 1789 bis 1800.* 1853–8 | German |

| Name | Birth and Death Dates | Selected Titles of Main Historical Work(s) | Nationality |
|---|---|---|---|
| Taine, Hippolyte | 1828–93 | *Les origines de la France contemporaine.* 1874–93 | French |
| Thierry, Augustin | 1795–1856 | *Essay on the Third Estate.* 1850 | French |
| Tocqueville, Alexis de | 1805–59 | *The Ancient Regime and the Revolution.* 1856 | French |
| Treitschke, Heinrich von | 1834–96 | *History of Germany in the 19th Century.* 1879–94 | German |
| Trescot, William Henry | 1822–98 | *The Diplomacy of the Revolution: An Historical Study.* 1852 | American |
| Trumbull, Benjamin | 1735–1820 | *Complete History of Connecticut,* 2 vols. 1797, 1818 *History of the United States of America.* 1810 | American |

| Name | Birth and Death Dates | Selected Titles of Main Historical Work(s) | Nationality |
|---|---|---|---|
| Tucker, George | 1775–1861 | *The Life of Thomas Jefferson*, 2 vols. 1837 *The History of the United States*, 4 vols. 1856–7 | Born in Bermuda |
| Warren, Mercy Otis | 1728–1814 | *History of the Rise, Progress and Termination of the American Revolution.* 1805 | American |
| **20th-Century Historians** | | | |
| Adams, James Truslow | 1878–1949 | *Revolutionary New England, 1691–1776.* 1923 | American |
| Ariès, Philippe | 1914–84 | *Centuries of Childhood.* 1962 | French |
| Andrews, Charles M. | 1863–1943 | *The Colonial Period of American History*, 4 vols. 1934–8 | American |
| Bailyn, Bernard | 1922– | *The Ideological Origins of the American Revolution.* 1967 | American |
| Barraclough, Geoffrey | 1908–84 | *The Origins of Modern Germany.* 1946 | English |

| Name | Birth and Death Dates | Selected Titles of Main Historical Work(s) | Nationality |
|---|---|---|---|
| Bassett, John Spencer | 1867–1928 | *A Short History of the United States.* 1913 | American |
| Beard, Charles A. | 1874–1948 | *An Economic Interpretation of the Constitution of the United States.* 1913 | American |
| Beard, Mary | 1876–1958 | *The Rise of American Civilization.* 1927 *Woman as Force in History.* 1946 | American |
| Becker, Carl | 1873–1945 | *The United States: An Experiment in Democracy.* 1920 *Everyman His Own Historian.* 1935 | American |
| Berr, Henri | 1863–1954 | *L'histoire traditionnelle et la synthèse historique.* 1921 | French |
| Bloch, Marc | 1886–1944 | *The Royal Touch.* 1924 | French |
| Boorstin, Daniel J. | 1914–2004 | *The Genius of American Politics.* 1953 | American |

| Name | Birth and Death Dates | Selected Titles of Main Historical Work(s) | Nationality |
|------|------|------|------|
| Braudel, Fernand | 1902–85 | *The Mediterranean and the Mediterranean World.* 1949 *Civilization and Capitalism.* 1967 | French |
| Bury, J. B. | 1861–1927 | *The Idea of Progress.* 1920 | English |
| Butterfield, Herbert | 1900–79 | *The Whig Interpretation of History.* 1931 | English |
| Carr, E. H. | 1892–1982 | *A History of Soviet Russia.* 1954–78 | English |
| Channing, Edward | 1856–1931 | *A History of the United States*, 6 vols. 1905–25 | American |
| Cochran, Thomas C. | 1902–99 | *The Age of Enterprise: A Social History of Industrial America.* 1942 | American |
| Collingwood, R. G. | 1889–1943 | *The Idea of History.* 1946 | English |
| Commager, Henry Steele | 1902–98 | *The American Mind: An Interpretation of American Thought and Character Since the 1880's.* 1950 | American |

| Name | Birth and Death Dates | Selected Titles of Main Historical Work(s) | Nationality |
| --- | --- | --- | --- |
| Craven, Avery | 1885–1980 | *The Coming of the Civil War.* 1942 | American |
| Croce, Benedetto | 1866–1952 | *The Theory and History of Historiography.* 1915 | Italian |
| Curti, Merle E. | 1897–1996 | *The Growth of American Thought.* 1943 | American |
| Curtin, Philip D. | 1922–2009 | *Cross-Cultural Trade in World History.* 1984 | English |
| Davis, David Brion | 1927– | *The Problem of Slavery in Western Culture.* 1966 | American |
| Davis, Natalie Zemon | 1929– | *Society and Culture in Early Modern France.* 1975 | American |
| Donald, David H. | 1920–2009 | *Lincoln.* 1995 *The Politics of Reconstruction, 1863–1867.* 1965 | American |
| Du Bois, W. E. B. | 1868–1963 | *Black Reconstruction in America.* 1935 | American |

| Name | Birth and Death Dates | Selected Titles of Main Historical Work(s) | Nationality |
|------|------------------------|--------------------------------------------|-------------|
| Dunning, William A. | 1857–1922 | *The Constitution of the United States in Civil War and Reconstruction: 1860–1867.* 1885. | American |
| Febvre, Lucien | 1878–1956 | *Philippe II et la Franche-Comté.* 1912 | French |
| Furet, François | 1927–97 | *La Révolution Française.* 1965 | French |
| Genovese, Eugene D. | 1930– | *The Political Economy of Slavery: Studies in the Economy and Society of the Slave South.* 1965 | American |
| Geyl, Pieter | 1887–1966 | *The Revolt of the Netherlands.* 1932 | Dutch |
| Gipson, Lawrence Henry | 1880–1971 | *The British Empire Before the American Revolution,* 15 vols. 1936, 1939–70 | American |
| Goubert, Pierre | 1915– | *Familles march-andes sous l' ancien régime.* 1959 | French |

| Name | Birth and Death Dates | Selected Titles of Main Historical Work(s) | Nationality |
|------|------------------------|-------------------------------------------|-------------|
| Handlin, Oscar | 1915–2011 | *The Uprooted.* 1951 | American |
| Hobsbawm, Eric | 1917– | *The Age of Revolution.* 1962 | English |
| Hofstadter, Richard | 1916–70 | *The American Political Tradition and the Men Who Made It.* 1948 | American |
| Huizinga, J. | 1872–1945 | *The Waning of the Middle Ages.* 1919 | Dutch |
| Jaurès, Jean | 1859–1914 | *Histoire socialiste de la Révolution française.* 1901–2 | French |
| Jensen, Merrill | 1905–80 | *The Articles of Confederation: An Interpretation of the Social-Constitutional History of the American Revolution, 1774–1781.* 1940 *The Making of the American Constitution.* 1964 | American |
| Laslett, Peter | 1915–2001 | *The World We Have Lost.* 1965 | English |

| Name | Birth and Death Dates | Selected Titles of Main Historical Work(s) | Nationality |
|---|---|---|---|
| Le Roy Ladurie, Emmanuel | 1929– | *The Peasants of Languedoc.* 1966 | French |
| Malone, Dumas | 1892–1986 | *Jefferson and His Time*, 6 vols. 1948–81 | American |
| McDonald, Forest | 1927– | *We the People: The Economic Origins of the Constitution.* 1958 | American |
| McNeill, William | 1917– | *The Rise of the West: A History of the Human Community.* 1963 | Canadian/ American |
| Meinecke, Friedrich | 1862–1954 | *Historism.* 1936 | German |
| Miller, Perry | 1905–63 | *The New England Mind: The Seventeenth Century.* 1939 *The New England Mind: From Colony to Province.* 1953 | American |
| Morgan, Edmund S. | 1916– | *The Stamp Act Crisis: Prologue to Revolution.* 1953 *The Puritan Dilemma: The Story of John Winthrop.* 1958 *Visible Saints: The History of a Puritan Idea.* 1963 | American |

| Name | Birth and Death Dates | Selected Titles of Main Historical Work(s) | Nationality |
|---|---|---|---|
| Morison, Samuel Eliot | 1887–1976 | *The Growth of the American Republic.* 1930 | American |
| Namier, Lewis | 1888–1960 | *England in the Age of the American Revolution.* 1930 | English b. Poland |
| Nevins, Allen | 1890–1971 | *The American States During and After the Revolution, 1775–1789.* 1924 *The Gateway to History.* 1938 | American |
| Nichols, Roy F. | 1896–1973 | *The Disruption of American Democracy.* 1948 | American |
| Niebuhr, Reinhold | 1892–1971 | *The Irony of American History.* 1952 | American |
| Parrington, Vernon L. | 1871–1929 | *Main Currents in American Thought: An Interpretation of American Literature From the Beginnings to 1920,* 3 vols. 1927, 1930 | American |

| Name | Birth and Death Dates | Selected Titles of Main Historical Work(s) | Nationality |
|---|---|---|---|
| Phillips, Ulrich B. | 1877–1934 | *Life and Labor in the Old South.* 1929 | American |
| Plumb, J. H. | 1911–2001 | *England in the 18th Century.* 1950 | English |
| Pocock, J. G. A. | 1924– | *The Ancient Constitution and the Feudal Law.* 1970 | English |
| Pollard, Albert | 1869–1948 | *England under Protector Somerset.* 1900 | English |
| Potter, David M. | 1910–71 | *People of Plenty: Economic Abundance and the American Character.* 1954 | American |
| Power, Eileen | 1889–1940 | *Medieval People.* 1924 | English |
| Randall, James G. | 1881–1953 | *The Civil War and Reconstruction.* 1937 *Lincoln, the President*, 4 vols. 1945–55 | American |
| Robinson, James Harvey | 1863–1936 | *The New History.* 1912 | American |

| Name | Birth and Death Dates | Selected Titles of Main Historical Work(s) | Nationality |
|---|---|---|---|
| Schlesinger, Arthur M., Jr. | 1917–2007 | *The Age of Jackson.* 1946 | American |
| Soboul, Albert | 1914–82 | *La Révolution française.* 1948 | French |
| Spengler, Oswald | 1880–1936 | *The Decline of the West.* 1918, 1922 | German |
| Stampp, Kenneth M. | 1912–2009 | *And the War Came: The North and the Secession Crisis, 1860–1861.* 1950 | American |
| Stone, Lawrence | 1919–99 | *The Crisis of the Aristocracy (1558–1641).* 1965 | English |
| Tawney, R. H. | 1880–1962 | *The Agrarian Problem in the Sixteenth Century.* 1912 | English |
| Taylor, A. J. P. | 1906–90 | *The Origins of the Second World War.* 1961 | English |
| Thompson, E. P. | 1924–93 | *The Making of the English Working Class.* 1963 | English |
| Toynbee, Arnold | 1889–1975 | *A Study of History.* 1934–61 | English |
| Trevelyan, George Macaulay | 1876–1962 | *England under the Stuarts.* 1904 | English |

| Name | Birth and Death Dates | Selected Titles of Main Historical Work(s) | Nationality |
|---|---|---|---|
| Trevor-Roper, Hugh | 1914–2003 | *The Last Days of Hitler.* 1947 | English |
| Turner, Frederick Jackson | 1861–1932 | *The Frontier in American History.* 1920 | American |
| Webb, Walter Prescott | 1888–1963 | *The Great Plains.* 1931 | American |
| Williams, William Appleman | 1921–90 | *The Contours of American History.* 1961 | American |
| Woodson, Carter G. | 1875–1951 | *The Education of the Negro Prior to 1861.* 1915 | American |
| Woodward, C. Vann | 1908–99 | *Origins of the New South, 1877–1913.* 1951 | American |

1    This table has been compiled with the aid of Caitlin Durham. The information provided has been taken from the following sources: D. R. Woolf, *A Global Encyclopedia of Historical Writing* (New York: Garland Publishing, 1998); John A. Garraty, *American National Biography* (New York: Oxford University Press, 1999); Clyde Norman Wilson, *American Historians, 1607–1865*, *Dictionary of Literary Biography*, vol. 30 (Detroit, MI: Gale Research Co., 1984); John Ashton Cannon, *The Blackwell Dictionary of Historians* (New York: Blackwell Reference, 1988); Clyde Norman Wilson, *Twentieth-Century American Historians*, *Dictionary of Literary Biography*, vol. 17 (Detroit, MI: Gale Research Co., 1983); *Oxford Dictionary of National Biography*, ed. H. C. G. Matthew and Brian Harrison (Oxford: Oxford University Press, 2004), online edn, edited by Lawrence Goldman.

# Suggestions for Further Reading

Readers wishing to do further reading will find below a selective list of some of the most important secondary sources on the topics covered in this book. The list is by no means comprehensive, and is aimed at highlighting for readers those books that would provide a valuable and accessible starting point for further study.

## GENERAL WORKS

Important works that provide an overview of Western historiography include Ernst Breisach, *Historiography: Ancient, Medieval, & Modern* (Chicago, IL: University of Chicago Press, 1983); J. W. Burrow, *A History of Histories: Epics, Chronicles, Romances and Inquiries from Herodotus and Thucydides to the Twentieth Century* (New York: Knopf, 2008), and the trilogy by Donald Kelley, *Faces of History: Historical Inquiry from Herodotus to Herder* (New Haven, CT: Yale University Press, 1998); *Fortunes of History: Historical Inquiry from Herder to Huizinga* (New Haven, CT: Yale University Press, 2003), and *Frontiers of History: Historical Inquiry in the Twentieth Century* (New Haven, CT: Yale University Press, 2006). For overviews of historiography that provide broader global coverage, see D. R. Woolf, *A Global History of History* (New York: Cambridge University Press, 2011), and Georg Iggers and Q. Edward Wang, *A Global History of Modern Historiography* (Harlow: Pearson Longman, 2008). Useful anthologies of primary sources include Donald Kelley, ed., *Versions of History from Antiquity to the Enlightenment* (New Haven, CT: Yale University Press, 1991); Fritz Stern, ed., *The Varieties of History: From Voltaire to the Present* (New York: World Publishing Co., 1956), and Adam Budd, ed., *The Modern Historiography Reader: Western Sources*

(New York: Routledge, 2009). For anthologies of modern scholarship on historiography, see Lloyd S. Kramer and Sarah Maza, eds., *A Companion to Western Historical Thought* (Oxford: Wiley-Blackwell Publishers, 2002), and Michael Bentley, ed., *Companion to Historiography* (New York: Routledge, 1997). For reference works on historiography, see D. R. Woolf, *A Global Encyclopedia of Historical Writing* (New York: Garland Publishing, 1998); D. R. Woolf, ed., *The Oxford History of Historical Writing* (New York: Oxford University Press, 2011); John Ashton Cannon, *The Blackwell Dictionary of Historians* (New York: Blackwell Reference, 1988), and Kelly Boyd, *Encyclopedia of Historians and Historical Writing* (London: Fitzroy Dearborn, 1999).

## CHAPTER ONE: ART AND SCIENCE IN RENAISSANCE AND EARLY MODERN HISTORICAL WRITING

For an overview of Renaissance historical thought, readers should begin with Peter Burke, *The Renaissance Sense of the Past* (London: Edward Arnold, 1969). On Jean Bodin and the *ars historica*, see especially Anthony Grafton, *What Was History?: The Art of History in Early Modern Europe* (New York: Cambridge University Press, 2007). Two important works on French Renaissance historical writing are George Huppert, *The Idea of Perfect History: Historical Erudition and Historical Philosophy in Renaissance France* (Urbana: University of Illinois Press, 1970), and Donald R. Kelley, *Foundations of Modern Historical Scholarship: Language, Law, and History in the French Renaissance* (New York: Columbia University Press, 1970). On English historical writing during this period, see F. Smith Fussner, *The Historical Revolution: English Historical Writing and Thought, 1580–1640* (New York: Columbia University Press, 1962), and D. R. Woolf, *The Idea of History in Early Stuart England: Erudition, Ideology, and "The Light of Truth" from the Accession of James I to the Civil War* (Toronto: University of Toronto Press, 1990). Finally, for two useful studies of Puritan historical writing, see Stephen Carl Arch, *Authorizing the Past: The Rhetoric of History in Seventeenth-Century New England* (DeKalb: Northern Illinois University Press, 1994), and Peter Gay, *A Loss of Mastery: The Puritan Historians in Colonial America* (Berkeley: University of California Press, 1966).

## CHAPTER TWO: ENLIGHTENMENT AND PHILOSOPHICAL HISTORY

Two works that provide a valuable starting point for further reading on Enlightenment historical writing are J. G. A. Pocock, *Barbarism and Religion* (Cambridge: Cambridge University Press, 1999–), and Karen O'Brien, *Narratives of Enlightenment: Cosmopolitan History from Voltaire to Gibbon* (Cambridge: Cambridge University Press, 1997). On Voltaire in particular, see Peter Gay, *Voltaire's Politics: The Poet as Realist* (Princeton, NJ: Princeton University Press, 1959), and J. H. Brumfitt, *Voltaire, Historian* (Oxford: Oxford University Press, 1958). For an important study of eighteenth-century British historical writing, see Mark Salber Phillips, *Society and Sentiment: Genres of Historical Writing in Britain, 1740–1820* (Princeton, NJ: Princeton University Press, 2000), and specifically on William Robertson, see Stewart J. Brown, ed., *William Robertson and the Expansion of Empire* (New York: Cambridge University Press, 1997). On Edward Gibbon, the most comprehensive study is Pocock's multi-volume work cited above. For further reading on Gibbon, see also David Womersley, *The Transformation of the Decline and Fall of the Roman Empire* (New York: Cambridge University Press, 1988). On the revolutionary historians, see Lester Cohen, *The Revolutionary Histories: Contemporary Narratives of the American Revolution* (Ithaca, NY: Cornell University Press, 1980), and Arthur Shaffer, *The Politics of History: Writing the History of the American Revolution, 1783–1815* (Chicago, IL: Precedent Publishing, 1975), as well as Peter Messer, *Stories of Independence: Identity, Ideology, and Independence in Eighteenth-Century America* (DeKalb: Northern Illinois University Press, 2005), on eighteenth-century American historical writing more generally.

## CHAPTER THREE: ROMANTIC AND CRITICAL HISTORY

Two important, though difficult, works on nineteenth-century European historical thinking and consciousness are Hayden V. White, *Metahistory: The Historical Imagination in Nineteenth-Century Europe* (Baltimore, MD: Johns Hopkins University Press, 1975), and Stephen Bann, *Romanticism and the Rise of History* (New York: Twayne Publishers, 1995). For further reading on Jules Michelet and French historical writing during this period, see Linda Orr, *Jules Michelet: Nature, History, and Language* (Ithaca, NY: Cornell University Press, 1976); Arthur Mitzman, *Michelet, Historian: Rebirth and Romanticism in Nineteenth-Century France* (New Haven, CT: Yale University Press, 1990), and Ceri Crossley, *French Historians and Romanticism: Thierry, Guizot, the Saint-Simonians, Quinet, Michelet* (New York: Routledge, 1993). On Thomas Macaulay and nineteenth-century English historical writing, see J. W. Burrow, *A Liberal Descent: Victorian Historians and the English Past* (New York: Cambridge University Press, 1983), and John Clive, *Macaulay: The Shaping of the Historian* (New York: Knopf, 1973). For further reading on Leopold von Ranke and nineteenth-century German historical writing, see Leonard Krieger, *Ranke: The Meaning of History* (Chicago, IL: University of Chicago Press, 1977), and Georg Iggers, *The German Conception of History: The National Tradition of Historical Thought from Herder to the Present* (1968; rev. edn, Middletown, CT: Wesleyan University Press, 1983). On American historical writing during this period, see David Levin, *History as Romantic Art: Bancroft, Prescott, Motley, and Parkman* (Stanford, CA: Stanford University Press, 1959), and Eileen K. Cheng, *The Plain and Noble Garb of Truth: Nationalism and Impartiality in American Historical Writing, 1784–1860* (Athens: University of Georgia Press, 2008). For further reading on George Bancroft, see especially Lilian Handlin, *George Bancroft: The Intellectual as Democrat* (New York: Harper & Row, 1984), and Russel Nye, *George Bancroft: Brahmin Rebel* (New York: Knopf, 1944). For a useful collection of documents by Karl Marx and an introduction to his ideas, see Karl Marx, *The Communist Manifesto: With Related Documents*, ed. John Toews (Boston, MA: Bedford/St. Martin's Press, 1999), and for a fuller account of his life, see David McLellan, *Karl Marx: His Life and Thought* (New York: Harper Collins, 1978). On Jacob Burckhardt, see White's *Metahistory* cited* above, and Felix Gilbert, *History: Politics or Culture?: Reflections on Ranke and Burckhardt* (Princeton, NJ: Princeton University Press, 1990).

## CHAPTER FOUR: SCIENTIFIC HISTORY AND ITS CHALLENGERS

A valuable starting point for further reading on professionalization, the rise of scientific history, and the later challenges to this ideal is Georg Iggers, *Historiography in the Twentieth Century: From Scientific Objectivity to the Postmodern Challenge* (Hanover, NH: Wesleyan University Press, 1997). On the professionalization of history in the United States, important works include Peter Novick, *That Noble Dream: The "Objectivity Question" and the American Historical Profession* (Cambridge: Cambridge University Press, 1988); Ian Tyrrell, *Historians in Public: The Practice of American History, 1890–1970* (Chicago, IL: University of Chicago Press, 2005), and John Higham, *History* (Englewood Cliffs, NJ: Prentice Hall, 1965). For further reading on British historical writing in this period, see Reba Soffer, *Discipline and Power: The University, History, and the Making of an English Elite, 1870–1930* (Stanford, CA: Stanford University Press, 1994), and Michael Bentley, *Modernizing England's Past: English Historiography in the Age of Modernism, 1870–1970* (New York: Cambridge University Press, 2005). On the Progressive historians and the rise of the New History in the United States, see especially Richard Hofstadter, *The Progressive Historians* (New York: Vintage Books, 1970), and Ernst Breisach, *American Progressive History: An Experiment in Modernization* (Chicago, IL: University of Chicago Press, 1993); and on Charles Beard and Carl Becker in particular, see Cushing

Strout, *The Pragmatic Revolt in American History: Carl Becker and Charles Beard* (New Haven, CT: Yale University Press, 1958).

## CHAPTER FIVE: SOCIAL HISTORY, FRAGMENTATION, AND THE REVIVAL OF NARRATIVE

For an overview of the challenges and problems created by the growing prominence of social and cultural history and the rise of postmodernism, see Iggers, *Historiography in the Twentieth Century*, cited above. A useful collection of essays on a wide range of recent developments in historical scholarship, including "history from below," microhistory, and the revival of narrative, is Peter Burke, ed., *New Perspectives on Historical Writing* (University Park: Pennsylvania State University Press, 1992). Specifically on the Annales school, a valuable starting point for further reading is Peter Burke, *The French Historical Revolution: The Annales School, 1929–89* (Stanford, CA: Stanford University Press, 1990). For further reading on the precursors to the "new" social history in the United States, see Ellen Fitzpatrick, *History's Memory: Writing America's Past, 1880–1980* (Cambridge, MA: Harvard University Press, 2002). For a useful analysis of the linguistic turn in the historical profession, see Elizabeth Clark, *History, Theory, Text: Historians and the Linguistic Turn* (Cambridge, MA: Harvard University Press, 2004). Readers wishing to do further reading on postmodernism should see the anthology by Keith Jenkins, *The Postmodern History Reader* (New York: Routledge, 1997). On the implications of all these developments for the ideal of objective truth, see Joyce Appleby, Lynn Hunt, and Margaret Jacob, *Telling the Truth about History* (New York: Norton, 1994), and Peter Novick, *That Noble Dream*, cited earlier.

CHAPTER SIX: HISTORY AND HISTORIOGRAPHY IN
GLOBAL PERSPECTIVE

For useful and important overviews on the rise of global history,
readers should begin with Jerry H. Bentley, *Shapes of World History
in Twentieth-Century Scholarship* (Washington, DC: American
Historical Association, 1996), http://www.historians.org/pubs/
free/BENTLEY.HTM, (accessed June 2011); Jerry Bentley, "The
New World History," in Lloyd Kramer and Sarah Maza, eds., *A
Companion to Western Historical Thought* (Oxford: Wiley-Blackwell,
2006), pp. 393–416, and Patrick Manning, *Navigating World History:
Historians Create a Global Past* (New York: Palgrave Macmillan,
2003). Important works that examine historiography from a global
perspective include Eckhardt Fuchs and Benedikt Stuchtey, *Across
Cultural Borders: Historiography in Global Perspective* (Lanham,
MD: Rowman & Littlefield Publishers, 2002); Benedikt Stuchtey
and Eckhardt Fuchs, *Writing World History, 1800–2000* (London:
German Historical Institute, 2003), as well as Woolf, *A Global
History of History*, and Iggers and Wang, *A Global History of Modern
Historiography*, cited earlier. For a useful overview of the different
approaches that have been taken to the study of African history,
see Joseph C. Miller, "History and Africa/Africa and History,"
*American Historical Review* 104, no. 1 (February 1999): 1–32. On
Samuel Johnson in particular, see Toyin Falola, *Pioneer, Patriot,
and Patriarchy: Samuel Johnson and the Yoruba People* (Madison:
University of Wisconsin-Madison, 1994), and Paul Jenkins, ed.,
*The Recovery of the West African Past: African Pastors and African
History in the 19th Century; C. C. Reindorf and Samuel Johnson*
(Basel: Basler Afrika Bibliographien, 1998). For further reading
on Hu Shi and the May 4 movement, readers should begin with
Q. Edward Wang, *Inventing China through History: The May Fourth
Approach to Historiography* (Albany, NY: State University of New
York Press, 2001).

# Bibliography

Abrams, M. H. *The Mirror and the Lamp: Romantic Theory and the Critical Tradition*. New York: Oxford University Press, 1953.

Appleby, Joyce, Lynn Hunt, and Margaret Jacob. *Telling the Truth about History*. New York: W. W. Norton, 1994.

Arch, Stephen Carl. *Authorizing the Past: The Rhetoric of History in Seventeenth-Century New England*. DeKalb: Northern Illinois University Press, 1994.

Bacon, Francis. *The History of the Reign of King Henry VII and Selected Works*, ed. Brian Vickers. New York: Cambridge University Press, 1998.

Bann, Stephen. *Romanticism and the Rise of History*. New York: Twayne Publishers, 1995.

Barnes, Harry Elmer. *A History of Historical Writing*. Norman: University of Oklahoma Press, 1937.

Bassett, John Spencer. *The Middle Group of American Historians*. New York: Macmillan, 1917.

Baym, Nina. "Mercy Otis Warren's Gendered Melodrama of Revolution." *South Atlantic Quarterly* 90 (summer 1991): 531–54.

—*American Women Writers and the Work of History*. New Brunswick, NJ: Rutgers University Press, 1995.

Beard, Charles Austin. *An Economic Interpretation of the Constitution of the United States*. New York: Free Press, 1986.

Becker, Carl. "What Is Historiography?" *American Historical Review* 44 (1938): 20–8.

Bender, Thomas. "Wholes and Parts: The Need for Synthesis in American History." *Journal of American History* 73, no. 1 (June 1986): 120–36.

—Wholes and Parts: Continuing the Conversation." *Journal of American History* 74, no. 1 (June 1987): 123–30.

—ed. *Rethinking American History in a Global Age*. Berkeley: University of California Press, 2002.

—*A Nation Among Nations: America's Place in World History*. New York: Hill & Wang, 2006.

Bentley, Jerry H. *Shapes of World History in Twentieth Century Scholarship*. Washington, DC: American Historical Association, 1996. http://www.historians.org/pubs/free/BENTLEY.HTM (accessed June 2011).

Bentley, Michael. *Companion to Historiography*. New York: Routledge, 1997.

Bercovitch, Sacvan. *The Rites of Assent*. New York: Routledge, 1993.

Berger, Stefan. *Writing the Nation: A Global Perspective*. Basingstoke: Palgrave Macmillan, 2007.

Berger, Stefan, Mark Donovan, and Kevin Passmore. *Writing National Histories: Western Europe since 1800*. London: Routledge, 1999.

Berkhofer, Robert F. *The White Man's Indian: Images of the American Indian from Columbus to the Present*. New York: Vintage Books, 1978.

Bernstein, Barton J. *Towards a New Past: Dissenting Essays in American History*. New York: Vintage Books, 1969.

Black, J. B. *The Art of History*. London: F. S. Crofts & Co., 1926.

Bloch, Ruth H. "The Gendered Meanings of Virtue in Revolutionary America." *Signs: Journal of Women in Culture and Society* 13 (1987): 37–58.

Bradford, William. *Of Plymouth Plantation, 1620–1647*. New York: Modern Library, 1981.

Breckman, Warren. *European Romanticism: A Brief History with Documents*. Boston, MA: Bedford/St. Martins Press, 2008.

Breisach, Ernst. *Historiography: Ancient, Medieval, & Modern*. Chicago, IL: University of Chicago Press, 1983.

—*American Progressive History: An Experiment in Modernization*. Chicago, IL: University of Chicago Press, 1993.

Brown, Stewart. "An 18th-Century Historian on the Amerindians: Culture, Colonialism and Christianity in William Robertson's

History of America." *Studies in World Christianity* 2 (1996): 204–22.

Brumfitt, J. H. *Voltaire, Historian.* London: Oxford University Press, 1958.

Burckhardt, Jacob. *The Civilization of the Renaissance in Italy.* New York: Modern Library, 2002.

Burke, Peter. *The Renaissance Sense of the Past.* London: Edward Arnold, 1969.

__*The French Historical Revolution: The Annales School, 1929–89.* Stanford, CA: Stanford University Press, 1990.

—*New Perspectives on Historical Writing.* University Park, PA: Pennsylvania State University Press, 1992.

Burrow, J. W. *A Liberal Descent: Victorian Historians and the English Past.* Cambridge: Cambridge University Press, 1981.

—*Gibbon.* New York: Oxford University Press, 1985.

—*A History of Histories: Epics, Chronicles, Romances and Inquiries from Herodotus and Thucydides to the Twentieth Century.* New York: A. A. Knopf, 2008.

Burstein, Andrew. "The Political Character of Sympathy." *Journal of the Early Republic* 21 (winter 2001): 601–32.

Butterfield, Herbert. *Man on His Past: The Study of the History of Historical Scholarship.* Boston, MA: Beacon Press, 1955.

—*The Whig Interpretation of History.* New York: Norton, 1965.

Callcott, George. *History in the United States, 1800–1860: Its Practice and Purpose.* Baltimore, MD: Johns Hopkins Press, 1970.

Canary, Robert. *George Bancroft.* New York: Twayne, 1974.

Chatterjee, Kumkum. "The King of Controversy: History and Nation-Making in Late Colonial India." *American Historical Review* 110, no. 5 (December 2005): 1454–75.

Cheng, Eileen. "Exceptional History? The Origins of Historiography in the United States," *History and Theory* 47 (May 2008): 200–28.

—*The Plain and Noble Garb of Truth: Nationalism & Impartiality in American Historical Writing, 1784–1860.* Athens, GA: University of Georgia Press, 2008.

Clark, Elizabeth A. *History, Theory, Text: Historians and the Linguistic Turn*. Cambridge, MA: Harvard University Press, 2004.

Clive, John. *Not by Fact Alone: Essays on the Writing and Reading of History*. Boston, MA: Houghton Mifflin, 1989.

Cohen, Lester. *The Revolutionary Histories: Contemporary Narratives of the American Revolution*. Ithaca, NY: Cornell University Press, 1980.

—"Explaining the Revolution: Ideology and Ethics in Mercy Otis Warren's Historical Theory." *William and Mary Quarterly* 37 (April 1980): 200–18.

Cohen, W.I. *The American Revisionists; The Lessons of Intervention in World War I*. Chicago, IL: University of Chicago Press, 1967.

Colbourn, H. Trevor. *The Lamp of Experience: Whig History and the Intellectual Origins of the American Revolution*. Chapel Hill: University of North Carolina Press, 1965.

Collingwood, R. G. *The Idea of History*, rev. edn 1946. Oxford: Clarendon Press, 1994.

Connolly, Brian. "Intimate Atlantics." *Common-Place: The Interactive Journal of Early American Life* 11, no. 2 (January 2011): 3.

Crowe, C. "The Emergence of Progressive History." *Journal of the History of Ideas* 27, no. 1 (March 1966): 109–24.

Dekker, George. *The American Historical Romance*. Cambridge and New York: Cambridge University Press, 1987.

den Boer, Pim. *History as a Profession: The Study of History in France, 1818–1914*. Princeton, NJ: Princeton University Press, 1998.

Elton, G. R. "Review Essay: Clio Unbound." *History and Theory* 20, no. 1 (1981): 83.

Evans, Richard J. *In Defense of History*. New York: W. W. Norton, 1999.

Ferguson, Arthur B. *Clio Unbound: Perception of the Social and Cultural Past in Renaissance England*. Durham, NC: Duke University Press, 1979.

Fitzpatrick, Ellen. *History's Memory: Writing America's Past, 1880–1980*. Cambridge, MA: Harvard University Press, 2002.

Fox, Richard Wightman. "Public Culture and the Problem of Synthesis." *Journal of American History* 74, no. 1 (June 1987): 113–16.

Fox-Genovese, Elizabeth, and Elizabeth Lasch-Quinn. *Reconstructing History: The Emergence of a New Historical Society.* New York: Routledge, 1999.

Fuchs, Eckhardt, and Benedikt Stuchtey. *Across Cultural Borders: Historiography in Global Perspective.* Lanham, MD: Rowman & Littlefield, 2002.

Fussner, F. Smith. *The Historical Revolution: English Historical Writing and Thought, 1580–1640.* New York: Columbia University Press, 1962.

Gay, Peter. *Voltaire's Politics: The Poet as Realist.* Princeton, NJ, Princeton University Press, 1959.

—*A Loss of Mastery: The Puritan Historians in Colonial America.* Berkeley: University of California Press, 1966.

—*The Enlightenment, an Interpretation.* New York: Knopf, 1966.

—*Style in History.* New York: Basic Books, 1974.

Gibbon, Edward. *The History of the Decline and Fall of the Roman Empire,* ed. David Womersley. London: Penguin, 2000.

Goldstein, Doris S. "J.B. Bury's Philosophy of History: A Reappraisal." *American Historical Review* 82, no. 4 (October 1977): 896.

Gooch, George Peabody. *History and Historians in the Nineteenth Century.* New York: P. Smith, 1959.

Grafton, Anthony. "The Footnote from De Thou to Ranke." *History and Theory* 33 (December 1994): 53–76.

—*The Footnote: A Curious History.* Cambridge, MA: Harvard University Press, 1997.

—*What Was History?: The Art of History in Early Modern Europe.* Cambridge and New York: Cambridge University Press, 2007.

Greene, Jack. *The Intellectual Construction of America: Exceptionalism and Identity from 1492 to 1800.* Chapel Hill: University of North Carolina Press, 1993.

Haines, D. L. "Scientific History as a Teaching Method: The Formative Years." *Journal of American History* 63, no. 4 (March 1977): 892–912.

Handlin, Lilian. *George Bancroft: The Intellectual as Democrat.* New York: Harper & Row, 1984.

Haskell, Thomas. "Objectivity Is Not Neutrality: Rhetoric and Practice in Peter Novick's *That Noble Dream.*" *History and Theory* 29 (1990): 129–57.

Haywood, Ian. *The Making of History: A Study of the Literary Forgeries of James Macpherson and Thomas Chatterton in Relation to Eighteenth-Century Ideas of History and Fiction.* Rutherford: Fairleigh Dickinson University Press, 1986.

Heffernan, James A. W. *Representing the French Revolution: Literature, Historiography, and Art.* Hanover, NH: Dartmouth College: University Press of New England, 1992.

Hexter, J. H. *On Historians: Reappraisals of Some of the Makers of Modern History.* Cambridge, MA: Harvard University Press, 1979.

Hicks, Philip. *Neoclassical History and English Culture: From Clarendon to Hume.* New York: St. Martin's Press, 1996.

Higham, John. *History: Professional Scholarship in America.* New York: Harper Torchbooks, 1973.

Himmelfarb, Gertrude. *The New History and the Old.* Cambridge, MA: Harvard University Press, 1987.

Hofstadter, Richard. *The Progressive Historians: Turner, Beard, Parrington.* New York: Knopf, 1968.

Hollinger, David. "Postmodernist Theory and Wissenschaftliche Practice." *American Historical Review* 96 (June 1991): 688–92.

Holt, W. Stull. "The Idea of Scientific History in America," *Journal of the History of Ideas* 1 (1940): 352–62.

Honour, Hugh. *Romanticism.* New York: Harper & Row, 1979.

Howard, Alan B. "Art and History in Bradford's 'Of Plymouth Plantation'." *William & Mary Quarterly* 28, no. 2 (April 1971): 237–66.

Huppert, George. *The Idea of Perfect History: Historical Erudition and*

*Historical Philosophy in Renaissance France.* Urbana: University of Illinois Press, 1970.

Hutchinson, William T., ed. *Marcus W. Jernegan Essays in American Historiography.* Chicago, IL: University of Chicago Press, 1937.

Iggers, G. G. "The Image of Ranke in American and German Historical Thought." *History and Theory* 2 (1962): 17–40.

—*New Directions in European Historiography*, rev. edn 1975. Middletown, CT: Wesleyan University Press, 1984.

—"Historicism: The History and Meaning of the Term." *Journal of the History of Ideas* 56, no. 1 (January 1995): 129–52.

—*Historiography in the Twentieth Century: From Scientific Objectivity to the Postmodern Challenge.* Middletown, CT: Wesleyan University Press, 1997.

Iggers, G. G., and James M. Powell, eds. *Leopold von Ranke and the Shaping of the Historical Discipline.* Syracuse, NY: Syracuse University Press, 1990.

Iggers, G. G., and Q. Edward Wang, with Supriya Mukherjee. *A Global History of Modern Historiography.* Harlow, England: Pearson Longman, 2008.

Jacob, Margaret C. *The Enlightenment: A Brief History with Documents.* Boston, MA: Bedford/St. Martin's Press, 2001.

Jameson, John Franklin. "The Future Uses of History." *American Historical Review* 65, no. 1 (1959): 61–71.

—*The History of Historical Writing in America*, 1891. Repr. Dubuque, IA: William C. Brown, 1972.

Jenkins, Keith. *The Postmodern History Reader.* London and New York: Routledge, 1997.

Jones, Howard Mumford. *O Strange New World: American Culture: The Formative Years.* New York: Viking Press, 1964.

Kant, Immanuel. *On History.* Indianapolis, IN: Bobbs-Merrill, 1963.

Kelley, Donald R. *Foundations of Modern Historical Scholarship: Language, Law, and History in the French Renaissance.* New York: Columbia University Press, 1970.

—*Versions of History from Antiquity to the Enlightenment*. New Haven, CT: Yale University Press, 1991.

—*Faces of History: Historical Inquiry from Herodotus to Herder*. New Haven, CT: Yale University Press, 1998.

—*Fortunes of History: Historical Inquiry from Herder to Huizinga*. New Haven, CT: Yale University Press, 2003.

—*Frontiers of History: Historical Inquiry in the Twentieth Century*. New Haven, CT: Yale University Press, 2006.

Kelley, Donald R. and Sacks, David. *The Historical Imagination in Early Modern Britain: History, Rhetoric and Fiction, 1500–1800*. New York: Cambridge University Press, 2002.

Kenyon, John. *The History Men: The Historical Profession in England since the Renaissance*, rev. edn 1983. London: Weidenfeld & Nicolson, 1993.

Kerber, Linda. *Women of the Republic: Intellect and Ideology in Revolutionary America*. New York: W. W. Norton, 1986.

Klein, M. M. "Everyman His Own Historian: Carl Becker as Historiographer." *History Teacher* 19, no. 1 (November 1985): 101–9.

Kloppenberg, James. "Objectivity and Historicism: A Century of American Historical Writing," *American Historical Review* 94 (October 1989): 1026–7.

Kramer, Lloyd, and Sarah Maza, eds. *A Companion to Western Historical Thought*. Oxford: Wiley-Blackwell, 2006.

Kraus, Michael. *A History of American History*. New York: Farrar & Rinehart, Inc., 1937.

—*The Writing of American History*. Norman: University of Oklahoma Press, 1953.

Krieger, Leonard. *Ranke: The Meaning of History*. Chicago, IL: University of Chicago Press, 1977.

Kupperman, Karen Ordahl. *America in European Consciousness, 1493–1750*. Chapel Hill: University of North Carolina Press, 1995.

Law, Robin. "How Truly Traditional is Our Traditional History? The Case of Samuel Johnson and the Recording of Yoruba

Oral Tradition." *History in Africa: A Journal of Method* 11 (1984): 195–221.

Lemisch, Jesse. "The American Revolution Seen from the Bottom Up," in *Towards a New Past: Dissenting Essays in American History*, ed. Barton Bernstein. New York: Pantheon Books, 1968, pp. 3–29.

—*On Active Service in War and Peace: Politics and Ideology in the American Historical Profession*. Toronto: New Hogtown Press, 1975.

Levin, David. *History as Romantic Art: Bancroft, Prescott, Motley, and Parkman*. Stanford, CA: Stanford University Press, 1959.

—*Forms of Uncertainty: Essays in Historical Criticism*. Charlottesville: University of Virginia Press, 1992.

Levine, Joseph. *Humanism and History: Origins of Modern English Historiography*. Ithaca: Cornell University Press, 1987.

—*The Autonomy of History: Truth and Method from Erasmus to Gibbon*. Chicago, IL: University of Chicago Press, 1999.

Lewis, Merill. "Organic Metaphor and Edenic Myth in George Bancroft's History of the United States." *Journal of the History of Ideas* 26 (1965): 587–92.

Lewis, R. W. B. *The American Adam: Innocence, Tragedy, and Tradition in the Nineteenth Century*. Chicago, IL: University of Chicago Press, 1955.

Loewenberg, Bert James. *American History in American Thought: Christopher Columbus to Henry Adams*. New York: Simon & Schuster, 1972.

Macaulay, Thomas Babington. *The History of England*, ed. Hugh Trevor Roper. New York: Penguin Books, 1979.

Manning, Patrick. *Navigating World History: Historians Create a Global Past*. New York, Palgrave Macmillan, 2003.

Marx, Karl. *Selected Writings*, ed. Lawrence Simon. Indianapolis: Hackett, 1994.

—*Communist Manifesto: With Related Documents*, ed. John Toews. Boston, MA: Bedford/St. Martin's Press, 1999.

Megill, Allan. "Fragmentation and the Future of Historiography." *American Historical Review* 96 (June 1991): 693–8.

Messer, Peter C. "Writing Women into History: Defining Gender and Citizenship in Post-Revolutionary America." *Studies in Eighteenth-Century Culture* 28 (1999): 341–60.

—*Stories of Independence: Identity, Ideology, and Independence in Eighteenth-Century America*. DeKalb: Northern Illinois University Press, 2005.

Michelet, Jules. *History of the French Revolution*. Chicago, IL: University of Chicago Press, 1967.

Mizruchi, S. L. T*he Power of Historical Knowledge: Narrating the Past in Hawthorne, James, and Dreiser*. Princeton, NJ: Princeton University Press, 1988.

Momigliano, A. D. "Ancient History and the Antiquarian." *Studies in Historiography*. New York: Harper & Row, 1966, pp. 1–39.

—"Gibbon's Contribution to Historical Method," in *Studies in Historiography* (New York: Harper & Row, 1966), pp. 40–55.

Monkkonen, Eric H. "The Dangers of Synthesis." *American Historical Review* 91, no. 5 (December 1986): 1146–57.

Muller, Jerry Z. *The Mind and the Market: Capitalism in Modern European Thought*. New York: Alfred A. Knopf, 2002.

Nadel, G. H. "Philosophy of History Before Historicism." *History and Theory* 3 (1964): 291–315.

Neem, Johann N. "American History in a Global Age." *History and Theory* 50 (February 2011): 41–70.

Noble, David. *Historians against History: The Frontier Thesis and the National Covenant in American Historical Writing since 1830*. Minneapolis: University of Minnesota Press, 1965.

Novick, Peter. *That Noble Dream: The "Objectivity Question" and the American Historical Profession*. Cambridge: Cambridge University Press, 1988.

Nye, Russel. *George Bancroft: Brahmin Rebel*. New York: Alfred A. Knopf, 1944.

O'Brien, Karen. *Narratives of Enlightenment: Cosmopolitan History from Voltaire to Gibbon*. New York: Cambridge University Press, 1997.

Outram, Dorinda. *The Enlightenment: New Approaches to European History*. New York: Cambridge University Press, 1995.

Painter, Nell Irvin. "Bias and Synthesis in History." *Journal of American History* 74, no. 1 (June 1987): 109–12.

Peardon, Thomas. *The Transition in English Historical Writing, 1760–1830*. New York: Columbia University Press, 1933.

Phillips, Mark Salber. "Macaulay, Scott, and the Literary Challenge to Historiography." *Journal of the History of Ideas* 50 (1989): 117–33.

—*Society and Sentiment: Genres of Historical Writing in Britain, 1740–1820*. Princeton, NJ: Princeton University Press, 2000.

Phillipson, Nicholas. "The Scottish Enlightenment," in *The Enlightenment in National Context*, ed. Roy Porter and Mikulas Teich. New York: Cambridge University Press, 1981, pp. 19–40.

__"Adam Smith as Civic Moralist," in *Wealth and Virtue: The Shaping of Political Economy in the Scottish Enlightenment*, ed. Istvan Hont and Michael Ignatieff. New York: Cambridge University Press, 1986, pp. 179–202.

Pocock, J. G. A. *The Ancient Constitution and the Feudal Law: A Study of English Historical Thought in the Seventeenth Century*, 1957. New York: W. W. Norton, 1967.

—*The Machiavellian Moment: Florentine Political Thought and the Atlantic Republican Tradition*. Princeton, NJ: Princeton University Press, 1975.

—*Barbarism and Religion*. New York: Cambridge University Press, 1999.

Poovey, Mary. *A History of the Modern Fact: Problems of Knowledge in the Sciences of Wealth and Society*. Chicago, IL University of Chicago Press, 1998.

Rathbun, John W. "George Bancroft on Man and History." *Transactions of the Wisconsin Academy of Sciences, Arts and Letters* 43 (1954): 51–73.

Ross, Dorothy. "Historical Consciousness in Nineteenth-Century America." *American Historical Review* 89 (October 1984): 909–28.

—*The Origins of American Social Science*. Cambridge: Cambridge University Press, 1991.

Rothberg, Morey. "'To Set a Standard of Workmanship and Compel Men to Conform to It': John Franklin Jameson as Editor of the American Historical Review." *American Historical Review* 89, no. 4 (1984): 957–75.

Sachsenmaier, Dominic. "Global History and Critiques of Western Perspectives." *Comparative Education* 42, no. 3 (2006): 451–70.

Shaffer, Arthur H. *The Politics of History: Writing the History of the American Revolution, 1783–1815*. Chicago, IL: Precedent Publishing, 1975.

Shapin, Steven. *The Scientific Revolution*. Chicago, IL: University of Chicago Press, 1996.

Shapiro, Barbara. *A Culture of Fact: England, 1550–1720*. Ithaca, NY: Cornell University Press, 2000.

Sheidley, Harlow. *Sectional Nationalism: Massachusetts Conservative Leaders and the Transformation of America, 1815–1836*. Boston, MA: Northeastern University Press, 1998.

Smith, Bonnie. *The Gender of History: Men, Women, and Historical Practice*. Cambridge, MA: Harvard University Press, 1998.

Smith, William Raymond. *History as Argument: Three Patriot Historians of the American Revolution*. The Hague: Mouton, 1966.

Smitten, Jeffrey. "Impartiality in Robertson's *History of America*." *Eighteenth-Century Studies* 19, no. 1 (1985): 56–77.

Somkin, Fred. *Unquiet Eagle: Memory and Desire in the Idea of American Freedom, 1815–1860*. Ithaca, NY: Cornell University Press, 1967.

Spickard, Paul R. *World History by the World's Historians*. Boston, MA: McGraw-Hill, 1998.

Stern, Fritz, ed. *The Varieties of History: From Voltaire to the Present*. New York: World Publishing, 1956.

Stone, Lawrence. "The Revival of Narrative: Reflections on a New Old History." *Past & Present* no. 85 (November 1979): 3–24.

Stromberg, R. N. "History in the Eighteenth Century." *Journal of the History of Ideas* 12 (1951): 295–301.

Stuchtey, Benedikt, and Eckhardt Fuchs. *Writing World History, 1800–2000.* London: German Historical Institute, 2003.

Thompson, James Westfall. *A History of Historical Writing.* New York: Macmillan, 1942.

Todorov, Tzvetan. *The Conquest of America: The Question of the Other.* New York: Harper & Row, 1984.

Trevor-Roper, H. R. "The Historical Philosophy of the Enlightenment." *Studies on Voltaire and the Eighteenth Century* 27 (1963): 1667–87.

Turnbull, Paul. "The 'Supposed Infidelity' of Edward Gibbon." *Historical Journal* 25, no. 1 (March 1982): 23–41.

Tuveson, Ernest Lee. *The Redeemer Nation: The Idea of America's Millennial Role.* Chicago, IL: University of Chicago Press, 1968.

Tyrrell, Ian. "American Exceptionalism in an Age of International History." *American Historical Review* 96, no. 4 (October 1991): 1031–55.

—"Making Nations/Making States: American Historians in the Context of Empire." *Journal of American History* 86, no. 3 (December 1, 1999): 1015–44.

—*Historians in Public: The Practice of American History, 1890–1970.* Chicago, IL: University of Chicago Press, 2005.

Van Tassel, David. *Recording America's Past; An Interpretation of the Development of Historical Studies in America, 1607–1884.* Chicago, IL: University of Chicago Press, 1960.

—"From Learned Society to Professional Organization: The American Historical Association, 1884–1900." *The American Historical Review* 89, no. 4 (October 1984): 929–56.

Vitzthum, Richard C. *The American Compromise: Theme and Method in the Histories of Bancroft, Parkman, and Adams.* Norman: University of Oklahoma Press, 1974.

Walker, L. D. "Qu' est-ce que l' histoire de l' historiographie?: The

History of Historical Research and Writing Viewed as a Branch of the History of Science [What is History of Historiography?]." *Storia della Storiografia* no. 2 (1982): 102.

Wang, Q. Edward. *Inventing China through History: The May Fouth Approach to Historiography.* Albany, NY: State University of New York Press, 2001.

Wang, Q. Edward, and Franz L. Fillafer, *The Many Faces of Clio: Cross-Cultural Approaches to Historiography.* New York: Berghahn Books, 2007.

White, Hayden. *Metahistory: The Historical Imagination in Nineteenth Century Europe.* Baltimore, MD: Johns Hopkins University Press, 1973.

—*Tropics of Discourse: Essays in Cultural Criticism.* Baltimore, MD: Johns Hopkins University Press, 1978.

White, M. *Social Thought in America: The Revolt Against Formalism,* 1947: New York: Oxford University Press, 1976.

Wiener, Jonathan M. "Radical Historians and the Crisis in American History, 1959–1980." *Journal of American History* 76, no. 2 (1989): 399–434.

Wish, Harvey. *The American Historian: A Socio-Intellectual History of the Writing of the American Past.* New York: Oxford University Press, 1960.

Womersley, David. *The Transformation of The Decline and Fall of the Roman Empire.* New York: Cambridge University Press, 1988.

Wood, Gordon. *The Creation of the American Republic, 1776–1787,* 1969. New York: W. W. Norton, 1972.

—*The Radicalism of the American Revolution.* New York: Alfred A. Knopf, 1992.

Woolf, D. R. "Erudition and the Idea of History in Renaissance England." *Renaissance Quarterly* 40 (spring 1987): 11–48.

—"Disciplinary History and Historical Culture. A Critique of the History of History: The Case of Early Modern England." *Cromohs* 2 (1997): 1–25.

—"A Feminine Past?: Gender, Genre, and Historical Knowledge

in England, 1500–1800." *American Historical Review* 102 (June 1997): 645–79.

—*Global Encyclopedia of Historical Writing.* New York: Garland, 1998.

—*A Global History of History.* Cambridge: Cambridge University Press, 2011.

Wootton, David. "Narrative, Irony, and Faith in Gibbon's Decline and Fall." *History & Theory* 33, no. 4 (December 1994): 77.

Zagarri, Rosemarie. *A Woman's Dilemma: Mercy Otis Warren and the American Revolution.* Wheeling, IL: Harlan Davidson, 1995.

—"The Significance of the ' Global Turn' for the Early American Republic: Globalization in the Age of Nation-Building." *Journal of the Early Republic* 31 (spring 2011): 1–37.

Ziolkowski, Theodore. *Clio the Romantic Muse: Historicizing the Faculties in Germany.* Ithaca, NY: Cornell University Press, 2004.

# Index

Abrams, M.H. 63
*Across Cultural Borders: Historiography in Global Perspective* (Fuchs and Stuchtey) 210
Act of Union (Scotland, 1707) 39
Acton, Lord John Emerich Edward Dalberg 93, 183
Adair, James 177
Adams, Hannah 177
Adams, Henry 183
Adams, Herbert Baxter 183
Adams, James Truslow 193
*Advancement of Learning* (Bacon) 15
African Americans 118–19, 121–2, 136
African history 140–1, 210
agency 30, 33, 129
*Age of Enterprise: A Social History of Industrial America, The* (Cochran) 195
*Age of Jackson, The* (Schlesinger) 202
*Age of Louis XIV, The* (Voltaire) 36–7, 41, 182
*Age of Revolution, The* (Hobsbawm) 198
*Agrarian Problem in the Sixteenth Century, The* (Tawney) 202
Allen, Ira 177
*American Annals: Or a Chronological History of America* (Holmes) 187
*American Archives* (Force) 185
American exceptionalism 77–9, 98–9

*American Geography* (Morse) 180
American Historical Association 97, 108, 119–20
*American Historical Review* 94, 96
*American Mind: An Interpretation of American Thought and Character Since the 1880's, The* (Commager) 195
*American Political Tradition and the Men Who Made It, The* (Hofstadter) 198
*American Progressive History: An Experiment in Modernization* (Breisach) 208
American Revolution 52–4, 56, 78–9, 119, 206
*American Revolution Considered as a Social Movement, The* (Jameson) 188
*American States During and After the Revolution, 1775–1789, The* (Nevins) 200
*Ancient Constitution and the Feudal Law, The* (Pocock) 201
*Ancient Regime and the Revolution, The* (Tocqueville) 192
Andrews, Charles M. 193
*And Still the Waters Run* (Debo) 117
*And the War Came: The North and the Secession Crisis, 1860–1861* (Stampp) 202

*Anglica historia* (Vergil) 175
Anglican Church 24–5
Annales school (France) 112–17, 209
anthropology 123
antiquarian tradition 9–10, 19–22, 28,
    33–4
*Antiquities of the Anglo-Saxon Church,*
    *The* (Lingard) 188
Appleby, Joyce 131–2, 209
archival research *see* primary and
    archival sources
Arch, Stephen Carl 205
Ariès, Philippe 193
Aristotle 8
*ars historica* 10–11, 205
*Articles of Confederation: An*
    *Interpretation of the Social-*
    *Constitutional History of the*
    *American Revolution, 1774–1781,*
    *The* (Jensen) 198
*Authorizing the Past: The Rhetoric of*
    *History in Seventeenth Century*
    *New England* (Arch) 205
Aztecs 45

Bacon, Francis 4, 13–19, 22, 25–6, 28,
    175
Bailyn, Bernard 193
Bancroft, George 61, 76–82, 134, 183,
    207
Bann, Stephen 207
barbarism and primitive societies
    concept 12–13, 45–50, 58
*Barbarism and Religion* (Pocock) 206
Barraclough, Geoffrey 193
Barthes, Roland 127
Bassett, John Spencer 194
Bayle, Pierre 175

Beard, Charles A. 91, 105–11, 194
Beard, Mary 194
Becker, Carl 1, 107–9, 194
*Behemoth* (Hobbes) 176
Belknap, Jeremy 53, 81, 177
Bender, Thomas 124, 139
Bentley, Jerry H. 139, 210
Bentley, Michael 205, 208
Berger, Stefan 138, 140
Berr, Henri 194
Beverley, Robert 177
Bible 11–13, 17–18
*Black Reconstruction in America* (Du
    Bois) 118, 196
*Blackwell Dictionary of Historians, The*
    (Cannon) 205
Blanc, Louis 184
Bloch, Marc 113–14, 194
Bodin, Jean 4, 10–19, 28, 174, 205
Bolingbroke, Henry St. John 32, 177
Book of Daniel 11–12, 17–18
Boorstin, Daniel J. 118, 194
Bossuet, Jacques-Bénigne 134, 176
bourgeoisie 85–7
Bowen, Francis 64
Boyd, Kelly 205
Bradford, William 4, 23–8, 176
Braudel, Fernand 112, 135, 195
Breisach, Ernst 204, 208
*Britannia* (Camden) 174
*British Empire Before the American*
    *Revolution, The* (Gipson) 197
Brown, Stewart J. 206
Brumfitt, J.H. 206
Bruni, Leonardo 174
Buckle, Henry 92, 184
Budd, Adam 204
Burckhardt, Jacob 61, 87–90, 184

Burke, Edmund 61
Burke, Peter 205, 209
Burk, John Daly 53–4, 184
Burnet, Gilbert 176
Burrow, J.W. 204, 207
Bury, J.B. 91, 100–2, 195
Butler, Nicholas Murray 109
Butterfield, Herbert 146, 195
Byrd, William, II 178

Camden, William 174
Cannon, John Ashton 205
Carlyle, Thomas 184
Carr, E.H. 195
Catholic Church 5, 21–2, 24
causation
   in nineteenth and twentieth
      centuries 73–4, 102, 143
   in Renaissance and
      Enlightenment 7, 24–7, 38, 43,
      47, 52, 60
*Causes of the Civil War in America*
   (Motley) 189
*Centuries of Childhood* (Ariès) 193
Chalmers, George 178
Channing, Edward 195
*Cheese and the Worms, The* (Ginsburg)
   123, 129
Cheng, Eileen K. 207
*Chronological History of New England*
   (Prince) 181
Church of Scotland 39, 41
citation and footnotes 42, 47, 82
*cité antique, La* (Fustel de Coulanges)
   186
civic humanism *see* republicanism
*Civil History of the Kingdom of Naples,*
   *A* (Giannone) 179

*Civilization and Capitalism* (Braudel)
   117, 195
*Civilization of the Renaissance in Italy,*
   *The* (Burckhardt) 88, 184
civil rights movement 119, 121
*Civil War and Reconstruction, The*
   (Randall) 201
Civil War (U.S.) 97
Clarendon, Edward Hyde 176
Clark, Elizabeth 209
*Class Struggles in France, The* (Marx)
   86–7
Clive, John 207
Cochran, Thomas C. 195
Cohen, Lester 206
Colden, Cadwallader 178
Collingwood, R.G. 195
colonialism and imperialism 4, 23,
   136–9
*Colonial Period of American History,*
   *The* (Andrews) 193
Columbus, Christopher 23
*Coming of the Civil War, The* (Craven)
   196
Commager, Henry Steele 195
*Commentarii Rerum in Ecclesia*
   *Gestarum* (Foxe) 174
commerce 40, 44, 136 *see also*
   economic theory
communism and socialism 83–7
Communist League 84
*Communist Manifesto: With Related*
   *Documents, The* (Marx and
   Engels, John Toews, ed.) 208
*Communist Manifesto, The* (Marx and
   Engels) 84–6
*Companion to Historiography* (Bentley,
   ed.) 205

*Companion to Western Historical Thought, A* (Kramer and Maza, eds.) 205

*Complete History of Connecticut* (Trumbull) 192

*Condition of the Working Class in England, The* (Engels) 185

Condorcet, Jean Antoine Nicolas de Caritat 31, 178

conjectural history 41

*Conquest of England, The* (Green) 186

consensus history 118

*Constitutional History of England, The* (Hallam) 187

*Constitutional History of Medieval England in Its Origin and Development, The* (Stubbs) 191

*Constitution of the United States in Civil War and Reconstruction: 1860–1867, The* (Dunning) 197

Constitution (U.S.) 105–7

*Contours of American History, The* (Williams) 203

Copernicus, Nicolaus 14–15

Craven, Avery 196

*Crisis of the Aristocracy (1558–1641), The* (Stone) 202

Croce, Benedetto 102, 110, 196

*Cross-Cultural Trade in World History* (Curtin) 196

Crossley, Ceri 207

Crusades 43

cultural history 122–5, 129 *see also* social and cultural history

Curti, Merle E. 196

Curtin, Philip D. 196

"Dangers of Synthesis, The" (Monkkonen) 125

Darnton, Robert 123

Davis, David Brion 196

Davis, Natalie Zemon 196

*Dead Certainties* (Schama) 112, 130–1

Debo, Angie 117

*Decline and Fall of the Roman Empire, The* (Gibbon) 46–52, 179

*Decline of the West, The* (Spengler) 202

deduction 15

*De falso credito et ementita Constantini donation* (Valla) 175

Deism 51

demography 122

Demos, John 129

*De nostri temporis studiorum ratione* (Vico) 182

Depression (1930s) 109

*De re diplomatic libri* (Mabillon) 176

Derrida, Jacques 127

*De viris illustribus* (Petrarch) 175

Dewey, John 143

*Dictionnaire historique et critique* (Bayle) 175

Diderot 31

*Diplomacy of the Revolution: An Historical Study, The* (Trescot) 192

Dirlik, Arif 138–9

*Discipline and Power: The University, History, and the Making of an English Elite, 1870–1930* (Soffer) 208

*Discourse on Universal History* (Bossuet) 176

*Discourses, The* (Machiavelli) 175

*Discoverie of the Large ... Empyre of Guiana, The* (Raleigh) 175

*Disruption of American Democracy, The* (Nichols) 200

Donald, David H. 196
Douglass, William 178
Droysen, Johann Gustav 184
Duara, Prasenjit 137
Du Bois, W.E.B. 117–18, 196
Dunlap, William 184
Dunning, William A. 197
Durham, Caitlin 203

École des Hautes Études en Sciences
    Sociales 113
*Economic Interpretation of the
    Constitution of the United States,
    An* (Charles Beard) 105–7, 194
economic theory 40, 44, 116, 122–3,
    136
educational system 93–4
*Education of the Negro Prior to 1861,
    The* (Woodson) 203
*Eighteenth Brumaire of Louis Bonaparte,
    The* (Marx) 86–7
Ellet, Elizabeth F. 185
Elton, G.R. 1
*Encyclopedia of Historians and
    Historical Writing* (Boyd) 205
Engels, Friedrich 83, 185
*England in the 18th Century* (Plumb) 201
*England in the Age of the American
    Revolution* (Namier) 200
*England under Protector Somerset*
    (Pollard) 201
*England under the Stuarts* (Trevelyan)
    202
*English Historical Review* 94–5
Enlightenment 29–60, 62–3, 127, 206
environmental history 136
érudits 33–4 *see also* antiquarian
    tradition

*Esquisse d' un tableau historique
    des progrès de l' esprit humain*
    (Condorcet) 178
*Essay on Manners and the Spirit of
    Nations* (Voltaire) 35–8, 42, 88, 182
*Essay on the History of Civil Society, An*
    (Ferguson) 179
*Essay on the Third Estate* (Thierry) 192
*Études critiques sur les sources de l'
    histoire mécrovingienne* (Monod)
    189
Eurocentrism 137–9
*Everyman His Own Historian* (Becker)
    108, 194
evidential scholars (Qing Dynasty,
    China) 144
*Expansion of England, The* (Seeley) 191

*Faces of History: Historical Inquiry from
    Herodotus to Herder* (Kelley) 204
Falola, Toyin 210
*Familles marchandes sous l' ancien
    régime* (Goubert) 197
Febvre, Lucien 113–14, 197
Ferguson, Adam 39–40, 179
fictional technique 130–1
Fitzpatrick, Ellen 209
footnotes and citation 42, 47, 82
Force, Peter 185
formalism and anti-formalism 103–4
Fortune concept 7
*Fortunes of History: Historical Inquiry
    from Herder to Huizinga* (Kelley) 204
Foucault, Michel 127–8
*Foundations of Modern Historical
    Scholarship: Language, Law, and
    History in the French Renaissance*
    (Kelley) 205

founding fathers (U.S.) 106–8
four empires theory 11–12
four-stage theory 39–45 *see also*
    stadial theory
Foxe, John 174
fragmentation and synthesis 124–6,
    130, 132, 136
*Francogallia* ( Hotman) 174
Frederick the Great (Prussia) 35
Freeman, Edward Augustus 185
*French Historians and Romanticism:*
    *Thierry, Guizot, the Saint-*
    *Simonians, Quinet, Michelet*
    (Crossley) 207
*French Historical Revolution: The*
    *Annales School, 1929–89, The*
    (Burke) 209
French Revolution (1789) 61–2, 66–8
*French Revolution, The* (Carlyle) 184
*Frontier in American History, The*
    (Turner) 203
*Frontiers of History: Historical Inquiry*
    *in the Twentieth Century* (Kelley)
    204
Froude, James Anthony 186
Fuchs, Eckhardt 140, 210
Furet, François 197
Fussner, F. Smith 205
Fustel de Coulanges, N.D. 186

Galloway, Joseph 179
Gardiner, Samuel Rawson 186
*Gateway to History, The* (Nevins) 200
Gatterer, Johann 134
Gayarré, Charles E.A. 186
Gay, Peter 206
Geertz, Clifford 123–4, 129
*Genealogical Dictionary of the First*

*Settlers of New England, A*
    (Savage) 190
*General History of Connecticut* (Peters)
    181
*General Laws of States and*
    *Constitutions* (Schlozer) 182
*Generall Historie of Virginia, New*
    *England, and the Summer Isles, The*
    (Selden) 176
*Genius of American Politics, The*
    (Boorstin) 194
Genovese, Eugene D. 118, 197
*George Bancroft: Brahmin Rebel* (Nye) 207
*George Bancroft: The Intellectual as*
    *Democrat* (Handlin) 207
*German Conception of History: The*
    *National Tradition of Historical*
    *Thought from Herder to the Present,*
    *The* (Iggers) 207
*German History in the Time of the*
    *Reformation* (Ranke) 70
*German Ideology, The* (Marx) 83, 189
*German Origin of New England Towns,*
    *The* (Adams) 183
German unification (1870) 75–6
*Geschichte der Hellenismus* (Droysen)
    184
*Geschichte der Revolutionszeit von 1789*
    *bis 1800* (Sybel) 191
Geyl, Pieter 197
Giannone, Pietro 179
Gibbon, Edward 29, 45–52, 59–60,
    179, 206
Gilbert, Felix 208
Ginsburg, Carlo 123, 129
Gipson, Lawrence Henry 197
*Global Encyclopedia of Historical*
    *Writing, A* (Woolf) 205

global history 133–40, 143, 210
*Global History of History, A* (Woolf)
139, 204, 210
*Global History of Modern
Historiography, A* (Iggers and
Wang) 139, 204, 210
globalization 133, 135, 138–9
Glorious Revolution (England, 1688)
69
golden age myth (Book of Daniel)
12–13
Gordon, Linda 129
Gordon, William 179
Göttingen school 34, 70–1, 81
Goubert, Pierre 197
Grafton, Anthony 205
*Great Arizona Orphan Abduction, The*
(Gordon) 129
*Great Cat Massacre, The* (Darnton) 123
*Great Plains, The* (Webb) 203
*Great Riots of New York, 1712–1873,
The* (Headley) 187
Greece 5, 44
Greenhow, Robert 186
Green, John Richard 186
Greven, Philip 121
*Growth of American Thought, The*
(Curti) 196
*Growth of the American Republic, The*
(Morison) 200
Guicciardini, Francesco 7–9, 174
Guizot, François 186
Gu Jiegang 145

Hallam, Henry 187
Handlin, Lilian 207
Handlin, Oscar 198
Harding, Warren 105

Hart, Albert Bushnell 187
Hartz, Louis 118
Haskell, Thomas 131
Headley, Joel T. 187
Heeren, A.H.L. 81
Hegel, G.W.F. 83–4, 140
Hening, William 81
Heussi, Karl 110
Hewatt, Alexander 179
Higham, John 208
Hildreth, Richard 187
Himmelfarb, Gertrude 125–6
*Histoire de France* (Michelet) 67, 189
*Histoire des Histoires* (La Popelinière)
174
*Histoire des origins du gouvernement
répresentatif en Europe* (Guizot)
186
*Histoire des républiques italiennes du
moyen age* (Sismondi) 191
*histoire événementielle* 114–15
*Histoire philosophique des deux Indes*
(Raynal) 181
*Histoire socialiste de la Révolution
française* (Jaurès) 198
*histoire totale* 114–15
*histoire traditionnelle et la synthèse
historique, L'* (Berr) 194
*Historians in Public: The Practice of
American History, 1890–1970*
(Tyrrell) 208
*Historiarum sui temporis* (de Thou) 175
*Historical Account of the Rise and
Progress of the Colonies of South
Carolina and Georgia* (Hewatt) 179
*Historical and Political Reflections on the
Rise and Progress of the American
Rebellion* (Galloway) 179

historical materialism 61, 90, 106

*Historical Revolution: English Historical Writing and Thought, 1580–1640, The* (Fussner) 205

Historical Social Science 113

historicism 73

*Historie of Tithes* (Selden) 19–21, 176

*Histories of the Florentine People* (Bruni) 174

*Histories of the Latin and Germanic Nations from 1494 to 1514* (Ranke) 70, 190

*Historiography: Ancient, Medieval, & Modern* (Breisach) 204

historiography concept 1–3, 133, 139–46, 204–5

*Historiography in the Twentieth Century: From Scientific Objectivity to the Postmodern Challenge* (Iggers) 208–9

*Historische Zeitschrift* (Germany) 94

*Historisch-Politische Zeitschrift* (Hamburg) 74

*Historism* (Meinecke) 199

*History* (Higham) 208

"History and Africa/Africa and History" (Miller) 210

*History and Present State of Virginia* (Beverley) 177

*History as Romantic Art: Bancroft, Prescott, Motley, and Parkman* (Levin) 207

history from below 113, 209

*History of America* (Robertson) 182

*History of Charles XII* (Voltaire) 35–6, 182

*History of Civilization in England, The* (Buckle) 92, 184

*History of England from the Accession of James I to the Outbreak of the Civil War* (Gardiner) 186

*History of England from the Accession of James II* (Macaulay) 68–9, 189

*History of England from the Fall of Wolsey to the Defeat of the Spanish Armada, The* (Froude) 186

*History of England from the Invasion of Julius Caesar to the Revolution in 1688, The* (Hume) 34, 180

*History of Germany in the 19th Century* (Treitschke) 192

*History of Henry VII, The* (Bacon) 18–19, 175

*History of Historical Writing in America, The* (Jameson) 96, 188

*History of Histories: Epics, Chronicles, Romances and Inquiries from Herodotus and Thucydides to the Twentieth Century, A* (Burrow) 204

*History of Louisiana* (Gayarré) 186

*History of New England* (Neal) 180

*History of New England* (Palfrey) 190

*History of New Hampshire* (Belknap) 53–4, 177

*History of New York, A* (Irving) 187

*History of North Carolina* (Williamson) 54

*History of Oregon and California, The* (Greenhow) 186

*History of Pennsylvania* (Proud) 181

*History of Plymouth Plantation* (Bradford) 24, 176

*History of Rome, The* (Niebuhr) 70, 189

*History of Scotland* (Robertson) 41, 182

*History of South Carolina* (Ramsay) 181

*History of South Carolina, The* (Simms)
191

*History of Soviet Russia, A* (Carr) 195

*History of the American Indians, A*
(Adair) 177

*History of the American Revolution*
(Ramsay) 181

*History of the American Theater, A*
(Dunlap) 184

*History of the Americas in Two Books*
(Morse) 180

*History of the Colony and Province of
Massachusetts Bay* (Hutchinson)
180

*History of the Dividing Line Betwixt
Virginia and North Carolina* (Byrd)
178

*History of the First Discovery and
Settlement of Virginia* (Stith) 182

*History of the Five Indian Nations*
(Colden) 178

*History of the Life and Death, Virtues,
and Exploits of General George
Washington, A* (Weems) 183

*History of the Political System of Europe*
(Heeren) 81

*History of the Popes* (Ranke) 70

*History of the Province of New York*
(Smith) 182

*History of the Rebellion and Civil War
in England, The* (Clarendon) 176

*History of the Reformation in England*
(Burnet) 176

*History of the Reign of the Emperor
Charles V* (Robertson) 41–3, 182

*History of the Revolution of South
Carolina* (Ramsay) 181

*History of the Rise and Progress of the*

*Arts of Design in the United States*
(Dunlap) 184

*History of the Rise, Progress, and
Establishment of the United States*
(Gordon) 179

*History of the Rise, Progress and
Termination of the American
Revolution* (Warren) 55–9, 193

*History of the States of Antiquity*
(Heeren) 81

*History of the United States, A*
(Channing) 195

*History of the United States* (Ramsay)
181

*History of the United States, The*
(Trumbull) 193

*History of the United States during
the Jefferson and Madison
Administrations* (Adams) 183

*History of the United States from
the Discovery of the American
Continent to the Present Time*
(Bancroft) 77, 81–2, 183

*History of the United States of America,
The* (Hildreth) 187

*History of the United States of America*
(Trumbull) 192

*History of Virginia* (Randolph) 181

*History of Virginia from its First
Settlement to the Commencement of
the Revolution* (Burk) 54, 184

*History: Politics or Culture?: Reflections
on Ranke and Burckhardt* (Gilbert)
208

*History's Memory: Writing America's
Past, 1880–1980* (Fitzpatrick) 209

*History, Theory, Text: Historians and the
Linguistic Turn* (Clark) 209

"History with the Politics Left Out"
  (Himmelfarb) 125–6
Hobbes, Thomas 176
Hobsbawm, Eric 198
Hofstadter, Richard 118, 198, 208
Holmes, Abiel 81, 187
Holy Roman Empire 12
Hotman, François 174
Huizinga, J. 198
humanism (Renaissance) 4–5
Hume, David 31, 34, 39, 180
Hunt, Lynn 131–2, 209
Huppert, George 205
Hu Shi 133, 143–5, 210
Hutchinson, Thomas 52, 180

idealism 61, 73–4, 79–81, 83
*Idea of History, The* (Collingwood) 195
*Idea of History in Early Stuart England:
  Erudition, Ideology, and "The
  Light of Truth" from the Accession
  of James I to the Civil War, The*
  (Woolf) 205
*Idea of Perfect History: Historical
  Erudition and Historical Philosophy
  in Renaissance France, The*
  (Huppert) 205
*Idea of Progress, The* (Bury) 195
*Ideological Origins of the American
  Revolution, The* (Bailyn) 193
Iggers, Georg 139, 204, 207–10
impartiality *see* objectivity
imperialism and colonialism 4, 23,
  136–9
Incas 45
individualism 89, 105
induction 15
Internet 139

*Introduction to the History of the
  Revolt of the American Colonies*
  (Chalmers) 178
*Introduction to the Study of History*
  (Langlois) 188
*Introduction to the Study of History*
  (Seignobos) 191
*Inventing China through History:
  The May Fourth Approach to
  Historiography* (Wang) 210
*Irony of American History, The*
  (Niebuhr) 200
Irving, Washington 187
*Itinerary* (Leland) 174
*Ius Possessionis of the Civil Law, The*
  (Savigny) 191

Jackson, Andrew 77
Jacob, Margaret 131–2, 209
James, William 104
Jameson, J. Franklin 91, 95–9, 111, 188
Jamestown 23
Jaurès, Jean 198
*Jefferson and His Time* (Malone) 199
Jefferson, Thomas 180
Jenkins, Keith 127, 209
Jenkins, Paul 210
Jensen, Merrill 198
Johns Hopkins University 94
Johnson, Obadiah 141
Johnson, Samuel (West African
  historian) 133, 141–3
*Journal of Global History* 135
*Journal of the Transactions and
  Occurrences in the Settlement
  of Massachusetts and the Other
  New-England Colonies* (Winthrop)
  177

*Journal of World History* 135
*Jules Michelet: Nature, History, and Language* (Orr) 207

Kant, Immanuel 30–1
*Karl Marx: His Life and Thought* (McLellan, ) 208
Kelley, Donald R. 204–5
Kloppenberg, James 131
Kramer, Lloyd S. 205
Krieger, Leonard 207

Lamprecht, Karl 102, 188
Langlois, Charles-Victor 93, 116, 188
La Popelinière, Henri Lancelot Voisin 174
Laslett, Peter 198
*Last Days of Hitler, The* (Trevor-Roper) 203
law 9–10
Lawson, John 180
*Leaders of Public Opinion in Ireland* (Lecky) 188
League of the Just 84
Lecky, William 188
*Lectures on Modern History* (Acton) 183
Leland, John 174
Lemisch, Jesse 112, 118–21
Le Roy Ladurie, Emmanuel 123, 129, 199
Levi, Giovanni 123–4
Levin, David 207
*Liberal Descent: Victorian Historians and the English Past, A* (Burrow) 207
liberalism 69
*Life and Labor in the Old South* (Phillips) 201

*Life of George Washington* (Irving) 187
*Life of George Washington* (Marshall) 189
*Life of Thomas Jefferson, The* (Randall) 190
*Life of Thomas Jefferson, The* (Tucker) 193
*Lincoln* (Donald) 196
*Lincoln, the President* (Randall) 201
Lingard, John 188
literary theory and language 126–7, 209 *see also* philology
*longue durée* 114–15
Lossing, Benson J. 188
*Loss of Mastery: The Puritan Historians in Colonial America, A* (Gay) 206
Lynd, Staughton 119

Mabillon, Jean 176
*Macaulay: The Shaping of the Historian* (Clive) 207
Macaulay, Catharine 55
Macaulay, Thomas 66, 68–70, 189, 207
McCall, Hugh 53
McDonald, Forest 199
Machiavelli, Niccolo 7–8, 32, 175
McLellan, David 208
McNeill, William 134–5, 199
*Magnalia Christi Americana* (Mather) 176
*Main Currents in American Thought: An Interpretation of American Literature From the Beginnings to 1920* (Parrington) 200
*Making of the American Constitution, The* (Jensen) 198
*Making of the English Working Class, The* (Thompson) 202

Malone, Dumas 199
manners *see* social and cultural history
Mannheim, Karl 110
Manning, Patrick 210
Marshall, John 53, 189
Marx, Karl 61, 83–7, 106–7, 189, 207–8
Massachusetts Bay colony 24
materialism 61, 83, 90, 106
*Mathematical Principles of Natural Philosophy* (Newton) 14
Mather, Cotton 24, 52, 176
May 4/New Culture movement (China) 143, 210
Maza, Sarah 205
*Medieval People* (Power) 201
*Mediterranean and the Mediterranean World, The* (Braudel) 195
Meinecke, Friedrich 199
Messer, Peter 206
*Metahistory: The Historical Imagination in Nineteenth-Century Europe* (White) 207–8
*Methodus ad facile historiarum cognitionem* (Bodin) 10–11, 174
*Michelet, Historian: Rebirth and Romanticism in Nineteenth-Century France* (Mitzman) 207
Michelet, Jules 66–7, 189, 207
microhistory 123–4, 129, 209
middle ages 4–7, 14, 19, 43, 65, 85, 89
migrations and diasporas 136
Millar, John 39
Miller, Joseph C. 210
Miller, Perry 199
Minot, George 53
Mitzman, Arthur 207

*Modern Historiography Reader: Western Sources, The* (Budd, ed.) 204
modernization 139
*Modernizing England's Past: English Historiography in the Age of Modernism, 1870–1970* (Bentley) 208
Mommsen, Theodor 189
monarchy and aristocracy 35–8, 74–5, 85
Monkkonen, Eric 125
Monod, Gabriel 189
*Montaillou* (Le Roy Ladurie) 123, 129
*Montcalm and Wolfe* (Parkman) 190
Morgan, Edmund S. 199
Morison, Samuel Eliot 200
Morse, Jedidiah 180
Motley, John Lothrop 189

Namier, Lewis 200
Napoleon, Louis 68
narrative history 112–13, 129–31, 209
*Narratives of Enlightenment: Cosmopolitan History from Voltaire to Gibbon* (O'Brien) 206
nationalism and nation concept
  and Enlightenment 37–8
  and Romanticism and scientific history 61, 65–7, 76–90, 95–6
  in twentieth century 117, 133, 137–9, 142, 145
National Studies project (Peking University) 145
Native Americans 44–5, 57–8, 117–18
*Natural and Political History of the State of Vermont* (Allen) 177
*Navigating World History: Historians Create a Global Past* (Manning) 210

Neal, Daniel 180
neoconservatism 125
Nevins, Allen 200
*New England Mind: From Colony to Province, The* (Miller) 199
*New England Mind: The Seventeenth Century, The* (Miller) 199
New Historians 91, 103–11, 117–18
*New History, The* (Robinson) 103, 201
New Left 118–21
*New Perspectives on Historical Writing* (Burke, ed.) 209
new social history 112–22, 128, 209 *see also* social and cultural history
Newton, Isaac 14
*New Voyage to Carolina Containing an Exact Description and Natural History of that Country* (Lawson) 180
"New World History, The" (Bentley) 210
Nichols, Roy F. 200
Niebuhr, Barthold Georg 70, 189
Niebuhr, Reinhold 200
*Norman Conquest of England, The* (Freeman) 185
*Notes on the State of Virginia* (Jefferson) 180
Novick, Peter 2, 108, 208–9
Nye, Russel 207

objectivity 79–80, 91–2, 95–103, 107–11, 119–20, 128
O'Brien, Karen 206
*On Active Service in War and Peace: Politics and Ideology in the*

*American History Profession* (Lemisch) 120
*On the Revolutions of the Heavenly Spheres* (Copernicus) 14
oral tradition 140–2
*Organisation de travail* (Blanc) 184
*origines de la France contemporaine, Les* (Taine) 192
*Origins of Modern Germany, The* (Barraclough) 193
*Origins of the New South, 1877–1913* (Woodward) 203
*Origins of the Second World War, The* (Taylor) 202
Orr, Linda 207
Otis, James, Jr. 54
*Oxford History of Historical Writing, The* (Woolf, ed..) 205

Palfrey, John G. 190
Parkman, Francis 190
Parrington, Vernon L. 200
Pasquier, Etienne 175
*Peasants of Languedoc, The* (Le Roy Ladurie) 199
Penn, William 79
*People of Plenty: Economic Abundance and the American Character* (Potter) 201
Peters, Samuel 181
Peter the Great (Russia) 35
Petrarch 5, 175
*Philippe II et la Franche-Comté* (Febvre) 197
Phillips, Mark Salber 206
Phillips, Ulrich B. 201
philology 20–2, 34, 70, 100
philosophe 31

philosophical history 29, 33, 35, 38–9, 45–7, 58–9, 100

*Pictorial Field-Book of the Revolution, The* (Lossing) 188

*Pioneer, Patriot, and Patriarchy: Samuel Johnson and the Yoruba People* (Falola) 210

Pitkin, Thomas 190

*Plain and Noble Garb of Truth: Nationalism and Impartiality in American Historical Writing, 1784–1860, The* (Cheng) 207

Plumb, J.H. 201

Plymouth colony 23–4

Pocock, J.G.A. 201, 206

*Political and Civil History of the United States of America, A* (Pitkin) 190

*Political Annals of the United Colonies* (Chalmers) 178

*Political Economy of Slavery: Studies in the Economy and Society of the Slave South, The* (Genovese) 197

political implications 146
    and Enlightenment 29, 37–40, 53–6
    of global history 133, 136–7, 142
    of New History 105–6, 108–9, 111
    of postmodernism 125, 128
    and Renaissance 8–9
    and Romanticism 61–2, 65–8, 70, 74–9, 83–8
    of scientific history 93, 98–9, 112
    of social and cultural history 112–15, 117–22

*Politics of History: Writing the History of the American Revolution, 1783–1815, The* (Shaffer) 206

*Politics of Reconstruction, 1863–1867, The* (Donald) 196

Pollard, Albert 201

positivism 100

*Postmodern History Reader, The* (Jenkins) 209

postmodernism 112, 126–9, 209

Potter, David M. 201

Power, Eileen 201

*Practical Essays on American Government* (Hart) 187

*Pragmatic Revolt in American History: Carl Becker and Charles Beard, The* (Strout) 209

pragmatism 104, 143

Prescott, William Hickling 190

"Present Mindedness Revisited: Anti-Radicalism as a Goal of American Historical Writing since World War II" (Lemisch) 119

primary and archival sources
    in nineteenth and twentieth centuries 67, 70–2, 76, 78, 81–2, 93
    in Renaissance and Enlightenment 18, 34, 42

*Prince, The* (Machiavelli) 175

Prince, Thomas 96, 181

*Problem of Slavery in Western Culture, The* (Davis) 196

professionalization of history
    in Enlightenment 34
    further reading on 208
    in nineteenth and twentieth centuries 71, 73, 77, 90–1, 93–6, 100, 145

progress as concept 2
    in Enlightenment 29, 31, 38–45, 47–50, 57–9
    in nineteenth and twentieth centuries 69, 79, 109–11, 127

*Progressive Historians, The*
    (Hofstadter) 208
Progressive history 104–5, 208–9
Progressive movement 104–5
*Prolegomena to Homer* (Wolf) 183
proletariat 85–7, 121
Proud, Robert 181
Providence concept 43–4, 59–60
psychology 122
publishing 99
*Puritan Dilemma: The Story of John
    Winthrop, The* (Morgan) 199
Puritanism 24–7, 205–6
Pyrrhonists 35

Québec siege (1759) 130

Raleigh, Walter 175
Ramsay, David 53, 181
Randall, Henry S. 190
Randall, James G. 201
Randolph, Edmund 53, 181
*Ranke: The Meaning of History*
    (Krieger) 207
Ranke, Leopold von 61, 69–76, 88,
    92–3, 100, 134, 190
    further reading on 207
Raynal, Guillaume Thomas François
    181
Reconstruction (U.S.) 117
*Recovery of the West African Past:
    African Pastors and African
    History in the 19th Century; C.C.
    Reindorf and Samuel Johnson, The*
    (Jenkins, ed.) 210
*Reflections on the Politics of Ancient
    Greece* (Heeren) 81
Reformation 43–4

Reign of Terror (French Revolution)
    62
relativism 107–11
religion
    and Enlightenment 29, 35–9, 41–4,
        47, 50–2, 59–60
    further reading 205–6
    in nineteenth and twentieth
        centuries 73–4, 78–80, 84, 133, 143
    and Renaissance 4–5, 7, 11–14,
        16–18, 21–8
*Remarks on the History of England*
    (Bolingbroke) 177
Renaissance 5–28, 88, 205–6
*Renaissance Sense of the Past, The*
    (Burke) 205
republicanism 32–3, 40, 49–50, 53,
    56–7
*Reserches de la France, Le* (Pasquier)
    175
revisionist history 146
*Revolt of the Netherlands, The* (Geyl)
    197
*Revolutionary Histories: Contemporary
    Narratives of the American
    Revolution, The* (Cohen) 206
*Revolutionary New England, 1691–1776*
    (Adams) 193
*Révolution Française, La* (Furet) 197
*Révolution française, La* (Soboul) 202
Revolutions of 1830 and 1848 68–9,
    74–5
*Revue historique* (France) 94–5
*Rise and Fall of the Choctaw Republic,
    The* (Debo) 117
*Rise of American Civilization, The*
    (Mary Beard) 194
*Rise of the West: A History of the*

*Human Community, The* (McNeill) 134, 199

Robertson, William 29, 39–45, 59–60, 182, 206

Robinson, James Harvey 103–4, 201

Romanticism 61–90, 104, 130, 207

*Romanticism and the Rise of History* (Bann) 207

Rome 5, 12, 44, 46–52, 56

*Romische geschichte* (Mommsen) 189

*Royal Touch, The* (Bloch) 194

Saussure, Ferdinand de 126

Savage, James 190

Savigny, Friedrich Karl von 191

scepticism 81

Schama, Simon 112, 130–1

Schlesinger, Arthur M., Jr. 202

Schlozer, August Ludwig 182

science and scientific method 13–14, 110, 143–5

*Science of History, The* (Bury) 100–2

scientific history 69–72, 79–81, 90–102, 111, 116–17, 144–5

challenges to 103, 107

further reading 208

Renaissance and Enlightenment precursors 9–11, 34

Scientific Revolution 4, 14–15, 31

Scott, Donald 121

Scottish Enlightenment 39–45 *see also* Enlightenment; stadial theory

Scott, Joan 121, 128

Seeley, J.R. 191

Seignobos, Charles 93, 116, 191

Selden, John 4, 19–22, 25–6, 28, 176

*Selected Writings on Economic and Cultural History and on*

*the Theory of Historiography* (Lamprecht) 188

Shaffer, Arthur 206

*Shapes of World History in Twentieth-Century Scholarship* (Bentley) 210

Shays Rebellion (U.S., 1786) 57

*Short History of the United States, A* (Bassett) 194

Simms, William Gilmore 191

Sismondi, Jean Charles Léonard Simonde de 191

skepticism 108

slavery and slave trade 136

Sleidan, Johann 175

Smith, Adam 39–40

Smith, John 176

Smith, William, Jr. 182

Soboul, Albert 202

social and cultural history 36–45, 87–8, 98–9, 102, 112–30, 135–6

further reading 209

socialism and communism 83–7

social science techniques 116, 121–3, 129

*Society and Culture in Early Modern France* (Davis) 196

*Society and Sentiment: Genres of Historical Writing in Britain, 1740–1820* (Phillips) 206

Soffer, Reba 208

Sparks, Jared 191

Spengler, Oswald 135, 202

stadial theory 39–45, 47–8, 57–8

*Stamp Act Crisis: Prologue to Revolution, The* (Morgan) 199

Stampp, Kenneth M. 202

Stern, Fritz 204

Stewart, Dugald 41
Stith, William 96, 182
Stone, Lawrence 128–30, 202
*Storia d'Italia* (Guicciardini) 174
*Stories of Independence: Identity,*
    *Ideology, and Independence in*
    *Eighteenth-Century America*
    (Messer) 206
Strout, Cushing 209
structuralism 126
Stubbs, William 191
Stuchtey, Benedikt 140, 210
Students for a Democratic Society
    (SDS) 119, 121
*Study of History, A* (Toynbee) 202
*Summary, Historical and Political . . .*
    *of the British Settlements in North*
    *America* (Douglass) 178
*Summary History of New England*
    (Adams) 177
Sybel, Heinrich von 191

Tacitus 32
Taine, Hippolyte 192
Tawney, R.H. 202
Taylor, A.J.P. 202
*Telling the Truth about History*
    (Appleby, Hunt, and Jacob)
    131–2, 209
"That Noble Dream" (Beard) 108
*That Noble Dream: The "Objectivity*
    *Question" and the American*
    *Historical Profession* (Novick)
    208–9
*Theory and History of Historiography,*
    *The* (Croce) 196
thick description 123–4, 129
Thierry, Augustin 192

Thompson, E.P. 113, 202
Thou, Jacques-Auguste de 175
Thucydides 12
time concepts 114–17, 139
tithes 19–22
*Titles of Honour* (Selden) 20–1
Tocqueville, Alexis de 192
*Towards a Democratic History*
    (Lemisch) 121
Toynbee, Arnold 135, 202
*Tracts and Other Papers Relating*
    *Principally to the Origin,*
    *Settlement, and Progress of the*
    *Colonies in North America, From*
    *the Discovery of the Country to the*
    *Year 1776* (Force) 185
*Transformation of the Decline and*
    *Fall of the Roman Empire, The*
    (Womersley) 206
Treitschke, Heinrich von 192
Trescot, William Henry 192
Trevelyan, George Macaulay 202
Trevor-Roper, Hugh 203
Trumbull, Benjamin 192
truth and objective reality *see also*
    materialism
  and Enlightenment 41, 59
  further reading 209
  and Renaissance 4, 10, 20–2,
    27–8
  and Romanticism 61, 63–4, 71–2,
    80, 88
  in twentieth century 104, 108–9,
    112, 126–8, 130–1
Tucker, George 193
Turkish Empire 12
Turner, Frederick Jackson 203
Tyrrell, Ian 208

*United States: An Experiment in Democracy, The* (Becker) 194
universal history 134
University of Berlin 70, 93–4
*Unredeemed Captive, The* (Demos) 129
*Uprooted, The* (Handlin) 198

Valla, Lorenzo 175
*Varieties of History: From Voltaire to the Present, The* (Stern, ed.) 204
Vergil, Polydore 175
*Versions of History from Antiquity to the Enlightenment* (Kelley, ed.) 204
Vico, Giambattista 182
Vietnam War protests 119
"View of the Progress of Society in Europe, A" (Robertson) 41–2, 44
*Visible Saints: The History of a Puritan Idea* (Morgan) 199
Voltaire 29, 31, 34–8, 42, 46, 59–60, 88, 134
  works by and about 182, 206
*Voltaire, Historian* (Brumfitt) 206
*Voltaire's Politics: The Poet as Realist* (Gay) 206

Wallerstein, Immanuel 135
Wang, Q. Edward 204, 210
*Waning of the Middle Ages, The* (Huizinga) 198
Warren, James 54
Warren, Mercy Otis 29, 53–60, 193
*Washington and His Generals* (Headley) 187
Webb, Walter Prescott 203
Weems, Mason Locke 183
Wehler, Hans Ulrich 113

Westernization 139
*We the People: The Economic Origins of the Constitution* (McDonald) 199
"What is Enlightenment?" (Kant) 30
*What Was History?: The Art of History in Early Modern Europe* (Grafton) 205
*Whig Interpretation of History, The* (Butterfield) 195
White, Hayden V. 127, 207–8
White, Morton 103–4
"Wholes and Parts: The Need for Synthesis in American History" (Bender) 124
*William Robertson and the Expansion of Empire* (Brown) 206
Williams, Roger 79
Williams, William Appleman 118, 203
Williamson, Hugh 53–4
Winthrop, John 24, 81, 177
Wolf, F.A. 183
*Woman as Force in History* (Mary Beard) 194
women 54–6, 118, 121–2, 128
*Women of the American Revolution, The* (Ellet) 185
Womersley, David 206
Wood, Gordon 131
Woodson, Carter G. 203
Woodward, C. Vann 203
Woolf, Daniel R. 139, 204–5, 210
world history 133, 135 *see also* global history
World War I 108–9
World War II 114–16
*World We Have Lost, The* (Laslett) 198
*Writings of George Washington, The* (Sparks) 191

*Writing the Nation: A Global Perspective* (Berger) 138

*Writing World History, 1800–2000* (Stuchtey and Fuchs) 210

"Written History as an Act of Faith" (Beard) 108, 110

Yoruba (West Africa) history 141–3

Zagarri, Rosemarie 138

Ziegler, Herbert 139

*Zwei Reden an Kaiser und Reich* (Sleidan) 175